The Place Vendôme

In *The Place Vendôme,* Rochelle Ziskin explores the sociological foundations of domestic design in eighteenth-century France, the acknowledged leader in domestic architecture during this period. Focusing on the Place Vendôme, which was developed by the financiers of Paris, she examines the representational strategies and dilemmas of French elites that were crucial to the formation of a French mode of design. These strategies are illuminated through a study of the socially mobile households of financiers, with their evolving but ambiguous social status. Through analyses of social distinctions and ambitions, Ziskin explores the manner in which the dwellings of the Place Vendôme embodied beliefs about the nature of society, the appropriate relations among social groups, as well as those between men and women, parents and children, and masters and domestics. This study also includes a wide range of illustrated material that is published here for the first time.

The Place Vendôme

———

Architecture and Social Mobility in Eighteenth-Century Paris

ROCHELLE ZISKIN

CAMBRIDGE
UNIVERSITY PRESS

PUBLISHED BY THE PRESS SYNDICATE OF THE UNIVERSITY OF CAMBRIDGE
The Pitt Building, Trumpington Street, Cambridge, United Kingdom

CAMBRIDGE UNIVERSITY PRESS
The Edinburgh Building, Cambridge CB2 2RU, UK http://www.cup.cam.ac.uk
40 West 20th Street, New York, NY 10011-4211, USA http://www.cup.org
10 Stamford Road, Oakleigh, Melbourne 3166, Australia

First published 1999

Printed in the United States of America

Typeface Sabon and Cochin, System DeskTopPro/ux®[RF]

A catalog record for this book is available from the British Library

Library of Congress Cataloging-in-Publication Data
Ziskin, Rochelle, 1954–
    The Place Vendôme : architecture and social mobility in 18th
  century Paris / Rochelle Ziskin.
      p.   cm.
    ISBN 0-521-59259-3 (hb)
    1. Place Vendôme (Paris, France)   2. Architecture and society –
    France – Paris – History – 18th century.   3. Paris (France –
    Buildings, structures, etc.   I. Title.
  NA9072.P37P589 1999
  944'.361033–dc21   98-25880
                                               CIP

ISBN 0 521 59259 3 hardback

For EZ, GZ, BZ, LZ, JZ, and MPF

Contents

List of Illustrations

Preface

IT WAS THROUGH the theoretical writings of Jacques-François Blondel that I first became interested in a study of the Place Vendôme. Among Blondel's goals was the codification of rules of representation in the realm of domestic design, an enterprise that revealed anxiety about social mobility in eighteenth-century France. I became interested in how financial families, with their ambiguous social identities, negotiated the rules of decorum in the domestic sphere. The Place Vendôme emerged as my focus because it formed a primary center of the financial quarter of Paris during most of the eighteenth century. Moreover, there had been no comprehensive architectural study of the square, despite its obvious importance, and questions about how it functioned as a site of social representation had rarely been raised.

Many scholars have appreciated the significance of the Place Vendôme, but the fundamental studies have not been architectural. Arthur de Boislisle's meticulous archival study of 1888 was enlarged upon by Maurice Dumolin, who made use of the papers of the archbishop of Paris to provide an outline of those who took up residence at the square (1927); drawing upon notarial documents not readily available to Boislisle and Dumolin, F. de Saint Simon has provided a fuller account of the square's residents (1983). The primary architectural studies had long been the work of Swedish scholars; they tended to focus on drawings housed in the Nationalmuseum, Stockholm, but nonetheless established an essential foundation. Most significant are Ragnar Josephson's study of facade drawings (1928), Erich Bier's catalogue providing a broader overview (1945), Eric Langenskiöld's monograph on Pierre Bullet (1959), and Runar Strandberg's articles on Jean-Baptiste Bullet de Chamblain, conveniently assembled in a published dissertation of 1971. The most significant recent work on the houses of the Place Vendôme has been that of the late Bruno Pons, who focused on interior decor; most important are his entries on Place Vendôme houses in *De Paris à Versailles 1699–1736: Les sculpteurs ornemanistes parisiens et l'art décoratif des Bâtiments du roi* (Strasbourg, 1986) and his accounts of decorative ensembles appearing in *Grands Décors Français* (published simultaneously as *French Period Rooms* in 1995), and the posthumously published catalogue of paneling installed at Waddesdon Manor (1996).

Acknowledgments

This study began as a Ph.D. dissertation at Harvard University, and I would like to express my deep gratitude to my advisers, James S. Ackerman and Neil Levine, for their incisive criticism and intellectual generosity. More recently, Robin Middleton, Myra Nan Rosenfeld, and the readers for Cambridge University Press have made valuable suggestions on manuscript versions of this book. Many scholars have offered valued suggestions during the research of this book, including Theda Shapiro, Allan Potofsky, Julia Adams, Jay Smith, and Thierry Claeys. Michael Dennis generously allowed me to reproduce his plan after Blondel, and Robert Neuman and Christopher Mead kindly permitted me to use their photographs.

Among the many museum and archival curators who have assisted my work, I would like to especially thank Börje Magnusson of the Nationalmuseum, Stockholm; Gillian Wilson, Brian Considine, and Jeffrey Weaver of the J. Paul Getty Museum; Bertrand Rondot of the Musée des Arts Décoratifs in Paris; Michel Le Moël and Nicole Felkay of the Archives Nationales; Nicole Ambourg of the Bibliothèque Marmottan and Madame Chauleur of the library of the Ministère de la Justice. I would like to express my deep appreciation to the enterprises and individuals permitting me to visit, study, and photograph their premises: Bank of India; Banque N.M.B.; Monsieur Jean-Louis du Boucheron; Chauderer; Chaumet; Crédit Foncier de la France; Monsieur Lucien Dana; Deutsche Banque; I.B.M.; La Minstère de la Justice; Morgan Guaranty Trust Company; the Ritz Hôtel; la Société des Centres Commerciaux; la Société KENLO; Union des Assurances de Paris; Van Cleef & Arpels; and Wella. I thank Gracie Luciani of the Ministère de la Justice for her exceptional generosity.

I am greatly indebted to Harvard University and the George C. Lurcy Trust for funding my dissertation research; to the J. Paul Getty Trust, for providing a postdoctoral fellowship that permitted extensive revision of that dissertation; and to Dean James Durig, the College of Arts and Sciences of the University of Missouri – Kansas City, and the Research Board of the University of Missouri for supporting this project with several generous grants. And I thank my colleagues Burton Dunbar, Marilyn Carbonell, and Sherry Best for their advice and support.

My greatest debt is to Michael P. Fitzsimmons. It is no exaggeration to say that without his encouragement, counsel, intellectual generosity, and friendship, this book could not have been written.

Introduction

Toward the end of the reign of Louis XIV, the French emerged as the undisputed European leaders in the realm of domestic design. French elites and their architects abandoned the style of planning and decoration associated with Versailles and turned to the development of the private realm. Together they "invented" a "new art" of domestic design, or so French theorists would later claim.

That refined "new art" emerged, I argue in this book, from the specific nature of French society, with its hierarchy of social estates and ranks, and from the representational, ceremonial, and functional needs of its elites. I explore this refined new mode of domestic design as it evolved during the course of the eighteenth century at the houses of the principal royal square in Paris dedicated to Louis XIV, the Place de Louis-le-Grand (Vendôme). Several factors coalesce to render the Place Vendôme a particularly fruitful context for these explorations. Initially planned in 1685 with a public program, this royal square was reconceived as a residential ensemble at the turn of the new century, during the period when the French were "inventing" domestic design. From the outset, the most mobile elite in France, the financiers of Paris, claimed the square as the center of what would become a predominantly financial quarter, and they remained the dominant presence until the Revolution. The significance of that presence appears in the equivocal reception of the houses of Place Vendôme. Architects and other cultivated observers lauded the elegance and modernity of the plans and the refinement of the interior decor, but others condemned the houses for breaches of representational decorum.

The conviction that representational codes had been transgressed reveals widely held beliefs about the true social station of financial families. In fact, the status of the first families to reside at the Place Vendôme was ambiguous, their identities fundamentally in transition. The most prominent among them were recently ennobled or rapidly ascending to such status, but they were widely perceived to be bourgeois by those above and below them in the social hierarchy. Integral to the functioning of the state, financiers were nonetheless socially disdained, in part due to the sources of their wealth, but primarily because of their mobility. The majority were perceived to be "outsiders" in several respects. Major financiers in Paris at the turn of the eighteenth century had risen to prominence, by and large, since Colbert's death in 1683. Most had been born in provincial cities, many to Protestant families that had converted to Catholicism during the years before or immediately following the revocation of the Edict of Nantes in 1685. Their identities were in flux. They were often "newly" rich, newly converted, and newly ennobled or on the most direct course to becoming so.

The high degree of social mobility among eighteenth-century financiers has attracted increasing attention during the last few decades from social, political, and economic historians who have produced subtle analyses of the status of financial families in French society.[1] Architectural historians, however, while usually conscientious in noting official titles and posts, have tended to employ a fairly generic notion of a French elite of wealth. This is understandable, finding support among some prominent historians who have stressed those aspects of social identity that the wealthiest members of sword, robe, and finance shared in common, arguing that a single elite of wealth dominated French society by the middle of the eighteenth century.[2] Leading financiers tended to be wealthier than all but the grandest seigneurs, and they hired the same architects, decorative artists, and craftsmen employed by members of court. Materially and representationally, they lived in dwellings akin to those of the upper ranks of the nobility.

So why do I insist on drawing distinctions, on questioning even subtle differences in social perceptions of members of different elites? I do so because other evidence – in memoirs, correspondence, comedies, and other texts – suggests that distinctions, most sharply drawn during the early decades of the century, continued to be made until the end of the Old Regime. Even in the eighties, as we shall see, when the comte d'Artois complained about the scale of the garden and villa that had been installed facing his own, at issue was not that *someone* had dared "compete" with him, but that a *financier* had done so. In penetrating the social meanings affixed to dwellings in Paris, it seems essential to delineate, with as much subtlety as possible, distinctions that never ceased to be made.

Among the principal arguments offered in this book is that houses of financiers were, for most of the century, *not* noble *hôtels*, in significant measure because they were *used* differently. This notion of use is broadly construed to refer to both function and representation. All eighteenth-century French dwellings were more than just residences. For each of the principal elites – the sword (with the court nobility at its summit), the robe (government officials and judges), and the top rungs of finance – houses were settings in which the social relations of a profoundly hierarchical society were represented and reenacted.

Two modes of social representation will be probed. The first is best considered strategic: the conscious manipulation of typologies, modes of planning, and decorative codes. The second is the ideological; through the workings of ideology, presuppositions and inchoate beliefs about the nature of society and relations among social groups – as well as those between men and women, parents and children, and servants and masters – were encoded into domestic design. Dwellings were complex signifying systems embodying both representational modes.

In analyzing these houses as complex organisms, I have selected certain families and dwellings to explore in depth, raising questions about the social and gendered meanings that adhered to specific spaces, locales, and decorative treatments. Most often, I limit my discussion of the household to family members, but at the end of Chapter 5, I examine the "*maison*" more broadly, considering all those who lived under a proprietor's roof – including domestics, retainers, relations, and friends.

I begin with the venture that built the Place Vendôme and a discussion of the place of the financier in French society. I then consider issues of typology, focusing on the urban dwellings of the court nobility and assessing the ways in which their houses traditionally had differed from those of the robe. Within that context, I explore the peculiar functional needs and representational dilemmas of financial families, examining in depth dwellings built for two leading men of finance, Poisson de Bourvalais and Antoine Crozat. Typological concerns reappear in Chapter 3, where I discuss many of the extant plans, and in Chapter 4, in the context of the Regency and its aftermath, when the court nobility established a significant presence at the square and the last houses were constructed. Following further consideration of the representational stratagems and quandaries of members of the Crozat clan, I turn in the final chapter to the dwellings of a more confident generation of financiers at the end of the Old Regime. In concluding remarks, I assess shifting social meanings attached to the status of the square as a *place royale*.

When I refer throughout this book to "the sword," "the court," "the robe," and "finance," I am using eighteenth-century labels that tend to mask individual differences of power, rank, and wealth, as well as a range of values. There were factions among sword and court nobles; men of the robe who directly served the Crown (ministers, secretaries of state, intendants) had interests and often outlooks that differed from those of magistrates. Among leading financiers in Paris, few actually resembled the endlessly repeated caricatures of arrogant, rapacious usurers, comic in their quest to appear noble. Real men of finance were, of course, far more complex. Some were clearly arrogant and ruthless in certain contexts, but the same men might be major patrons of the arts and renowned in other situations for their charity. Most quite clearly pursued noble status for their families, but others built dynasties that remained engaged in finance long after it was necessary to do so, and some even left the dignity of the robe to pursue finance. Finance may have been inherently "parasitic," but it is essential to remember that others in Old Regime France were *equally* "parasitic" (and, no doubt, as arrogant) – courtiers enjoying royal pensions spring first to mind.[3] Within each category, individuals absorbed the ideological structures characteristic of their group to varying degrees. Familial goals might be similar, but they were not homogeneous. Nonetheless, within the corporate society of Old Regime France, our understanding seems furthered by such categories as "noble of the court," "man of the robe," and "financier."

4

My aim has not been to produce a *catalogue raisonné* of the dwellings of the Place Vendôme. I do not discuss every house, nor do I provide a comprehensive list of residents. The nature of the questions raised means that some inhabitants mentioned in this book will not have appeared in prior accounts, but readers should consult the works cited in the preface for a fuller enumeration. This study focuses on those dwellings and select moments that provide the best context for an exploration of social representation. It has been my intention, however, to illustrate and discuss a majority of the extant plans, as well as the most significant extant ensembles of interior decor.

Throughout this book, I employ the French measure of the *toise*, equivalent to six French *pieds* (each *pied* approximately equal to an English foot) and French usage in referring to stories in buildings (so that the first floor is one flight up). Unless otherwise specified, all numbers of houses refer to those that exist today.

Louis XIV's Parisian *place royale* Reconceived

ɪN 1685, at the height of French power during the reign of Louis XIV, the Crown announced its intention to build a royal square in the capital – the Place de Nos Conquêtes. Larger than any other *place royale* in Paris, more magnificent and triumphal in its imagery, it was to accommodate and display the royal academies, the royal library, and the mint, and to provide a residence for special visits of foreign dignitaries. The square glorified French "conquests" in various realms – military, religious, and cultural.

The assembling of a suitable site near the city's western boundary had entailed considerable expense: the purchase and razing of the large Hôtel de Vendôme along the north side of the rue Saint-Honoré, as well as the demolition and reconstruction of a neighboring Capuchin convent (Fig. 1). By 1691, a continuous facade bearing a giant Ionic order and flat cornice had been built around three sides of the large rectangular space. In the center of its northern range, the facade projected to form a triumphal arch, which served as the backdrop for a colossal equestrian statue of the king when it was viewed from the main east–west artery of the quarter (Fig. 2).

But military reversals and defeat during the long War of the League of Augsburg (1688–97) eroded the king's enthusiasm for a large public square dedicated to his conquests. Construction stopped in 1691 after the death of the marquis de Louvois, the Secretary of State for War and Superintendent of Royal Building Works who had promoted the project. By 1699, the king wanted to efface all memory of the square, to pave streets over the site and to store the statue permanently out of public view.[1] When leading ministers and city councilors lobbied to preserve the *place royale*, the king agreed that the statue might be displayed, but only if the square was reconceived. The new square was to be residential, like the two other royal squares in the capital: the Place Royale (des Vosges) (Fig. 3), built for Henri IV, and the diminutive Place des Victoires (Fig. 4), conceived in tandem with the Place de Nos Conquêtes.[2]

The Crown gave the Place de Nos Conquêtes to the city of Paris, on the condition that it be sold to a group of investors charged with constructing the new square according to a design by Louis's trusted new Superintendent of Royal Building Works Jules Hardouin-Mansart, architect of the Place de Nos Conquêtes and the Place des Victoires. In August 1699, the city councilors and the governor of Paris celebrated the installation of the colossal equestrian statue at the Place de Nos Conquêtes, but demolition began within weeks. On its site, the investors built a residential square with a new form, a new imagery, and a new name – the Place de Louis-le-Grand (more popularly known as the Place Vendôme).

Mansart and his collaborators, most importantly Robert de Cotte (who would succeed him as First Architect to the King in 1708), shaped a new square that withdrew from the urban fabric, canting the corners of the reduced public space to enhance its sense of enclosure and to provide gentler transitions that better accommodated the needs of residences (Figs. 5 to 8).[3] The smaller public space freed more land for sale to individuals and shrank the area to be paved and maintained by the city. Retaining a giant order and an arcuated ground floor, Mansart replaced the public, open loggia with a blind arcade that marked new boundaries between public and private realms. Above the new cornice, Mansart added a tall French roof, suited both functionally and representationally to the residential program. He abandoned the triumphal arch, replacing it with one of two short "streets," extensions of the square sharing its facade and linking the main public space with important urban arteries. Mansart punctuated the newly canted corners and central pa-

Figure 1

De Fer plan, 1690s, detail of northwest Paris [photo: after *Atlas des anciens plans de Paris*, eds. A. Alphand, Michaux, and L.-M. Tisserand (Paris, 1880)].

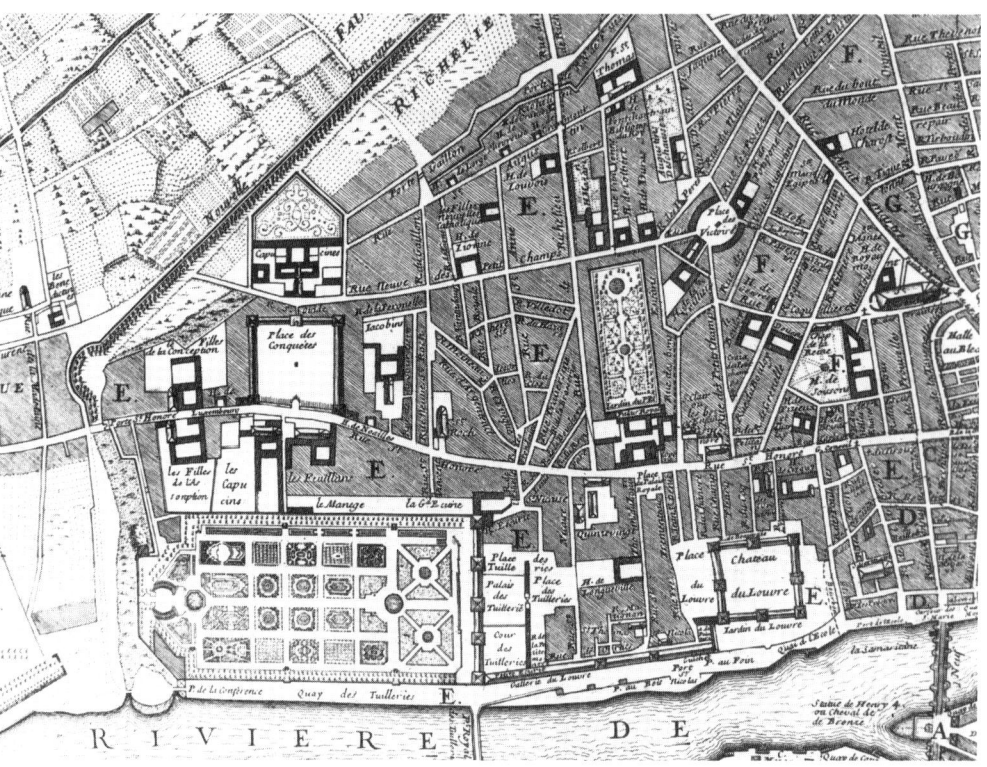

Figure 2
Place de Nos Conquêtes, inauguration of François Girardon's
statue of Louis XIV, August 1699, engraving, Almanac, 1700
[photo: Bibliothèque Nationale, Est., Va 234].

Figure 3
Place Royale (des Vosges) [photo: author].

8

vilions with temple fronts bearing the king's arms, flanking the east and west pediments with reclining figures holding royal crowns aloft (Fig. 6). The square was still quite grand, but no longer imperial in its imagery; it had a more domestic character, akin to that of the Place des Victoires.

The public space of the reconceived square retreated from life along the streets that connected it with the rest of the city, its newly self-referential quality reinforced by the subsidiary axes. As recast, the form of the square served a domestic program at the expense of its public character. That reconception coincided with a less confident moment in the reign, when the focus of architectural interest turned inward toward the private realm.

Investors and Proprietors

A la place Royale, on a placé ton père
Parmi les gens de qualité.
On voit, sur le Pont-Neuf ton aïeul débonnaire,
Près du peuple qui fut l'objet de sa bonté.
Pour toi, des partisans le prince tutélaire,
A la place Vendôme – entre eux – on t'a placé.[4]

Most of the investors and the heads of the first families to take up residence at the Place Vendôme were, as this epigram pointedly observed, financiers. General tax farmer Alexandre Luillier, who had begun negotiations with the Crown as early as May 1698, directed the partnership and assembled it weekly

Figure 4
Place des Victoires (nos. 4 *bis* – 12) [photo: courtesy of Christopher Mead].

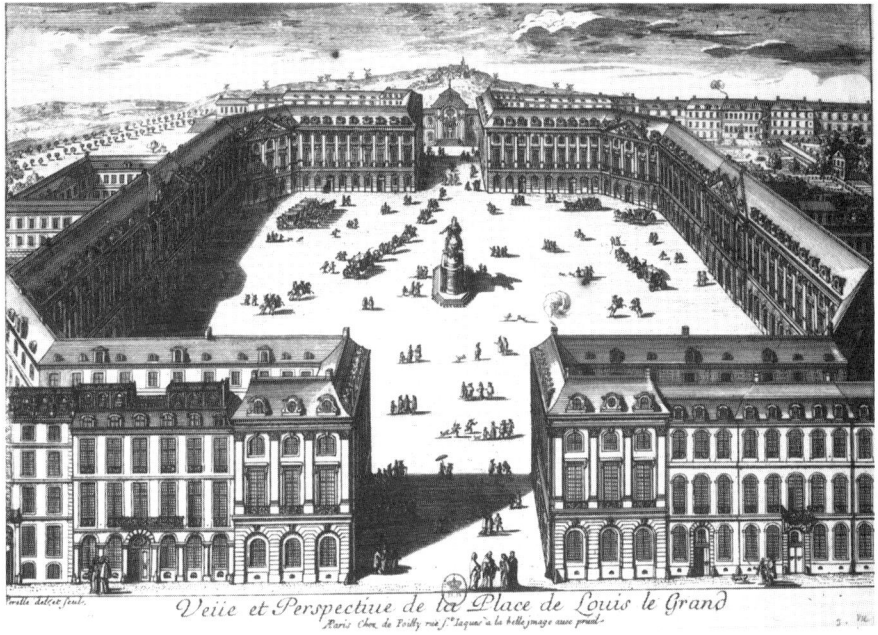

Figure 5

Perelle, engraving, "View and perspective of the Place de Louis le Grand" [photo: Bibliothèque Nationale, Est., Va 234].

Figure 6

Place de Louis-le-Grand (Vendôme), study, central pavilion [photo: Nationalmuseum, Stockholm, THC 2683].

in his house on the nearby rue Sainte-Anne.[5] Several of the investors owed their fortunes to the sponsorship of Louis II Phélypeaux de Pontchartrain, Controller General of Finance from 1689 to 1699. In 1699, Pontchartrain's son Jerôme was Secretary of State in charge of the Maison du Roi, which carried with it responsibility for the capital city; like his father, he was anxious to see the project successfully completed.

Four investment partners held financial offices, and each committed one-sixth (16.7 percent) of the purchase price. They were, in addition to Luillier, Moïse-Augustin Fontanieu, Receiver General of Finance for La Rochelle;[6] Extraordinary Treasurer of War Jean de Sauvion, related by marriage to both Mansart and Claude Bosc; and Nicolas-Hiérosme Herlaut, a receiver at the *siège présidial de Beauvais*, who would become Treasurer General of French and Swiss guards in 1702. The lawyer Mathurin Besnier, who invested heavily in extraordinary finance and was the new father-in-law of the architect Jacques V Gabriel (a member of Mansart's extended clan), had the largest interest – 21 percent.[7] The royal architect Pierre Bullet took a 13 percent share. Profit motives and dynastic ambitions prompted a reshuffling of shares among

Figure 7
Air view toward east and north ranges of Place Vendôme [photo: Préfecture de Police de Paris].

the investment partners shortly before and immediately after the inauguration of the king's statue.[8]

A key event in the shaping of the social composition of the square occurred a month after the inauguration of the statue, as demolition of the Place de Nos Conquêtes began, when the king named Pontchartrain the Chancellor of France. The new Controller General of Finance, Michel Chamillart, planned a special tax on financiers (who had just lost their patron), and the king gave him an advance of 500,000 *livres* from anticipated revenues to build a new residence in Paris, at the Place Vendôme or in its vicinity.[9] The king's gift and instructions suggest that Louis may have intentionally sought to define the social profile of the new *place royale*. Financiers often clustered near the Controller General of Finance, whose patronage was essential for success. Chamilliart, who apparently wanted more palatial accommodations than the square permitted, assembled a huge site along the north side of the rue Neuve-des-Petits-Champs, immediately east of the Capuchin Convent, and extending all the way to the boulevard.[10]

Leading financiers soon began acquiring lots at the Place Vendôme (Fig. 9). Antoine Crozat, Receiver General of Finance for Bordeaux since 1689, purchased parcel no. 17 along the west range. His powerful former mentor and business associate, Pierre-Louis Reich de Pennautier, Treasurer General of the Bourse of Languedoc and Receiver General for the Clergy of France, followed

Figure 8
Place Vendôme, west range (nos. 13–23) [photo: courtesy of Robert Neuman].

suit, buying a large contiguous parcel (no. 19). Soon after, Thomas Quesnet, first *commis* (assistant) of Chamillart, bought no. 24, extending from the square to the rue Neuve-des-Petits-Champs.

Mansart and members of his clan extended their significant financial interest in the quarter, which had probably influenced the initial choice of the site and the survival of the *place royale*. When Luillier's initiative first appeared in journals and correspondence in July 1698, it was already connected with re-

Figure 9

Pierre Bullet (attrib.), drawing prepared for dissolution of Place Vendôme partnership, late 1704 (with parcels numbered as they are today and in text) [photo: Bibliothèque Nationale, Est. Va 441].

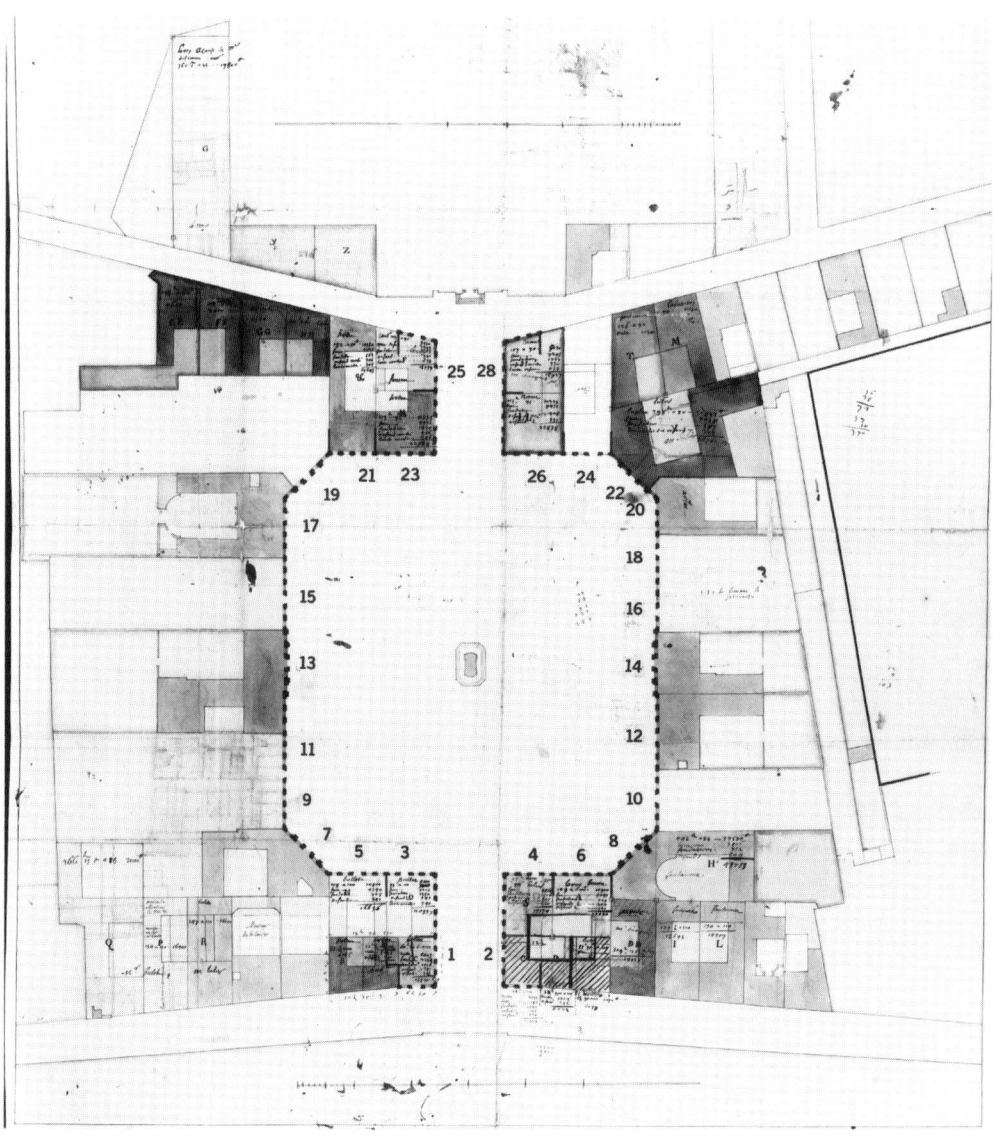

building the square according to a new octagonal plan by Mansart.[11] Mansart's speculative interest had emerged as early as 1677, when he formed a partnership with five others to buy the Hôtel de Vendôme and its gardens; the group intended to raze the dwelling and open new streets.[12] That project was never realized, but Mansart soon began to acquire land in the vicinity, along the rue Neuve-des-Petits-Champs and near the porte Gaillon.[13] In the reconceived project, the king gave Mansart almost 579 square *toises* along the south side of the rue Neuve-des-Petits-Champs, immediately northeast of the square, removed from the land sold to the Luillier group (Fig. 9).[14]

Less than two months after Chamillart's initial land purchase, however, the political landscape radically changed. Charles II of Spain died, leaving his entire empire to Louis XIV's second grandson, the duc d'Anjou, a legacy that made military conflict almost inevitable. The threat of war dampened enthusiasm for tying up capital at the Place Vendôme. Purchases of parcels effectively ceased, but Mansart and his clan continued to increase their stake in the project.[15]

Mansart enlarged his holdings when Charles Renouard de La Touanne and his brother-in-law Sauvion, Extraordinary Treasurers of War who had never recovered from the War of the League of Augsburg, declared bankruptcy in June 1701.[16] The Crown seized their assets, including the large parcel Sauvion bought in 1699. In early 1703, when a grant of Sauvion's parcel was imminent, Mansart purchased an adjacent lot (no. 7) in the southwest corner. By then, Mansart owned more land at the Place Vendôme than some of the investment partners. These investments and those in the vicinity constituted a significant share of the real estate speculation engaged in by Mansart and his clan, but they also invested considerable sums in other quarters of Paris.

The partners envisaged selling the lots quickly, and they had negotiated to pay a single fee covering seigneurial taxes until January 1, 1704.[17] By early 1704, the partnership had invested about 250,000 *livres* more than it recovered from sales.[18] Requesting an extension of the exemption, the society blamed "the times, the war, the lack of resources . . ." for its failure to sell the lots.[19] The partners decided to divide the remaining parcels, apportioning them into shares of approximately equal value.[20]

The investment partners had a plan prepared delineating the parcels to be divided. It is now lost, but an extant drawing is clearly an advanced study for it (Fig. 9).[21] Its author, most likely Bullet, indicated the massing of six dwellings built by late 1704 and some others that were never realized. In early 1705, the association dissolved, each partner receiving four to seven parcels, at the square and along the streets immediately north and south of it – the rue Neuve-des-Petits-Champs, the rue Neuve-des-Capucines, and the rue Saint-Honoré.

Anticipated political and financial advantages and a representational dignity otherwise beyond their reach initially drew leading financiers to the Place Vendôme. The outbreak of the War of the Spanish Succession shifted the equation, draining resources until the middle of the second decade of the century. Still, in spite of the war, some financiers proceeded to build dwellings and install their families at the new Place de Louis-le-Grand.

The "Lackey-Financier"[22]

Financiers formed the most socially mobile elite in French society. The majority were office holders, and there was a certain dignity attached to the posts they held in the state's bureaucracy. Most financiers purchased offices that provided opportunities to administer the Crown's finances and to advance funds to the government at highly profitable rates of interest. At the top of the hierarchy were three principal groups of financiers: the *receveurs généraux* (receivers general), administering the collection and distribution of direct taxes on property; *trésoriers généraux* (general treasurers) responsible for paying out funds (the most profitable posts associated with war, the navy, colonial trade, and certain provincial estates like Languedoc); and the more autonomous *fermiers généraux* (general tax farmers), who directed the collection of indirect consumption tariffs and customs duties. Key to the relative lucrativeness of a post was the amount of funds that passed through a financier's hands, less because of handling fees than because he used funds at his disposal for short-term investments and loans. Even more lucrative was "extraordinary" finance, generally called upon only when France was at war; in exchange for advances of anticipated revenues, often tied to sales of new offices or special taxes (*traités*), financiers could earn substantial returns in a relatively short time. From *traités* and *partis* (contracts) came the derogatory terms *traitants* and *partisans* (outside fiscal agents) so often affixed to financiers.[23]

Bankers were somewhat different. They worked in tandem with financiers, helping them to secure credit among French and foreign investors. The Crown had long relied upon Italian bankers, established in Lyon since the fifteenth century, but by the middle of the seventeenth century, it increasingly turned to Swiss and German agents. The revocation of the Edict of Nantes in 1685 theoretically left no place for Protestant bankers in France, but the War of the Spanish Succession made them essential to raising sufficient capital and conveying funds to military fronts. By 1705, Protestant bankers, many of them Swiss, returned to Paris; they would dominate banking later in the century, but some powerful Catholic clans, several formerly Protestant, were also active. Considered *négociants*, wholesale merchants dealing in currency rather than goods, bankers did not share in the prestige enjoyed by office holders during most of the century. The exceptions were the court banker, always Catholic and one of the wealthiest and most powerful financial figures of the realm, and bankers whose clans participated in royal finance.[24]

There is an astonishing consistency to representations of financiers, from fairly early in the reign of Louis XIV until well into the eighteenth century, in texts that range from comedies to personal memoirs and even correspondence; the same stock types appeared in popular prints. A dominant mythology emerged, with origins that could be traced to the interests of the nobility – both sword and robe. Both groups found their social positions significantly threatened by mobile financiers. Sword nobles, including courtiers, were increasingly forced to marry younger sons to daughters of rich financiers, in order to maintain the leisured and opulent lifestyle that had become a primary sign of their stature; when they sold the seigneuries so fundamental to their identities, the lands from which they took their names, it was very often to men of finance.[25] Robe nobles, whose social status could remain relatively stagnant over generations (especially in the provinces), often resented financiers who purchased offices for their sons that equalled or superseded those robe clans had toiled long to achieve.[26] Nobles of the blood, and to a lesser extent those of the robe, found solace in their pedigrees and in the antiquity of their nobility, and they often exaggerated the "base" origins of financiers. Their attitudes were so pervasive that even solidly bourgeois contemporaries, among them Robert Challes and Edmond Barbier, regularly described leading financiers and their sons as *hommes de rien* ("men of nothing").[27]

Stock characterizations went further. Not only did men and women of financial families have lowly origins, but they lacked that prime noble trait that wealth could not buy – taste. The concept was, of course, intimately and inextricably linked to social position.[28] The classic parody of the most ambitious among the ranks of the bourgeoisie, including many elements that became standard features in the representation financiers, was Molière's *Le Bourgeois gentilhomme* of 1670. Monsieur Jourdain (apparently a *négociant* or financier) hired instructors in the arts, fencing, and philosophy; commissioned tailors who outfitted the nobility; pursued noble women (and, presumably, would have hired the architects and decorative artists who worked for the court) – but he consistently revealed himself to be bourgeois to the core.[29] However overdrawn, Jourdain embodied traits that were recognizable, at least to an extent; his uninformed taste emerged not from the lack of a noble pedigree, but from inadequate access to the quickly changing codes of a relatively closed societal elite. The popularity of the comedy, however, reveals anxiety among the court nobility, probably stemming from the degree to which financial families *could*, in fact, *convincingly* represent themselves as noble.

The financier who rose "out of the mire" and the crude usurer were ubiquitous types.[30] Despite the endlessly repeated portrait of the "lackey-financier," those who occupied the top ranks in Paris at the turn of the century were largely the progeny of generations engaged in finance in provincial centers, where clans established the credit networks to amass sizable sums to lend to the Crown. Sons often learned their professions from fathers or uncles, and they frequently served as assistants to other financiers early in their careers. Far from indicating "vile" origins, such a background constituted the best sort of professional training. Many leading financiers at the turn of the eighteenth century, including several of the first residents at the Place Vendôme, were – in fact – legally noble.

The Ideal: The Noble Hôtel

Residences take different names according to the different estates of those who occupy them. One speaks of the *maison* of a bourgeois, the *hôtel* of a noble, the *palais* of a prince or a king.[31]

An analysis of the first houses of the Place Vendôme must first assess the type that architects emulated for their clients but could adapt only to a degree: the aristocratic *hôtel*. In the first volume of his *Cours d'architecture* (1691–3), Augustin-Charles Daviler presented a model urban dwelling for a *grand seigneur*, exemplifying conventions of *hôtel* design about a decade before the first houses of the Place Vendôme (Figs. 10 to 13). Daviler's model is illuminating, but it was already rather old-fashioned by 1700. To supplement my discussion of it, I will consider two *hôtels* built for court nobles at the turn of the new century (Figs. 14 to 18).

In an urban context, signification began with the type itself. Cities were not the principal sphere of the feudal nobility; the power of the landed nobility was based in the rural seigneuries from which it reigned. Often, however, it was desirable or necessary to have an urban residence. Such was the case in Paris when it served, periodically, as the center of court life. To represent their power within an urban context, feudal noblemen adopted a rather straightforward strategy: They brought their *châteaux* with them.[32]

The seigneurial manor house, necessarily reduced, provided the basic type that endured for centuries. Just as the *château* traditionally withdrew from its surroundings, at one time detached from them by a moat and fortified wall, architects removed the *corps-de-logis* (principal living quarters) of the noble *hôtel* from the street, and they set it between a court and a garden. Subsidiary wings connected the *corps-de-logis* with a lower range screening the house from the street.[33] Along the street, the facade was treated simply. The weight of representational display was borne by the entrance portal, often treated grandly as a triumphal arch of sorts; it was inscribed with the name of the house and frequently embellished with applied columns and trophies alluding to military service (Figs. 12 and 15).[34]

Architects typically set stables and carriage stalls in or near the range along the street. Ample provision in that realm and such a placement identified the dwelling as noble. Real estate along an urban street was valuable, especially in bourgeois quarters where it might be used for shops or, among wholesale merchants, for offices of cashiers and accountants (*caisses* and *bureaux*) (Figs. 19 and 20).[35] The locating of the most mundane of functions along the public realm was a sign that no commercial value was attached to the street frontage, because the proprietors were noble – or, at least, living nobly.[36]

The procession of entry that began at the street portal typically extended across a court of honor and along a direct axis to a centrally placed entrance vestibule, a space frequently left fairly open to the elements. The axis often continued through a *salle* to a garden beyond, and apartments (the traditional units of French planning) often extended to either side of that principal axis.[37]

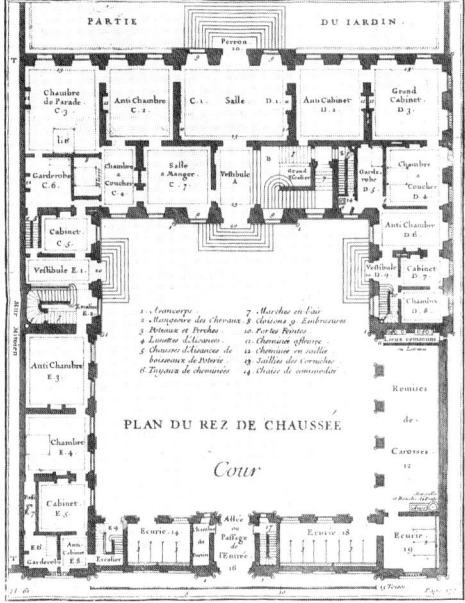

Figure 10

Augustin-Charles Daviler, ground-floor plan, *hôtel* for a *grand seigneur*, from *Cours d'architecture*, I (Paris, 1691) [photo: 1720 ed., University of Florida, Gainesville].

Figure 11

Augustin-Charles Daviler, first-floor plan, *hôtel* for a *grand seigneur*, from *Cours d'architecture*, I (Paris, 1691) [photo: 1720 ed., University of Florida, Gainesville].

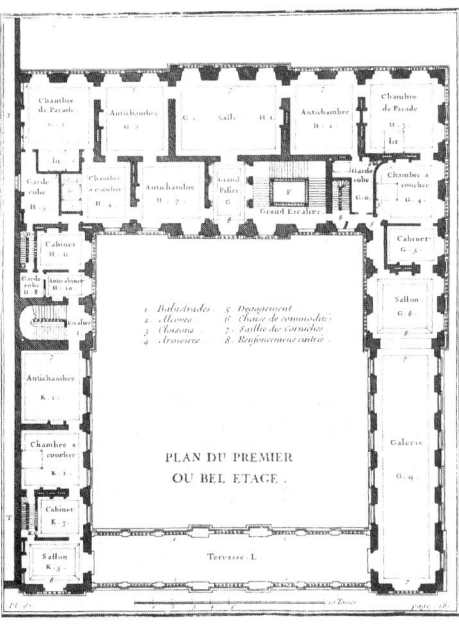

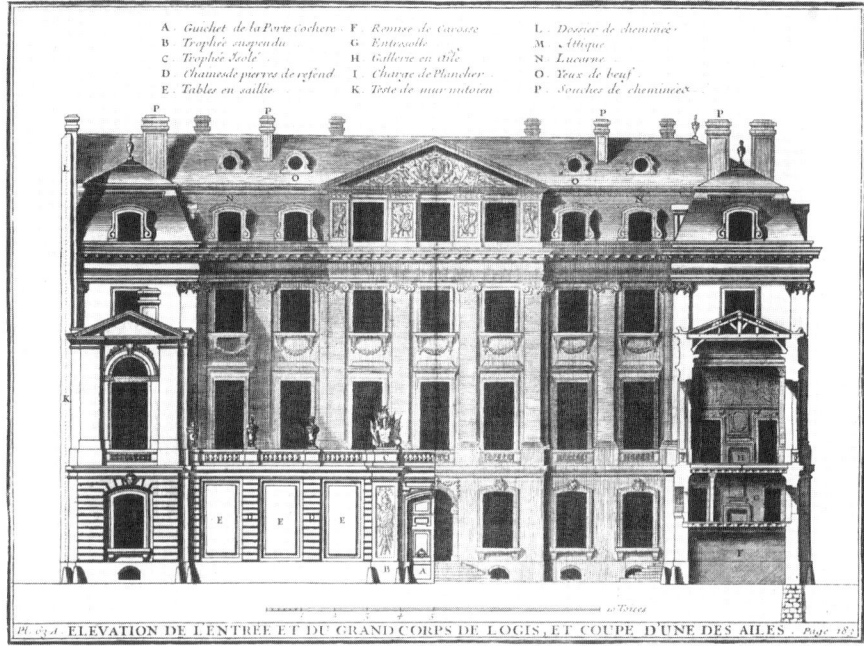

Figure 12

Augustin-Charles Daviler, court elevation, *hôtel* for a *grand seigneur*, from *Cours d'architecture*, I (Paris, 1691) [photo: 1720 ed., University of Florida, Gainesville].

Figure 13

Augustin-Charles Daviler, elevation of wing and section, *hôtel* for a *grand seigneur*, from *Cours d'architecture*, I (Paris, 1691) [photo: 1720 ed., University of Florida, Gainesville].

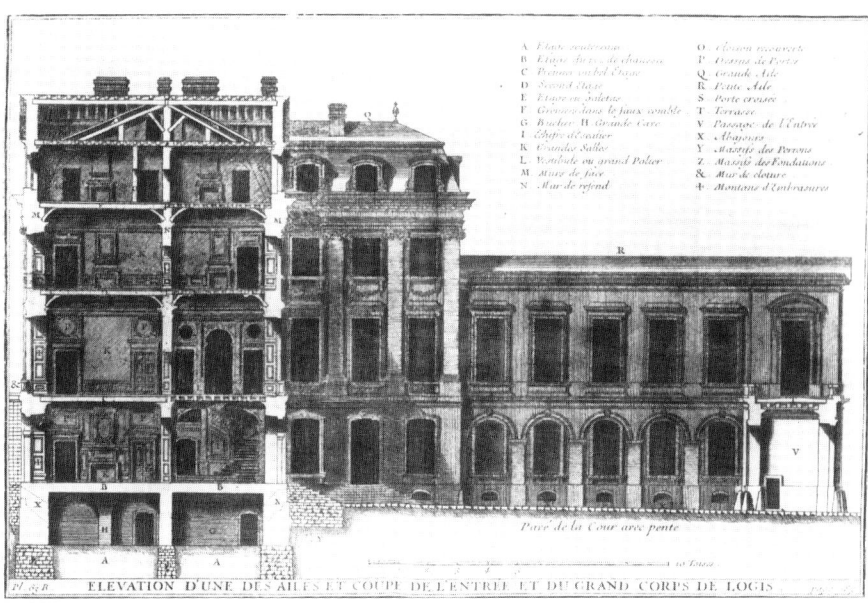

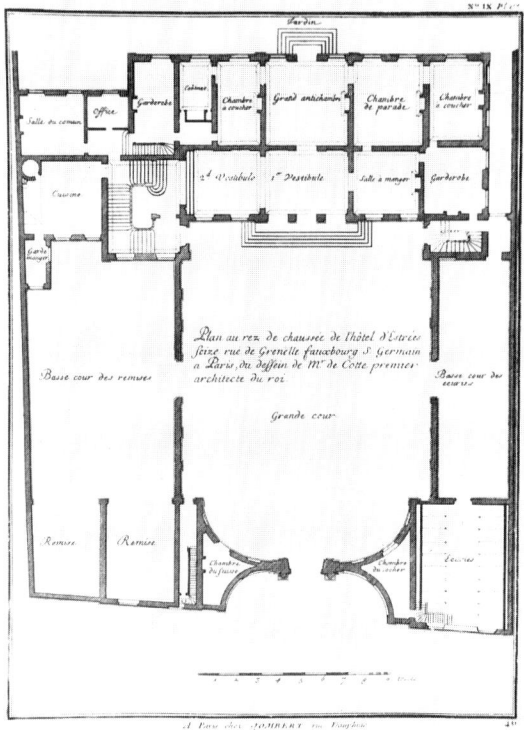

Figure 14

Robert de Cotte, ground-floor plan, Hôtel d'Estrées, rue de Grenelle, Faubourg Saint-Germain, built c. 1711–13, engraving in Jacques-François Blondel, *Architecture Française*, I (Paris, 1752) [photo: after reprint ed., Paris, 1904].

At the turn of the century, there were two types of apartments: ceremonial *appartements de parade*, incorporating large public rooms of reception; and private *appartements de commodité*, consisting of smaller rooms that were "the most lived-in," as Daviler explained. Each suite typically included at least one waiting room for visitors and servants (*antichambre*); a bedroom (*chambre*); a more private room for conversation, writing or study (*cabinet*); and a *garderobe* where clothes were stored, where a domestic might sleep to be more readily available, and where toilet facilities were often placed. Daviler tucked *chaises de commodité* (also called *chaises percées*) into corners off subsidiary stairs, presumably screened by curtains;[38] in his revised edition of Daviler's treatise, published in 1710, Jean-Baptiste-Alexandre Le Blond wrote that architects currently installed a "very new" means for flushing these *lieux de commodité* (or *aisances*) with water.[39] But such new facilities were still a rarity in elite residences;[40] throughout the century, water closets (also called *cabinets à l'angloise*) were often supplemented by *chaises de commodité*.[41]

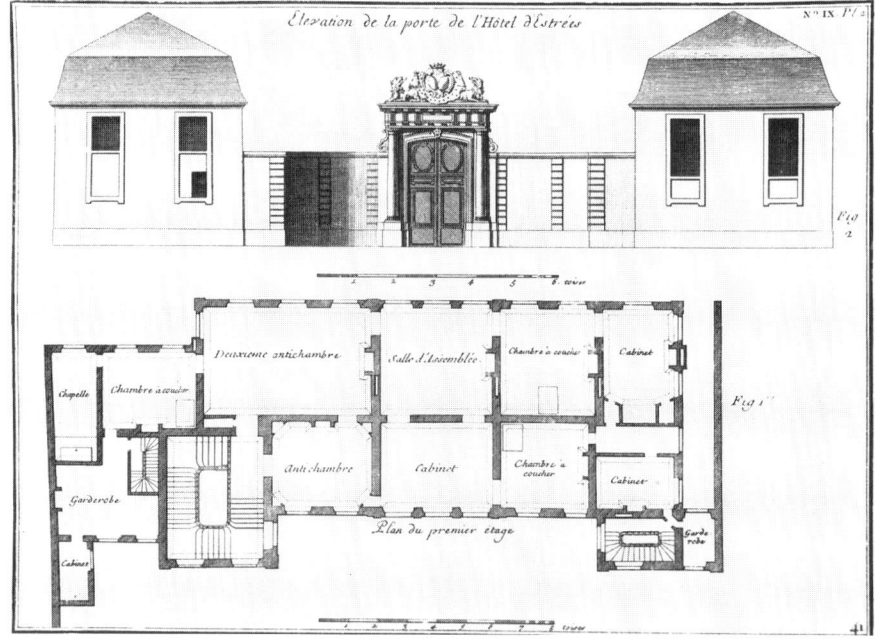

Figure 15
Robert de Cotte, first-floor plan and street elevation, Hôtel d'Estrées, rue de Grenelle, Faubourg Saint-Germain, built c. 1711–13, engraving in Jacques-François Blondel, *Architecture Française*, I (Paris, 1752) [photo: after reprint ed., Paris, 1904].

Figure 16
Robert de Cotte, court elevation, Hôtel d'Estrées, rue de Grenelle, Fauborg Saint–Germain, built c. 1711–13, engraving in Jacques-François Blondel, *Architecture Française*, I (Paris, 1752) [photo: after reprint ed., Paris, 1904].

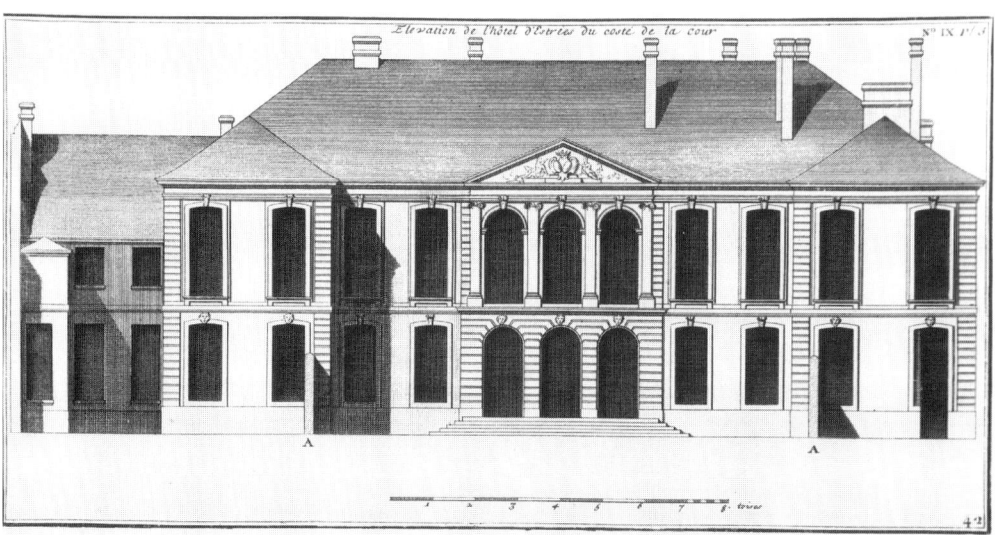

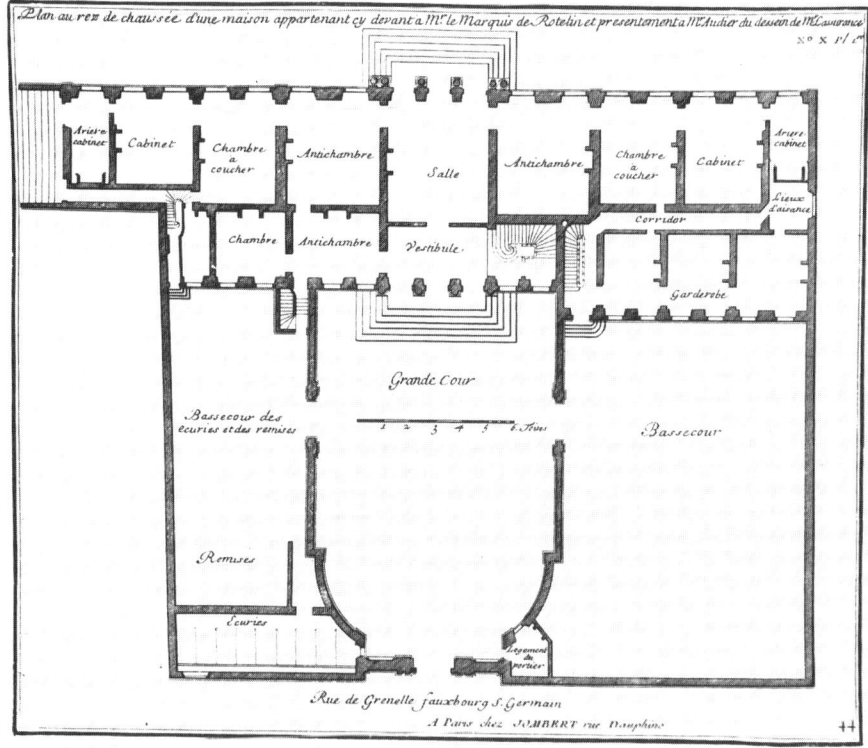

Figure 17

Lassurance, ground-floor plan, Hôtel de Rothelin, rue de Grenelle, Faubourg Saint-Germain, built c. 1703–4, engraving in Jacques-François Blondel, *Architecture Française*, I (Paris, 1752) [photo: after reprint ed., Paris, 1904].

Figure 18

Lassurance, court elevation, Hôtel de Rothelin, rue de Grenelle, Faubourg Saint–Germain, built c. 1703–4, engraving in Jacques-François Blondel, *Architecture Française*, I (Paris, 1752) [photo: after reprint ed., Paris, 1904].

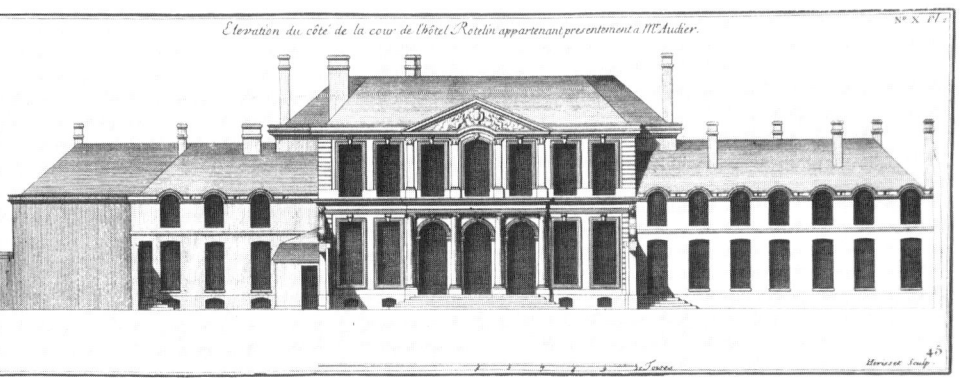

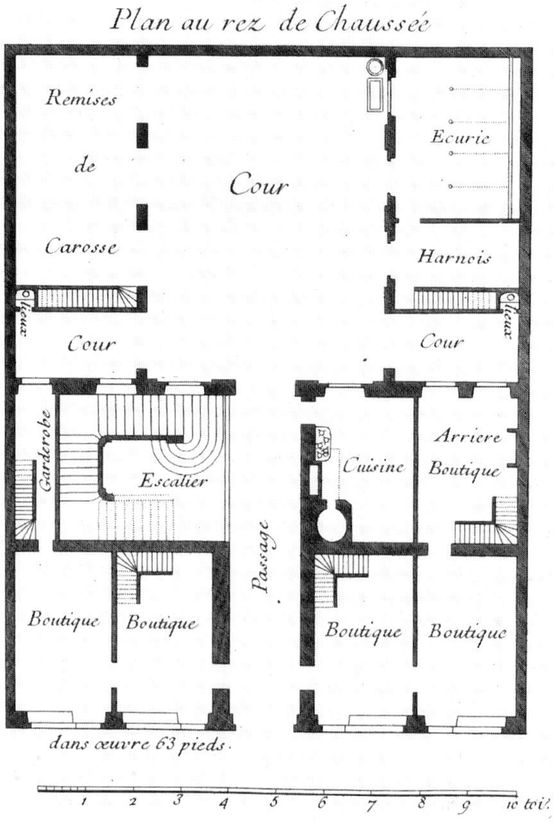

Plan au rez de Chaussée

Figure 19

Tiercelet, ground-floor plan, house of a bourgeois type, *Architecture moderne, ou l'art de bien bâtir pour toutes sortes de personnes* . . . I, pl. 49 (Paris, 1728), ("distribution 29") [photo: University of Florida, Gainesville].

Ceremonial apartments typically stretched along the garden in an *enfilade*, with doorways aligned to maximize display. At the end of the seventeenth century, the principal ceremonial apartments were usually reached by ascending the grand stair to the first floor. That was the case in Daviler's project, but there were also two such apartments on the ground floor, opening to either side of the central hall (*salle*) and perhaps intended for summer use (Fig. 10). The large *salle* functioned in the late seventeenth and early eighteenth centuries as an ample first waiting room for visitors and as a place where liveried servants might assemble awaiting instructions; it also served a variety of ceremonial uses.[42] Le Blond replaced *salles* with *salons* in the model plans published in 1710. The *salon* was no longer conceived as a waiting room, but instead as among the most distinguished rooms of the ceremonial suite; it absorbed many functions of the *salle*, and it served as a room in which to receive guests, where a table might be set up for dining on special occasions,

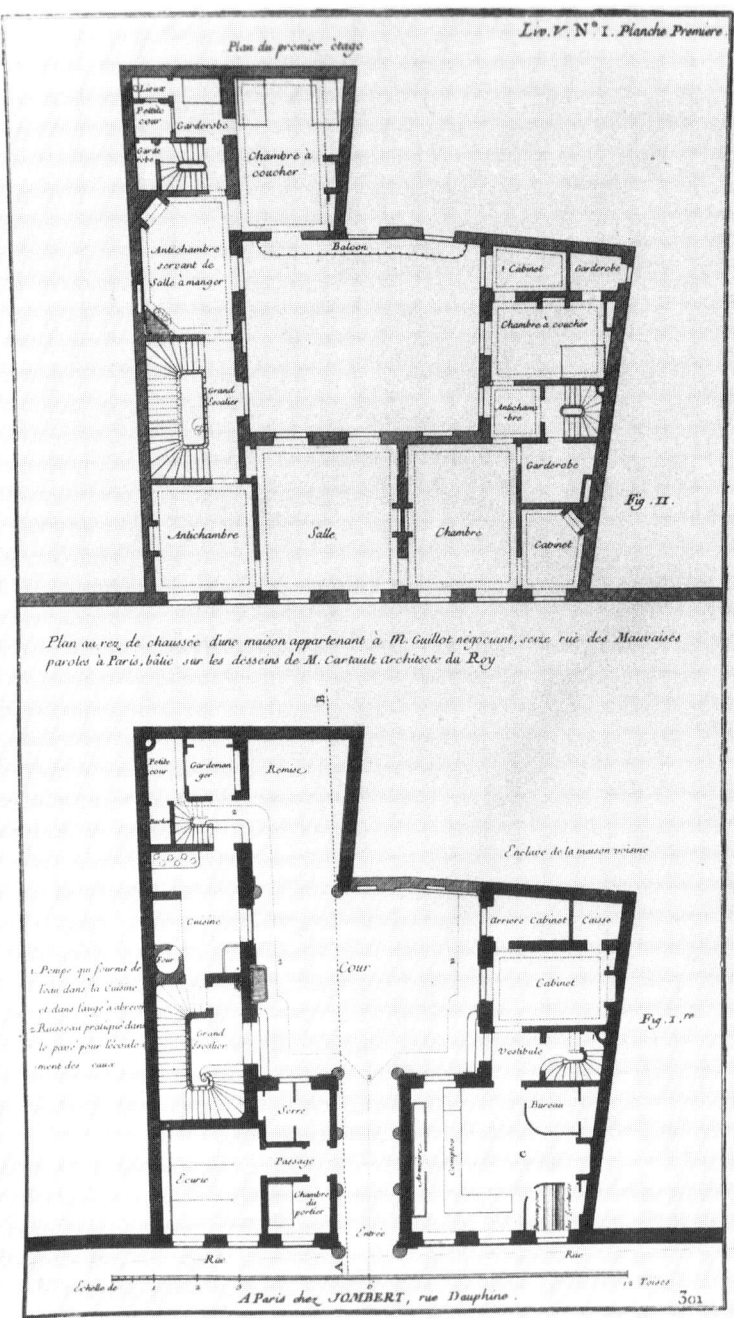

Figure 20

Jean-Sylvain Cartaud, ground- and first-floor plans, *maison* of *négociant* M. Guillot (with "*bureau pour le change*" and "*caisse*"), rue des Mauvaises paroles, Paris, built c. 1723–4, engraving in Jacques-François Blondel, *Architecture Française*, III (Paris, 1754) [photo: after reprint ed., Paris, 1904].

and as a space for concerts and games.[43] The *salle à manger* (dining room) was most often placed to the left of the entrance vestibule, off the main enfilade. But many elite dwellings at the turn of the century still lacked separate dining rooms, and mobile tables continued to be set up in anterooms.[44]

Here the grand stair opened to the right of the vestibule, providing an impressive prelude to the main ceremonial apartments on the first floor.[45] The first-floor plan of the *corps-de-logis* was nearly identical to that of the ground floor, but an important addition was the gallery, here stretching along six bays of the right wing (Figs. 11 and 13). The gallery had become the most distinguished representational space in a noble dwelling, in emulation of its prestige in royal palaces and in the houses of first ministers.[46] Attached to the apartment of the master of the house, it was considered a male space; early in the seventeenth century, decorative programs of galleries often celebrated lineage, carried through the male line.[47]

Another sign of a noble *hôtel* was the presence of a chapel. In Daviler's dwelling, a terrace above the range along the street connected the gallery with a *salon* that, he explained, might also function as a chapel (Fig. 11). Private chapels in urban residences derived, once again, from norms set in rural seigneuries, where *châteaux* might be located at some distance from local churches. In urban centers, private chapels were functionally unnecessary, imbuing them with even greater power as social signs. To have a chapel in a private residence was a privilege limited to the nobility, and it required application to the archbishop of Paris and the consecration of the site. In eighteenth-century urban dwellings, chapels usually opened off the apartments of women, traditionally considered "the devout sex."[48]

> These noblemen . . . even in the extreme poverty to which a great number find themselves reduced, obstinately . . . [regard] idleness as their handsomest privilege and as the most essential distinction between them and the bourgeoisie, with whom, if it were possible, they would like to have nothing in common.[49]

"Idleness" (*l'oisiveté*), as Genevan Béat-Louis de Muralt observed at the turn of the century, formed an essential component of self-definition among sword nobles. A group that had traditionally defined itself through military service to the Crown represented itself by the turn of the new century through its leisure. Nobles of the blood did not work, and leisure became not just a privilege, but a requirement, especially among courtiers; the Crown cooperated through laws of derogation that forbade most gainful employment to those of the second estate. Professionalization of the army had to some extent undermined the traditional calling of the *noblesse d'épée*; when they were not called upon for military service, the daily lives of sword noblemen focused on the reception of a variety of official visitors at their places of residence and on social activities within their circle.[50]

Official reception constituted "the 'business' of court life," Norbert Elias has argued; nobles of the blood received visitors "as representatives of their 'houses,' " using the ceremonial apartments of their city and country houses.[51] When there was more than one anteroom preceding the ceremonial apartment, lackeys dressed in recognizable household livery assembled in the first, often simply decorated, with the lackeys themselves serving as the chief element of display. Visitors of a stature lower than that of the proprietor waited for an audience in a first or second anteroom, according to rank; those of equal or higher status were led directly into one of the reception rooms.

Rank determined the locale of official reception, which might take place in the *grand cabinet*, where a nobleman often kept a desk, or in another of the ceremonial rooms. For special distinction, reception might occur in the most lavishly decorated room, the ceremonial bedchamber, distinguished by its canopied bed and the privileged zone around it. That zone of distinction might be raised above the rest of the room, and princes of the blood and dukes had the privilege of emulating the king by demarcating it with a balustrade, sometimes flanked by columns.[52] Antoine de Courtin's popular late seventeenth-century guidebook, *Nouveau Traité de la Civilité*, specified the sort of respectful behavior to be observed in the ceremonial bedchambers of the king, the queen, and persons of high rank.[53]

Noble men and women lacking the privilege of the balustrade often defined the zone around the bed by lining its walls with tapestries; during the eighteenth century, these were often (and increasingly) replaced by hangings of the same opulent fabric employed for the crown and draperies of the bed. The stature of the ceremonial bed in a noble dwelling derived from the dignity of the royal bed, which shared the status of the throne and was the site of the two most important daily rituals at court, the *lever* and the *coucher*.[54] In noble households, the master and mistress maintained separate state bedrooms; in each, the ceremonial bed was, in a sense, vestigial, since it was rarely slept in, but its representational importance persisted. By the turn of the century, men no longer received guests while reclining on the ceremonial bed, but noble women sometimes returned to that archaic practice, for added prestige.[55]

A related room was the *salle du dais*, and only princes or princesses of the blood and dukes or duchesses enjoyed the privilege of setting up a canopied dais decorated with the family arms. It was a mark of high distinction, even among the court nobility, and Daviler did not include one. Jean Courtonne placed a large *salle du dais* on axis with the entrance vestibule at the Hôtel de Matignon in the Faubourg Saint-Germain, which he designed in 1722 for the prince de Tingry, of the distinguished Montmorency clan.[56] A prelate or an ambassador might install such a room, the latter placing an image of the king whom he served under the canopy.[57] By the middle of the eighteenth century, these rooms were rarely used for ceremonial audiences, but they continued to appear for representational reasons.[58]

The first floor of the noble dwelling was ordinarily occupied by the mistress, according to Daviler, but in his model *hôtel*, both the proprietor and his wife had grand ceremonial apartments on that floor, opening to either side of the central *salle* (Fig. 11). Daviler did not delineate those who might inhabit the second floor, but typically they included children, relations, and the upper domestic staff. Noble proprietors lodged lower-ranking domestics in modest rooms in the mansard roofs or in *entresols* (mezzanines) between the floors; those at the bottom of the hierarchy were squeezed into rooms with multiple beds, and stable hands slept on mattresses or hammocks in the stables. A chambermaid usually slept next to the bedroom of her mistress, to be available during the night.

When Daviler's treatise was reprinted in 1710, the publisher considered it necessary to include a supplement to show "the new manner of planning."[59] For our purposes, Daviler's conventions are best examined in light of noble dwellings constructed during the first decade and a half of the eighteenth century. They formed a type, but were distinguished by the flexibility with which the formula could be adapted to contingencies of site, prior construction, households of different size, and a host of other factors.[60]

It is illuminating to examine two *hôtels* built within a decade of one another for members of the court (Figs. 14 to 18), the elite that established the domestic fashions emulated to varying extents by robe and financial clans. Both were sited along the rue de Grenelle in the Faubourg Saint-Germain. Pierre Cailleteau (called Lassurance), employed by Mansart in the Bâtiments du Roi, was perhaps the most active architect to the court nobility at the end of the reign of Louis XIV; in 1703–4, he designed one of these houses for Philippe d'Orléans, the marquis de Rothelin. De Cotte designed the second for the widowed duchesse d'Estrées in about 1711, for a parcel of 1,750 square *toises* (its garden extending to the rue de Varenne), more than double the size of the largest lots at the Place Vendôme.[61]

The massing of each departed from that of Davilier's enormous dwelling for a *grand seigneur*, which had clung to the party walls of an atypically regular rectangular lot. In their more modern plans, Lassurance and de Cotte broke up that monolithic massing. Each recessed the *hôtel* entry from the street, increasing the legibility of the noble portal and providing space for carriages to turn. In that recessed zone, carriages were screened by a porter, often labeled "Suisse" in plans of noble dwellings (Fig. 14). Swiss guards, stationed at royal palaces and public buildings, were also employed by the highest ranking families in the capital, but by the eighteenth century, *grands seigneurs* engaged them less for protection than as signs of stature.[62] Beyond each portal, visitors found themselves in a court with a curved end, which reversed and answered the concavity of the entry; this was a common means of masking asymmetries that might arise from the irregular shape of the lot or the angle of the street.[63] Both plans were still largely symmetrical, but most important was the perception of symmetry. A decade later, when massing was even freer with respect to the party walls of the site, Courtonne still found symmetry one of the principal beauties of architecture, but he argued that it was neither necessary nor desirable unless perceived by the visitor.[64]

The courtyard shape was conventional by the first decade of the eighteenth century. By that time, subsidiary courts had long been considered important features of noble dwellings. When there were two, which was considered preferable, one normally housed stables and the other typically the kitchens (although Lassurance and de Cotte devoted both to stables and carriages).[65] Lassurance placed the kitchens of the Hôtel de Rothelin in a subterranean story, as Daviler had done; in a more modern arrangement, de Cotte situated those rooms on the ground floor, off one of the secondary courts.[66] Soon it seemed essential to include one or two service entries from the street, screening the activities of servants from noble proprietors and their guests. Increasingly, court nobles wanted some service to be invisible in their dwellings. But service could also be an important element of display, for example, when liveried domestics served the principal dishes at meals. The importance of that spectacle is especially evident at the Hôtel d'Estrées, where servants would have transported food – prepared in the kitchen, along one of the party walls – beneath the grand stair and through two entry vestibules to the dining room. De Cotte devoted about a third of the *corps-de-logis* to an ensemble of vestibules and the grand stair, revealing their importance as noble signs.

Both dwellings were lower in height than Daviler's *hôtel*, each rising two stories plus a mansard roof, dimensions that remained the norm for much of the century. The articulation of facades during the early years of the eighteenth century tended to be simpler than Daviler's ideal with its giant pilaster order. At the Hôtel de Rothelin, Lassurance limited embellishment of the court facade to simple channeled rustication demarcating a central pavilion and a two-story frontispiece at the entrance, with a single-story Ionic order on the ground floor and a Corinthian pilaster order above; a pediment bore the family's coat of arms. Such armorial emblems were traditionally associated with the nobility, having been first employed on the battlefield.[67] De Cotte's design for a widowed duchess was even simpler, with just a single-story pilaster order applied to the central bays on the first floor.

These noble dwellings were, in fact, closer to each other in type than many variations built during the first decades of the eighteenth century. Still, there were noteworthy differences between them. At the Hôtel de Rothelin, two ample and virtually identical ground-floor apartments (presumably for the master and mistress of the house) diverged from the central axis. De Cotte retained the central axis, but dispensed with identical ground-floor apartments that would not have served the needs of his client, who was a widow with a reduced household; he provided, nonetheless, a large ceremonial apartment on the first floor (Fig. 15). The Hôtel d'Estrées was thus not entirely "typical," but its prominent female patron must have been far from unique during this period when France was almost constantly at war; many *hôtels* would have been shaped by women rather than men of court – by widows and noble women whose husbands were at military fronts.

The robe nobility typically built houses of a similar type, although it was considered appropriate for the dwellings of all but the highest robe to be less

28

grand than those of their court counterparts. There were two principal kinds of high robe offices: those directly in the service of the Crown (with royal ministers and the Chancellor of France at the summit) and magistrates in the sovereign courts (at their apex, the *présidents* of Parlement of Paris).[68] Since the mid-seventeenth century, Louis XIV had selected his ministers not from the oldest and most powerful military families, but among sons of newly ennobled families that had been engaged in trade or finance during the sixteenth or even seventeenth century.[69] At the turn of the eighteenth century, most magistrates in the Parlement of Paris had similar backgrounds.[70] The dignity attached to robe offices, coupled with a tendency to intermarry, promoted a corporate identity (especially among magistrates).[71]

Ministers built magnificently, but their dwellings, and those of magistrates, differed functionally and, to some extent, representationally from those of the *noblesse d'épée*. Most importantly, the robe *worked* at official tasks, even if venality resulted in many less-than-dedicated officeholders, but their efforts were considered service.[72] Official duties required certain sorts of spaces, and as rooms became more specialized, one of these would be called an audience hall (*salle d'audience*); by the fifties, the term referred to a room that, "in the house of a Minister or Magistrate, serves to receive persons from outside who come to present petitions, where he listens to their grievances and learns of disputes which emerge in families and among Citizens."[73] Theoretically, the decor of public rooms in the residences of ministers differed from comparable rooms among courtiers, but when Blondel warned, "it is not appropriate to decorate an apartment destined for the residence of a prelate, or for that of a Minister, as that of a *personne du monde*," he seems to have been railing against prevailing practice.[74] In some robe dwellings, there was a room called a "*bureau*" (or "*les bureaux*"), which should not be confused with *bureaux* where clerks kept accounts in the houses of financiers; in robe dwellings, *bureaux* tended to be more grandly furnished and used for official business.[75]

Finally, a feature distinguishing high-robe dwellings was often an unusually ample library; court nobles, too, sometimes assembled large and impressively installed collections of books, but considerable libraries were more often associated with magistrates and high-ranking clerics. Court noblemen aspired to participate with wit and polish in polite society, but rarely did they seek erudition. Ministers, magistrates, and prelates, on the other hand, were expected to be learned.[76]

Values traditionally considered exemplary among the robe appear in reminiscences of his father by a Place Vendôme resident, Henri-François d'Aguesseau, the Chancellor of France. His father had served as a royal intendant, then, from 1683 until the death of Louis XIV, as a *conseiller d'État*. "He always remembered that he was born to be a magistrate," the Chancellor recalled. "His house, open to everyone, but much more for official business than for pleasure, presented to all who approached the image of the most respectable magistracy. No luxury, no ostentation offended the eyes of even the most modest; honorable without being magnificent, it was grand because of he who lived there. . . . [He maintained] a table . . . sufficient without being sumptuous, expressing, like all the rest, his natural moderation. . . ."[77] More-over, "the application with which he worked was almost incredible."[78] And within their household, the future Chancellor's mother – who shared with her husband intellect, charity, and piety – was "more dominant . . . born to gov-ern."[79] Both were devoted to family life and the education of their children.

Many of the qualities d'Aguesseau presented – including thrift and the in-terest taken by the mistress in running the household – were, in fact, widely considered bourgeois. Significantly, it was common to refer to the dwellings of all but the highest robe as *maisons* (the term for bourgeois houses) and not *hôtels*.[80] Theoretically, houses of financiers were, properly, more unassuming than robe dwellings. The reality among both groups was quite different. Under Louis XIII and Louis XIV, royal ministers, despite some relatively new claims to nobility, maintained palatial dwellings; houses of leading judicial clans tended to be akin to those of court families.

The wealthiest financial families emulated not the traditional (and rapidly disappearing) modesty of magistrates, but the magnificence of court nobles and the highest robe. Leading financiers had done so for more than a century, building houses of the noble type, with a *corps-de-logis* that withdrew from the street.[81] In fact, *most* prominent men of finance during the seventeenth and eighteenth centuries built such dwellings, including many in the vicinity of the Place Vendôme. The question that arises at the turn of the eighteenth century is why a number of financiers were willing to forego the noble type in favor of residence at the new royal square – in a context that made the realization of that type almost impossible to achieve.

Social Representation at the Place Vendôme

> It remains for me to tell you in brief what I mean by *convenance* to the estate of persons . . . [it is] the science of putting nothing in a building which might be above the dignity or condition of the Master. . . . [82]

Financiers amassed great wealth, bought ennobling titles and large country estates, but they were still considered bourgeois by those above and below them in the social hierarchy. Residence in the new Faubourg Saint-Germain was probably attractive to many, but convenience in transacting business, benefits attached to proximity to centers of power, and social pressures kept financiers, with a few exceptions, from penetrating that noble quarter. The Place Vendôme, situated just beyond the locale financiers had already claimed, allowed the most socially ambitious among them to appropriate the represen-tational grandeur of the royal square.

Emulation of the nobility entailed some level of "conspicuous consump-tion," of living nobly, but there may have been a variety of motives for such imitation.[83] For many financiers, it was apparently understood as an essential element in their quest for acceptance as noblemen, but it also made excellent business sense. As the center of a credit network, the financier's ability to attract investments meant the need to inspire confidence in his personal wealth. Whatever seigneuries he purchased, the center of his business and social worlds was Paris. The setting provided by Mansart at the Place Vendôme was representationally far nobler than any financier would have dared to build for himself at the turn of the eighteenth century.

In what sense were the facades representationally noble? The notion arose that the use of the orders to embellish facades was appropriate only for noble dwellings. Architectural theorists increasingly sought to codify rules offering a hierarchical and carefully calibrated system for the decoration of domestic facades, intended to make legible to all the estate and rank of the proprietor. Jacques-François Blondel, professor at the Academy of Architecture, later offered this theory in its most proscriptive form: "From the diversity of ranks and the dignity of the subjects of the Prince, must necessarily emerge the different characters that it is appropriate to give each of these edifices," he declared. "The rank of the proprietor is, thus, the source from which the Architect must derive the genre of his decoration." That hierarchy of representation in the embellishment of facades had a specific social goal. It was meant to "offer to the eyes of foreigners and citizens the image of the different orders of a civilized State (*État policé*)."[84]

The Place Vendôme bore a giant Corinthian order, making its facades among the noblest that adorned dwellings, particularly in the years around 1700, when house facades became simpler and a colossal order was almost never employed. Moreover, it was a *place royale*, and it derived dignity from its association with the Crown. But residence at the square meant adopting a high profile in the capital, which left financial families vulnerable – and not only to ridicule.[85]

The very nature of communal living at the square was an atypical mode in France, one encumbered with contradictory signs of social status. It was not, however, without precedent as a manner of living among Parisian elites. The Place Royale had been built almost a century earlier (Fig. 3), and by 1700, its residents were predominantly of robe families, several quite high-ranking, joined by some prominent court nobles.[86] By the time the Place Vendôme was reconceived, the Place des Victoires had been recently completed; there, behind facades articulated with a giant order (making them representationally nobler than those of the Place Royale), financiers and bankers occupied smaller houses built on very restricted sites (Figs. 4 and 21). Dwellings at each of those squares tended to be close in type to those along major thoroughfares and along the quais of the Seine – where the principal living quarters were often placed along the street.[87] At each royal square, relations between public and private domains were more complex and ambiguous than they were in the Faubourg Saint-Germain. Even the "noble" setting of a royal square was subject to multiple readings, since distinction was so powerful an indicator of status among the court nobility, the group that tended to define the values other elites emulated.[88]

At each *place royale*, the public space of the square functioned in part as a

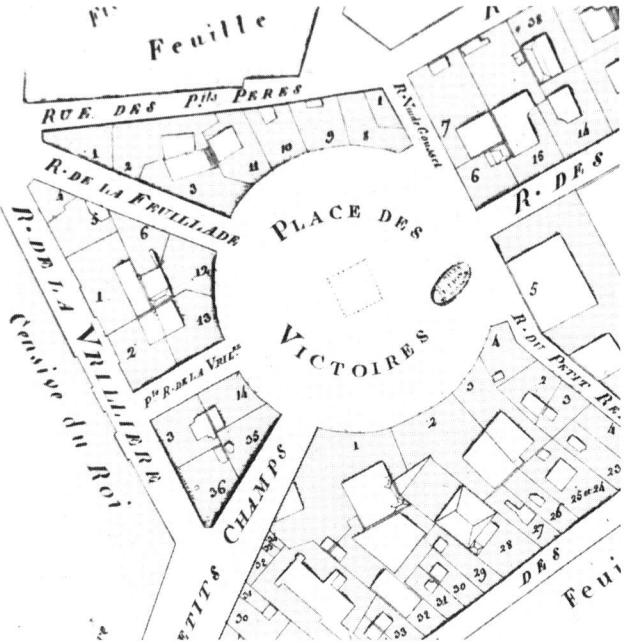

Figure 21

Place des Victoires, *Atlas de la censive de l'archevêché dans Paris*, detail, *feuille* 22 (Paris, 1786); *no. 1 = no. 3 today* (Maison Crozat); *no. 2 = no. 5 today* (Hôtel de Bauyn, leased by Bernard); *no. 3 = no. 7 today* (Hénault, proprietor); *no. 4 = no. 9 today* (Hénault, proprietor); *no. 8 = no. 12 today* (Maison Cornette); *no. 9 = no. 10 today* (Maison Rolland); *no. 10 = no. 8 today* (Maison Pellé); *no. 11 = no. 6 today* (leased by Crozat, 1690); *no. 12 = no. 4 today* (Maison de Monchy); *no. 14 = no. 1 Place des Victoires today* (Maison Edme-Firmin Pellé); *no. 35 rue Croix-des Petits Champs = no. 1 bis Place des Victoires today* (Maison Le Gras) [photo: after reprint ed., Paris, 1906].

kind of forecourt to the private residences, compounding the ambiguities between public and private realms that typified all eighteenth-century dwellings. At the Place des Victoires and Place Vendôme, financial dwellings accommodated a wide range of callers. During the day, most of those traversing the squares were paying official or social visits, transacting business, or making deliveries. In the evenings, residents reclaimed these public spaces and were joined by neighbors from adjoining streets for strolls around the squares.[89] Occasionally, special events brought a more diverse cross-section of Paris into these royal squares, and at the Place Vendôme, those occasions included periodic large-scale military reviews, festivities connected with celebrations of royal marriages, and, later in the century, the Foire Sainte-Ovide.[90]

Why were financial families attracted to the Place Vendôme at a time when nobles of the sword and robe were far less eager to reside there? Certainly, for financiers at the Place Vendôme, as well as for financiers and bankers at the Place des Victoires, proximity made for ease in transacting business.[91] But financiers could have, as easily, built houses of the noble type on nearby streets where land was far less costly – and many did. The dignity of the setting was, presumably, the principal lure for leading financial clans, who may have been less troubled than their aristocratic counterparts by representational ambiguities and spatial constraints. That explanation may not be sufficient, however, in accounting for the almost complete absence, during the first decade and a half of the new century, of court nobles, who were busy building new *hôtels* in the Faubourg Saint-Germain (and, a bit later, in the Faubourg Saint-Honoré); also missing were magistrates, who often preferred to remain in the older noble quarter of the Marais, although some moved to the more fashionable faubourgs.[92] A more compelling answer must consider the relations of the three principal Parisian elites with the Crown. Two of them had seen their power significantly eroded during the reign of Louis XIV. The Crown had subdued magistrates in the Parlement of Paris, where the Fronde began, revoking their power of remonstrance. Similarly, the role of leading court families had diminished as that of "bourgeois" ministers grew. During Louis's lifetime, both groups were conspicuously absent from the square that bore the king's name, presided over by his equestrian statue.

Financiers who inhabited the Place de Louis-le-Grand, however, had a very different relationship with the Crown. It was the Crown that offered them ennoblement during their own lifetimes and conferred the distinction that came from proximity to power. The plethora of royal symbols may well have seemed less signs of domination than emblems of status, pointing to the source of their prestige. The stature of the financiers grew at the expense of the other elites: They married their daughters to sons of a court nobility that Louis XIV had helped to impoverish; they bought the seigneuries that the *noblesse d'épée* could no longer afford to maintain; and they purchased for themselves and their sons the ennobling offices created to finance Louis's wars. The colossal equestrian statue dominating the square served, moreover, as a kind of permanent reenactment of the royal entry ceremony; it was a ritual that had traditionally functioned, one scholar has argued, as a kind of "pact between the monarch and the urban bourgeoisie, who grew in parallel to the detriment of the feudal seigneurs and peasants."[93] Financiers, who emerged from that bourgeoisie, benefited handsomely from this "pact" with the king.

The nobility of the setting clearly appealed to financiers. They did not, however, rush to build private houses at the Place de Louis-le-Grand until the Crown opened its purse and perhaps flexed its political muscle to make the venture a success. The king's presence, embodied principally in the centrally placed equestrian statue, suggests a "domesticating" of residents in a manner analogous to the Louis XIV's "domestication" of the highest nobility at Versailles. The statue originally embodied the pivotal role of the king in France's military, religious, and cultural "conquests," and its quality of authoritarian power, albeit diluted, still dominated the reconceived square. Residents lived in the shadow of the colossal statue, its central position suggesting the centrality of the king's power. It carried a sense of "surveillance," but if financiers found the metaphorical gaze of the king oppressive, the dignity of the royal square and the political benefits of residence outweighed their unease, at least in several prominent cases. The nobility of the setting did not, however, resolve the many representational and typological dilemmas posed by the goal of building aristocratic types of residences on parcels extending behind the noble facades.

Social Representation and Gendered Realms

> The city has sold the parcels to several rich individuals, for whom blind,
> unjust and bizarre fortune has, during these last years of war, procured the
> faculties to lodge themselves as *grands seigneurs* and men of importance.[1]

The paradox of residence at the Place Vendôme was that the very facades
that lent it such dignity also virtually excluded dwellings of the ideal noble
type. The aristocratic mode of living in the city, with the principal living
quarters set between court and garden, was almost impossible to achieve. At
the Place Vendôme, Mansart's noble facades dictated that there be three stories plus a mansard along the public realm, fundamentally conflicting with the
noble ideal. Living along the public realm was considered a bourgeois mode,
although that association was tempered in certain contexts – along some major streets and at the royal squares, especially the Place Royale. Still, the
houses of the Place Vendôme were inherently ambiguous in the social signs
they incorporated. Representationally noble facades were wed to houses of a
fundamentally bourgeois type.

Other essential features of the noble *hôtel* were difficult to achieve. Space
available for stables and carriage stalls was typically quite modest, and rarely
were parcels ample enough to accommodate more than small gardens. Finally,
certain refinements of aristocratic planning, such as subsidiary courts for stables and kitchens, were nearly impossible to incorporate.

During the first decade, two of the most powerful financiers in France established residence at the square. Both were closely associated with the Controller General of Finance Pontchartrain, who had played a key role in the
survival of the Place Vendôme, and both were among the financiers his successor Chamillart would rely upon most heavily. Installing their families in two
of the largest dwellings, both expanded their dynastic households, absorbing
contiguous parcels in the process. They were Paul Poisson de Bourvalais and
Antoine Crozat.

The Maison de La Vieuxville-Bourvalais (No. 13)

Shortly after the inauguration of the statue, Luillier's son-in-law, Joseph Guillaume de La Vieuxville, *maître des requêtes* and *secrétaire des commande-*

ments of the duchesse de Bourgogne, purchased the first parcel.[2] It extended behind eight bays, including the grand central pavilion of the west range (Figs. 6 and 8). La Vieuxville chose as his architect the supervisor of construction at the new square, Robert de Cotte.[3]

La Vieuxville died suddenly five months after building began, and Luillier, who probably directed the purchase of the parcel and the selection of the architect, oversaw the completion of the house.[4] He apparently installed his daughter and her children there in 1702, when the dwelling was not yet complete.[5] In 1704, Luillier arranged marriages for his two granddaughters, allying both with clans involved in general tax farming; on the same day as the second marriage, he purchased lifetime use of the dwelling from La Vieuxville's heirs.[6] Perhaps unwilling to tie up funds during the War of the Spanish Succession, Luillier sold the large house to the most active and prominent financier at the end of Louis's reign – Paul Poisson de Bourvalais.[7]

In designing the first residence of the square, de Cotte utilized a T-shaped massing akin in overall disposition to a dwelling prepared for a different site by his brother-in-law and mentor Hardouin-Mansart (Fig. 22). In Mansart's plan, an elongated *corps-de-logis* between court and garden stretched from party wall to party wall; a perpendicular range separated a court of honor from the stables. The type was not new, but it was a bit unusual, and more than one member of their extended clan experimented with it at the turn of the eighteenth century. In 1704, Jacques V Gabriel adopted the disposition in a house for a noble widow in the Faubourg Saint-Germain, the Maison de Varangeville (Fig. 23). There, on a relatively narrow site, Gabriel used it to provide an impressive *enfilade* along the garden and a secondary court. Contemporaries called both of these houses *maisons*, not *hôtels*, implying a certain modesty (despite Mme de Varangeville's rank).

De Cotte adapted the type to the square. The principal *enfilade* of ceremonial rooms – along the garden in Mansart's dwelling – were here placed along the square, but the type was so attractive because it allowed de Cotte to introduce a second important suite of rooms between court and garden (Fig. 9). Such a range was a key sign of a noble dwelling, but it was a feature initially lacking in all except the largest *hôtels* at the Place Royale (and often introduced there in later renovations). The type allowed de Cotte to provide both a court of honor and a smaller service court, and he even adopted details of planning akin to Mansart's model, including placement of a stair at the intersection of the wings. In 1706, Luillier lived in this house with his wife Jeanne Boussingault, their daughter Marie, and eldest grandson Alexandre, the latter occupying the important first-floor suite along the terrace and garden.[8]

The earliest extant plans are those prepared by Bullet de Chamblain in 1708–9 for Poisson de Bourvalais, who enlarged the house (Figs. 24 and 25).[9] Expansive stables and carriage stalls were prime features of noble dwellings, and among Chamblain's principal modifications was more ample provision in

36

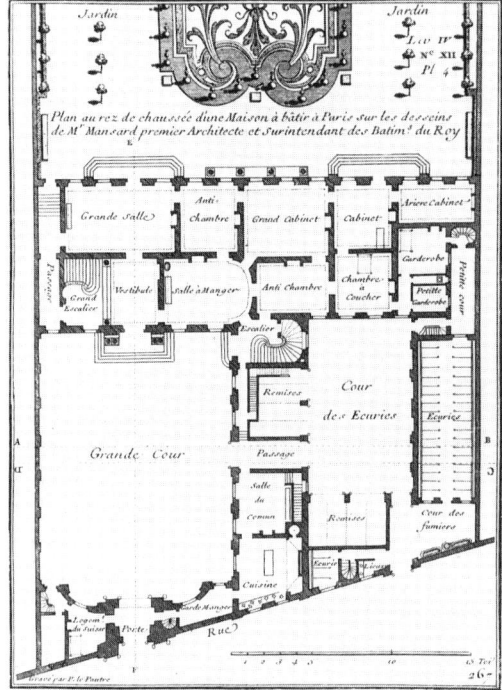

Figure 22
Jules Hardouin-Mansart, ground-floor plan, "Maison à bâtir à Paris," c. 1700, engraving in Jacques-François Blondel, *Architecture Française*, II (Paris: 1752) [photo: after reprint ed., Paris, 1904].

that realm. De Cotte probably had placed the stables of the original house in spaces along the square that Chamblain labeled *bureaux*. It may seem curious that architects placed stables and kitchens along the public space of the square (a location now valued as a prime commercial site), but it was the norm among the early dwellings. In adapting the noble type to the square, most architects placed the most mundane functions on the ground floor along the public realm. That devaluation was a sign of a noble dwelling, but so were extensive stables; in late 1708, when Bourvalais's nephew purchased the adjoining three-bay lot (acting for his uncle), Chamblain designed a small house along the square and Bourvalais appropriated the space behind it for stables.

Entry to a dwelling at the square was necessarily different from the entrance to a noble *hôtel*. It was more compressed, lacking passage through a grand portal adorned with the family arms. In compensation, the square served as a kind of forecourt, from which visitors entered a passage screened by a porter (not the Swiss guard a real *grand seigneur* might employ); his room was within the envelope of the house itself, not set at a remove across the court.

At the Maison Bourvalais, visitors disembarked in the main court, but

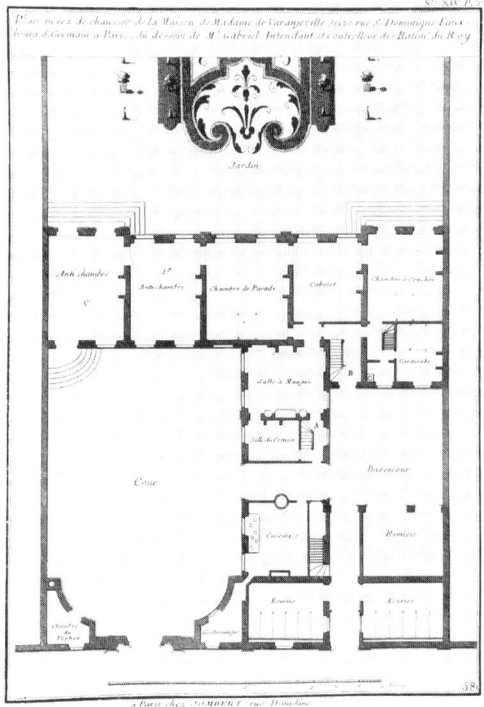

Figure 23
Jacques V. Gabriel, ground-floor plan, Maison de Madame de Varangeville, rue Saint-Dominique, Faubourg Saint-Germain, 1704, engraving in Jacques-François Blondel, *Architecture Française*, I (Paris: 1752) [photo: after reprint ed., Paris, 1904].

coachmen and carriages then traversed a passage to the stables of the subsidiary court. In the wing, just beyond the passage connecting the courts, de Cotte placed the main entrance to the house, opening onto a grand stair hall that extended the full width of that range; Brice found it "one of the most beautiful and best imagined that we have at the present time."[10] To the rear of the stair, on both the ground and first floors, were important L-shaped apartments. The axes of each suite intersected in large light-filled *grand cabinets*, enjoying garden views along two walls, and the one on the ground floor had a French door opening directly onto the terrace. Bourvalais extended his garden in late 1708 and had a small pavilion with a *salon*, an ice-storing facility (*glacière*) and a reservoir built along its new western edge – a kind of miniature "Trianon."[11]

The grand stair extended only to the first floor, where two ceremonial apartments overlooked the Place Vendôme and a third faced the garden; private apartments were lit along the courts. Just off the landing of the stair, one

38

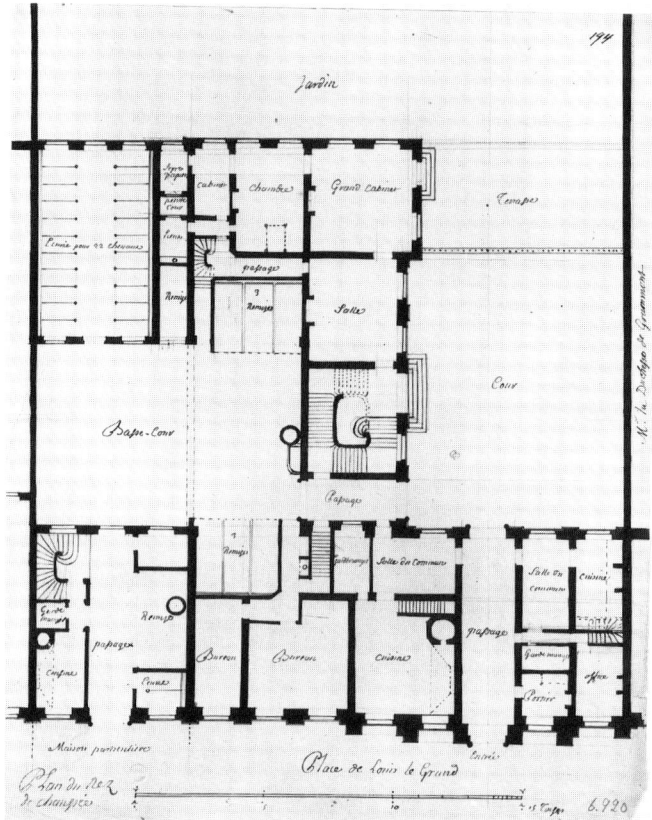

Figure 24

Jean-Baptiste Bullet de Chamblain, ground-floor plan, Maison Bourvalais, nos. 11–13 Place Vendôme, 1709; extension and modification of Maison de La Vieuxville (no. 13), Robert de Cotte, 1699 [photo: Nationalmuseum, Stockholm, THC 6920].

anteroom straddled the intersection of the wing with the range along the square, and a second (doubling as a *salle à manger*, according to Chamblain's plan) preceded the important suite along the garden.

Contemporaries were impressed. According to Brice, "although it was already sufficient to lodge a very important nobleman (*très grand seigneur*), the new master further augmented it in 1709 with three windows along the square, so that it has presently eleven facade windows, which appears in almost no other bourgeois house (*maison particulière*) in this great city. The rich furnishings and the magnificent fittings appear above all in the apartment of Marie-Suzanne Guihou, his wife."[12] Her suite included the ceremonial "*chambre parée*" and *cabinet* on the first floor along the square; the large chamber with two beds may have accommodated one of her nephews and his wife.

One crucial feature distinguished this and other financial houses from their noblest counterparts. This was the presence of *bureaux*. The term allerts us that houses of financiers were also places of work. The ground-floor plan (Fig.

Social Representation and Gendered Realms

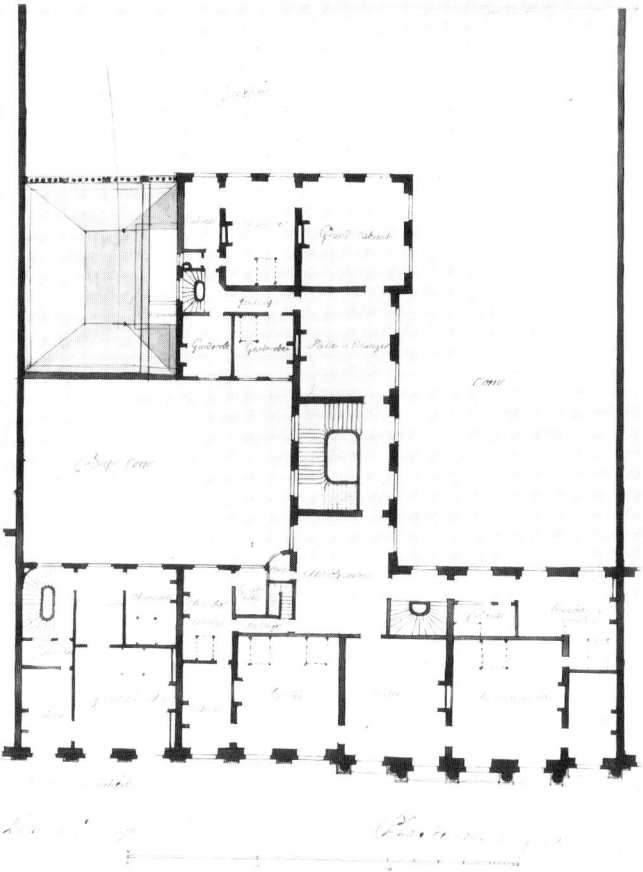

Figure 25
Jean-Baptiste Bullet de Chamblain, first-floor plan, Maison Bourvalais, nos. 11–13 Place Vendôme, 1709; extension and modification of Maison de La Vieuxville (no. 13), Robert de Cotte,
1699 [photo: Nationalmuseum, Stockholm, THC 6351].

24) reveals Bourvalais's *bureaux* to be spartan spaces without fireplaces, and
inventories confirm the modesty with which such rooms were furnished. It
was here clerks kept accounts and transacted daily business, so they had to be
easily accessible, but architects tried to make them "invisible" to important
callers. Chamblain's solution, once the stables had been removed to the adjacent parcel, was to install them on the ground floor along the square, entered
from a passage between the two courts. That locale was akin to one often
employed in financial dwellings, but less common among the early houses of
the Place Vendôme or those of the Place des Victoires (completed in the
1690s). Early in the century, at both squares, *bureaux* were most often situated in the *entresol* between the ground and first floors in the range along the
square (Fig. 26), a placement that may have had its roots in Italian banking
customs.[13]

Figure 26
Place Vendôme, west range nos. 9–13 (partial views of nos. 7 and 15) [photo: author].

Bourvalais himself used the ground-floor apartment along the garden for daily reception. It was easily accessible from the main stair hall, as well as from *bureaux* where assistants worked. According to a highly polemical pamphlet of 1716, this *grand cabinet* was stuffed (beyond capacity, it would seem) with expensive objects – paintings by Old Masters, including Raphael and Rubens; chests and furnishings of Chinese and Japanese lacquer; alabaster and jasper vases; rare porcelain; small bronzes; and cases of engraved stones.[14] An interpretation was offered of a series of paintings supposedly on view there, each conveniently symbolizing a facet of Bourvalais's contemptible character or his wife's humble origins.[15]

The list of riches should not be taken literally, but the evocation of Bourvalais's treasures is confirmed, to an extent, by Brice's account of Bourvalais's house on the rue des Petits-Champs, shortly before he moved to the Place Vendôme. According to Brice, Bourvalais became an art collector overnight, purchasing the paintings of general tax farmer Louis Bauyn de Cormery; residing at the Place des Victoires at the end of his life, Bauyn had owned over a hundred works, including many Old Master paintings.[16] Among the opulent furnishings were marquetry pieces by Boulle *père*, whose clients included the royal family, court nobles, ministers, and leading men of finance; figuring among them were Bourvalais and his neighbor Le Bas de Montargis (no. 7).[17]

If contemporaries frequently reiterated the stereotype of lackey turned financier, they applied it most harshly to Bourvalais, a barometer of social resentment.[18] In fact, Bourvalais had worked with the leading financier Jean Thévenin the Elder not as his lackey but as his principal financial assistant. When Bourvalais applied to the Crown to purchase the post of *secrétaire du roi* in

1695, Thévenin appeared among the witnesses to his character, testifying that he came "from a good family, son and grandson of . . . royal notaries at La-val" and was related to important families in Laval, Vitré, and Angers.[19] Through Thévenin, Bourvalais met Pontchartrain, and later became his trusted counselor.

In December 1688, Bourvalais had made a very unusual marriage among leading financiers of his generation. According to contemporaries, Marie-Suzanne de Guihou had been the chambermaid of Mme de Pontchartrain's friend, the marquise de Sourches (some said of Mme de Pontchartrain herself).[20] Legal challenges to the settling of Bourvalais's estate seem to confirm Mme Bourvalais's modest lineage.[21] Mme de Pontchartrain, known for her charity, often took particular interest in arranging marriages for young women without resources.[22] Marie-Suzanne de Guihou's extremely modest dowry – just 16,000 *livres* – and the arrangement in which property was not held commonly, give further credence to these accounts.[23]

Normally, when financiers accepted small dowries, the attraction was the nobility of their wives – obviously not the case here. Pontchartrain, of course, had the power to reward Bourvalais many times over through participation in extraordinary finance. During the wars between 1688 and 1714, Bourvalais was more active in extraordinary finance than any of other financier.

The modesty of her background left Mme Bourvalais subject to particularly savage attacks by those enraged by her husband's fortune. One pamphleteer called her a peasant, "very ugly but a schemer (*intriguante*)"; another cast her as "an ape" (*une guenuche*) so miserly she became enraged when servants did not "collect all the ends of candles and . . . separate egg yolks into two for adding to the soup the next day."[24] Since financial wives were typically casti-gated for unrestrained opulence, this critique seems rather ironic. It was in-tended, of course, to reveal the baseness of her pedigree.

Whatever were the bonds in this childless marriage, Bourvalais sponsored his wife's relations on a remarkable scale. By 1703, he had brought her brother Charles Guihou de Marcois and at least three of five nephews (Guihou de Boislarcher, Guihou de Montlevaux, and François de Chendret) into the world of arms provision and extraordinary finance. Nephew Guihou de Brus-lon purchased the adjoining three-bay parcel (no. 11) in 1708, but his aunt paid for the house built on it; a fifth nephew, Guihou de Villamur, resided with them until about 1712.[25] In 1714, Mme Bourvalais's niece, who had recently become the comtesse de Simiane, acquired the smaller dwelling at no. 11 with funds from the dowry provided by her aunt, but it is not clear whether she ever lived there.[26] In that house, royal painter Bon Boullongne seems to have resided (probably as a tenant, but perhaps as part of this extended house-hold), from 1712 until his death in 1717.[27]

There would be other instances at the Place Vendôme when childless cou-ples brought nephews into their households and sponsored them, but never again a financial dynasty as extensive as the one built by Bourvalais. In addi-tion to his wife's relations, some financial assistants also lived in Bourvalais's house.[28] His *commis* Pierre Duquesnoy might have had a bedroom or small suite there, too; for a few years before 1716, Duquesnoy leased his own dwelling at the square, "one of the most commodious houses," Brice remarked (without indicating which one it was), "in which all glitters with gold and large mirrors, and where the furnishings have all the richness and magnificence that could be desired in the palaces of the greatest princes."[29]

De Cotte's design had solved the primary dilemma in adapting the aristocratic type to the square – the introduction of a range between court and garden; it also provided a subsidiary court, removing servants from proprietors and their guests. Mansart would experiment with the same type in an unrealized design for the contiguous parcel (nos. 9 to 11), but de Cotte's disposition remained unique. In a design conceived a few months later, Bullet offered a solution that also proved exceptional – for a six-bay parcel owned by the powerful financier Antoine Crozat.

The Maison Crozat (No. 17)

Antoine Crozat had been born in Toulouse in 1655 and had held the major financial post of Receiver General for Bordeaux since 1689. Popular gossip claimed, once again, the humblest of origins – in Crozat's case as "lackey" of the financier Pierre-Louis Reich de Pennautier. This was more outrageous in Crozat's case than it had been for Bourvalais, since Crozat's father had been a wealthy banker and *capitoul* in Toulouse, a title that conferred nobility.[30] The Crozat brothers had, indeed, worked with Pennautier, but as his chief financial assistants. When they came to Paris, they brought considerable financial resources and a credit network, and they worked together closely, in a manner similar to the Thévenin brothers and the Pâris frères.

Antoine Crozat arrived in Paris in 1684, and, with his brother Pierre, he lived for a period in Pennautier's house.[31] A key event shaping his career was his marriage in 1690 to Marie-Marguerite Legendre. Her father François Legendre, a leading general tax farmer, munitions dealer, and *capitoul*, was a converted Protestant (prompting Challes's remark that he had "no more religion than a dog"), but members of his wife's family emigrated and formed an important base in Amsterdam.[32] Crozat's marriage significantly extended his web of contacts in banking, finance, and colonial trade. Such alliances were typical of the first generation at the Place Vendôme, providing access to the vast resources that secured familial advances.[33] Crozat would become a leading figure in royal finance.

Crozat's house, designed in early 1700, occupied a site with five bays along the west range plus a sixth in the northwest corner. Bullet grappled with the challenge of adapting the noble type in a manner akin to that of de Cotte (Figs. 9, 27 to 29). He began with the standard aristocratic type, then rotated it 180 degrees, so that living quarters were set along the public realm and two wings extended back for stables and carriages, just as they might have extended toward the street in a noble dwelling (Fig. 14). Bullet

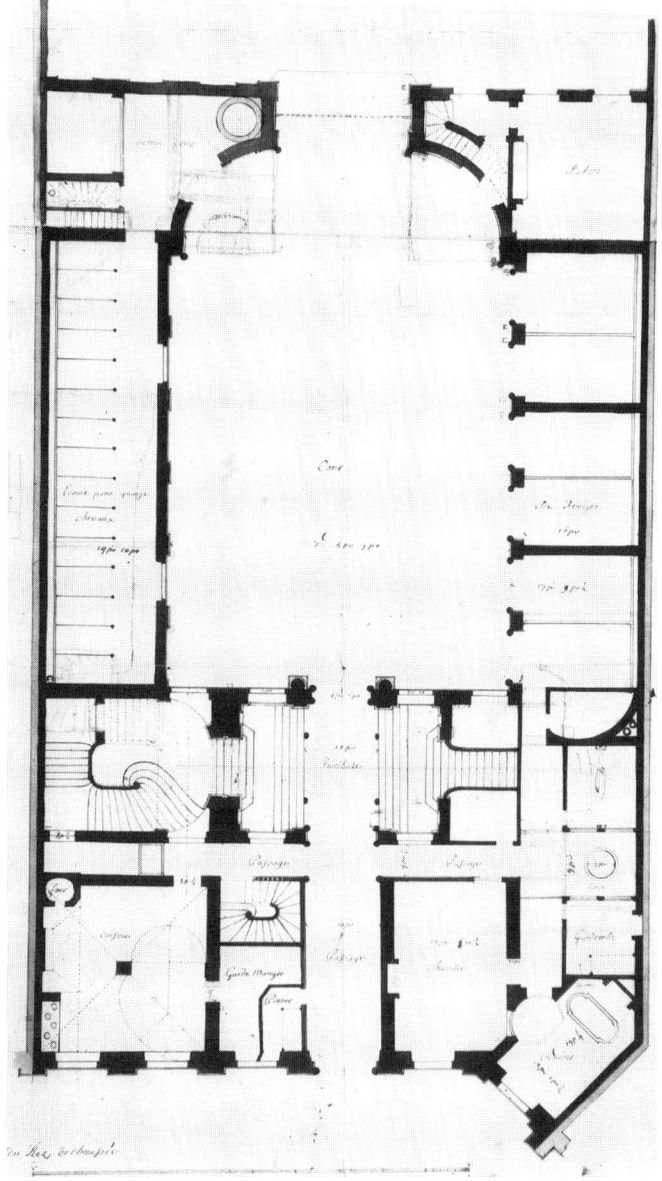

Figure 27
Pierre Bullet (drawing by Chamblain) ground-floor plan, Maison
Crozat, no. 17 Place Vendôme, "seen and approved 29 April
1700 AC" [photo: Nationalmuseum, Stockholm, THC 6916].

retained the conventional courtyard shape, "vestigial" here since there was
no need to mask irregularities arising from the angle of the street. But it
was far from functionless, since it embodied the form associated with the
noble type.

The procession of arrival was more condensed here than at the Maison

44

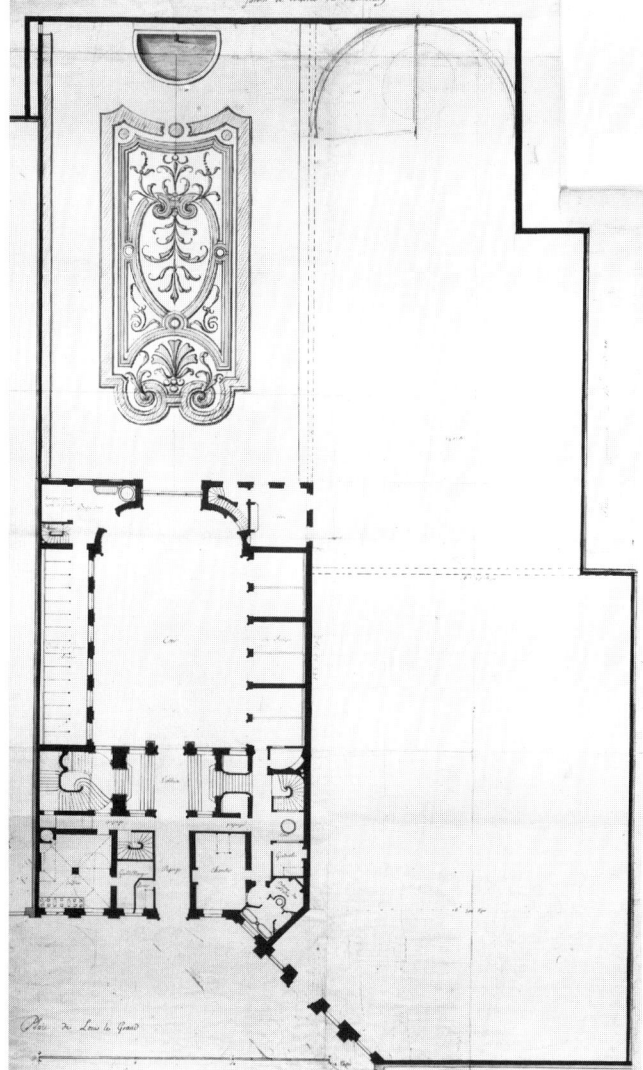

Figure 28
Pierre Bullet (drawing by Chamblain), ground-floor plan, Maison Crozat, no. 17 Place Vendôme, c. 1706, with windows of "*salon*" overlooking garden of no. 19 [photo: Nationalmuseum, Stockholm, THC 6332].

Bourvalais, since visitors disembarked beneath the main living rooms, within the dwelling. Carriages traversed a passage leading to an enormous grand stair, treated with a Doric pilaster order – an indoor–outdoor zone grander than its counterpart at no. 13. The vestibule and two stair halls extended almost the entire width of the dwelling, separated by a corridor from service rooms. The grand stair opened to the left and an important secondary stair to

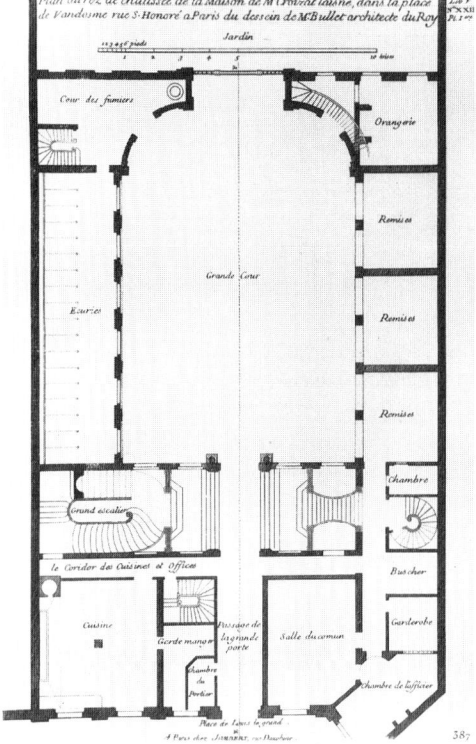

Figure 29
Pierre Bullet, ground-floor plan, Maison Crozat, no. 17 Place Vendôme, c. 1706–7, engraving in Jacques-François Blondel, *Architecture Fran-çaise*, III (Paris, 1754) [photo: after reprint ed., Paris, 1904].

the right. The latter probably always functioned as a business entry, providing access to the *entresol* (Fig. 31). Like most financiers at the square, Crozat used it in part for his *caisse* (cashier's office), lit by a single lunette window overlooking the Place Vendôme. Along with a counter and a pair of scales, Crozat provided some inexpensive chairs, a wooden table, and a bed for his cashier, who slept there, presumably to safeguard funds.[34]

On the first floor, Bullet placed the major ceremonial apartment of Mme Crozat along the square and a secondary suite for her husband behind it, bisecting the mass along its full extent with a corridor (Fig. 32). The corridor connected the stair with an oval vestibule functioning as both an anteroom and an elegant circulatory joint. Accessible from the smaller stair that assistants and business callers presumably used, the vestibule also provided access to the second floor and connected the ceremonial rooms overlooking the square with the gallery.

Such an extensive use of a corridor was unusual, especially on the *noble*

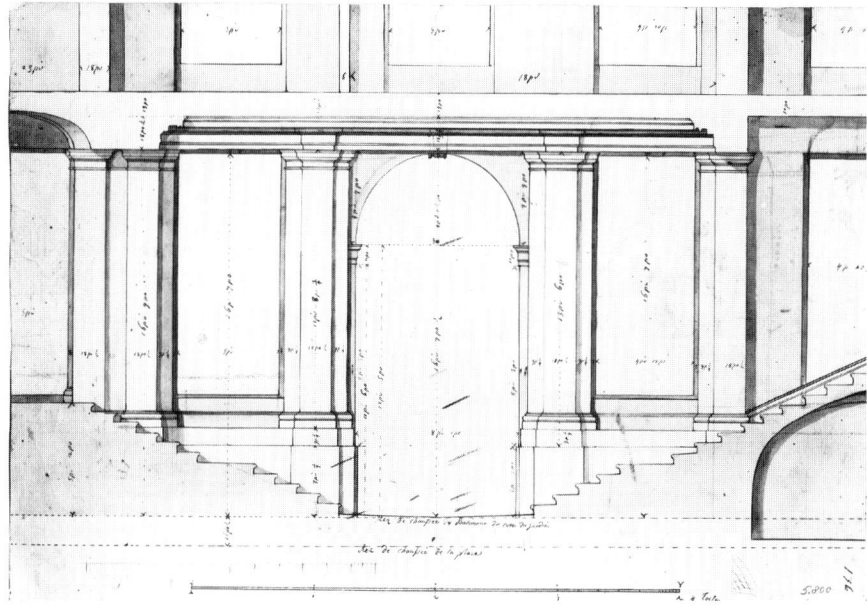

Figure 30
Pierre Bullet, section through entrance vestibule and stair, Maison Crozat, no. 17
Place Vendôme, c. 1700 [photo: Nationalmuseum, Stockholm, THC 5800].

étage. It was all but invisible to most visitors, however, providing instead a
route for servants to perform their tasks unseen, probably a path family
members took to avoid the ceremonial rooms, and – most importantly – a
means of segregating business callers from official or social visitors. Double-
loaded corridors were rare, in part because they were so difficult to illuminate; here the only natural light would have been indirect light from the oval
vestibule.[35]

Bullet employed the oblique bay to provide certain spaces with more privacy. In two projects for the ground floor, he used it for a pentagonal bathing
room (Figs. 27 and 28). For nearly a century, some elite urban dwellings had
been equipped with rooms devoted to bathing. In revisions to Daviler's treatise
published in 1710, Le Blond provided his largest *hôtel* with a bathing apartment (including a small anteroom, a *salle des bains*, and a wardrobe) opening
onto a walled private garden, but extended bathing suites were rarely realized
on urban sites early in the century. At the Place Vendôme, with its less expansive parcels, placement of so "private" a function along the public realm may
seem curious, but it faced southeast (preferred for morning light), and it was
near the kitchen, where water could be heated; in fact, eighteenth-century
bathing rooms were often placed in locales that now strike us as unusually
public.[36] Here the bathing room was expendable; Crozat replaced it with a
bedroom for the *officier* who kept watch over the household's silver (Fig. 29).
On the first floor, Bullet used the bay for an *arrière cabinet* (possibly used by
Crozat, but later clearly part of his wife's apartment).

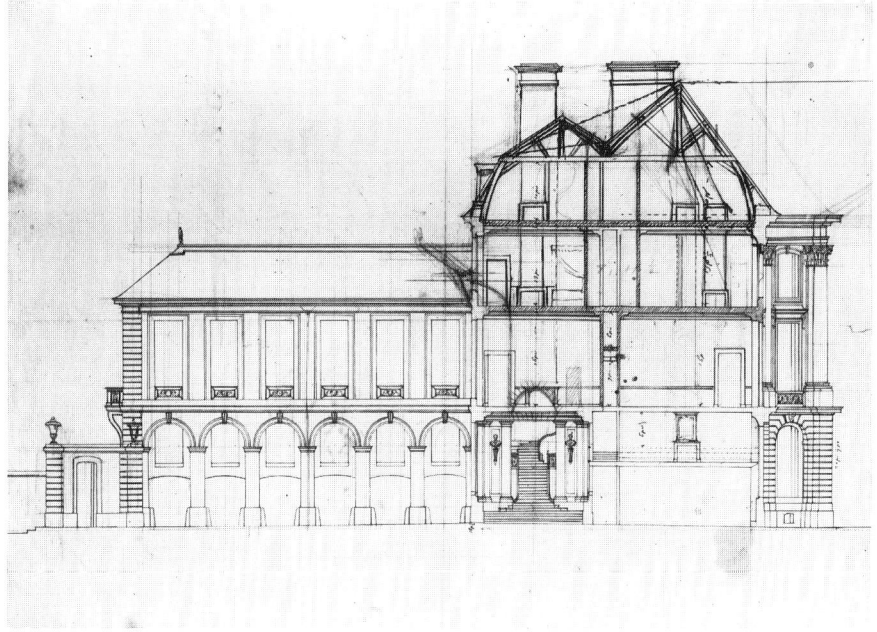

Figure 31
Pierre Bullet, section, view to north (toward subsidiary stair), Maison Crozat, no. 17
Place Vendôme, c. 1700 [photo: Nationalmuseum, Stockholm, THC 6791].

The most important ceremonial room was the gallery. It faced south, and
eight large mirrors reflected the gilded moldings and expensive furnishings.[37]
Easily accessible from Crozat's suite and from the secondary stair, the gallery
opened onto a balcony with stairs to a terrace overlooking the garden (Figs.
31 to 33); a small stair from the terrace descended to a ground-floor "*salon*"
in early plans (Figs. 27 and 28). The placement of ceremonial apartments on
the first floor deprived financiers of the close relationship between those rooms
and the garden, which was just emerging as the ideal in noble dwellings. The
salon provided a compact substitute, but it may have proved impractical, since
the room is labeled *orangerie* in engravings later published by Mariette and
Blondel (Fig. 29). In the opposite wing on the first floor, Bullet shaped another
fairly independent and important apartment, giving its most private rooms
(the *cabinet* and *garderobe*) access to a balcony facing the garden.

Just as Crozat was completing his house in 1702, the comte d'Estrées, a
commander in the French navy and a lieutenant general of the king of Spain,
brought to France painter Paolo de Matteis, whom he had met at the Spanish
court in Naples. Crozat had Matteis paint the ceiling of his gallery, as well as
those of the stair hall and some other rooms. The commission brought high-
ranking visitors into Crozat's new house, including the prince de Conti and
the duc d'Orléans (the future Regent); they were apparently impressed, since
d'Orléans figured among Matteis's clients.[38] Brice sharply criticized Matteis's

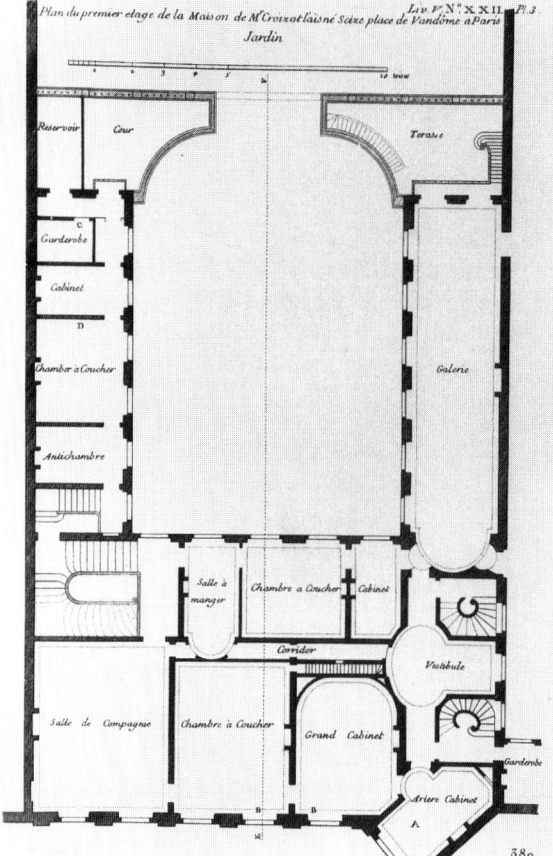

Figure 32

Pierre Bullet, first-floor plan, Maison Crozat, no. 17 Place Vendôme, c. 1706–7, engraving in Jacques-François Blondel, *Architecture Française*, III (Paris, 1754) [photo: after reprint ed., Paris, 1904].

work, but his tone suggests the real offense was Crozat's pretension in employing an Italian painter – a princely custom, even if the height of its prestige as a practice had long since passed.[39]

Brice's critique was not the only censure of Crozat's gallery. Crozat had the gallery gilded in 1703, circumventing extant but slackly enforced luxury laws. In expressing his disapproval, the king singled out the contraventions of Crozat and Thévenin.[40] Bourvalais's mentor Thévenin had also commissioned paintings from Matteis, and some high-ranking "connoisseurs" who came to see them presumably complained to the king. At a time when the *style moderne* relied heavily upon gilding, the real issue must have been a breach of decorum, too conspicuous a display of social pretensions. These financiers had the audacity to emulate the king himself, each installing a kind of gilded and mirrored "Galerie des glaces."

Figure 33
Pierre Bullet, garden facade, Maison Crozat, no. 17 Place Vendôme, c. 1700, engraving in Jacques-François Blondel, *Architecture Française*, III (Paris, 1754) [photo: after reprint ed., Paris,
1904].

Blondel did not publish the plan of the second story. That was where
Crozat's three sons, all born during the last decade of the seventeenth century,
probably had modest suites, perhaps accompanied by a room for their preceptor and a room for study. By the time the Maison Crozat was built, at least
two of Crozat's sons were of school age; sons of elite families typically resided
at school, but in Paris, they could attend a day school and live at home.[41]
Crozat's daughter Marie-Anne, born in 1695, was probably less in evidence
in this house, although she may have been educated at home for a period,
since the abbé Le Français dedicated to her his popular *Traité de géographie*
(a primer known as the "*Géographie de Crozat*").[42] Soon after, however, she
would have been sent to a local convent; that was the norm among financial
families, who typically followed this custom established by noble families of
the sword and robe.[43] Along with Crozat's children, some high-ranking domestics may have had rooms on the second floor.[44]

Some financiers among the first generation at the Place Vendôme, while
adopting many public symbols of the nobility, apparently retained certain
customs considered to be bourgeois. Among these may have been the sharing
of a bedroom by husband and wife. Crozat's 1738 inventory reveals that there
were then two beds in Mme Crozat's private bedroom. More intriguing was

the transfer of that practice to the representational sphere, since there were two beds, as well, in the *chambre de parade* overlooking the square on the first floor.[45] Chambers with two beds also appear in Chamblain's plans of 1709 for Bourvalais and Villemaré (Figs. 25, 76, and 78). At the Maison Bourvalais, the first-floor chamber along the square may have served a married niece and nephew; two beds appeared in an *entresol* chamber at the Maison Villemaré, in what may have been the private sleeping room of Villemaré and his wife.[46] Saint-Simon would register surprise that Chancellor Pontchartrain and his wife had retained the bourgeois practice of a shared private bedroom.[47] Certain financiers may have also retained this bourgeois custom, but it seems possible that they were emulating the former Controller General of Finance, just as court nobles imitated the king. It is difficult to assess how common the practice may have been, but it disappeared after the first generation at the Place Vendôme, as financiers universally adopted noble norms mandating separate bedrooms for husband and wife.[48]

The overall form of Bullet's design was ingenious in providing many amenities difficult to achieve at the square, including ample stables and carriage stalls, as well as the most potent sign of a noble dwelling – the gallery. But the spatial constraints of the site meant that these came at a cost. Brice, while commending the great "quantity of large and small rooms, among which some are very beautiful and richly furnished," found the court "very narrow and very gloomy because of the excessive height of the buildings on each side, the facades of which are not at all extraordinary."[49] It was probably, above all, Crozat's desire to incorporate a gallery that resulted in the cramped court. Important guests, however, disembarked in the range along the square, and they would have descended to the garden from Crozat's gilded gallery (Figs. 32 and 33).

The Maison Reich de Pennautier and the Hôtel d'Évreux (No. 19)

People are talking a good deal today about the marriage of the comte d'Évreux with Mlle Crozat, to whom her father gave one and a half million *livres* in silver; besides that, he gave the comte d'Évreux 100,000 *livres* to pay his debts; he [Crozat] is obligated to feed him [d'Évreux] and his wife and all their domestics for six years, to build him a house next to his own at the Place Vendôme, according to a design that he himself will have chosen, and to furnish it appropriately for his dignity.[50]

In 1706, four years after the completion of his own house, Crozat acquired the much larger lot, contiguous with his own, in the northwest canted corner, where his mentor Reich de Pennautier had begun to build a dwelling. Crozat bought the lot to build a large *hôtel* for his daughter and her prospective new husband, Henri-Louis de La Tour d'Auvergne, the comte d'Évreux.

The marriage of Crozat's daughter to the comte d'Évreux was a truly remarkable one. The comte d'Évreux was the heavily indebted twenty-eight-year-old son of the duc de Bouillon; Crozat managed the finances of Bouillon and his cousin, the duc de Vendôme.[51] Marriages of daughters of financiers with impoverished nobles had long been a means of social advancement, but a leap into the upper reaches of the court was unusual and widely criticized. The marriage took place in 1707, shortly before Marie-Anne Crozat turned twelve, and the building of the house was part of the marriage agreement.[52] Dwellings at the Place Vendôme were often dynastic investments.

Bullet and his son had just begun to build a house on the site for Pennautier, whose long career had been punctuated by the sorts of perils financiers could face. In 1672, shortly after he wed Madeleine Le Secq, daughter of his co-treasurer at the Bourse of Languedoc, the marquise de Brinvilliers implicated him in poisoning her father and two brothers; she recanted, but a few years later more charges emerged, apparently originating with those who coveted his lucrative offices.[53] It was during the following decade that Pennautier sponsored the Crozat brothers, and Pierre remained his assistant for twenty years.

Bullet had taken the aristocratic *hôtel* type and rotated it 180 degrees at the Maison Crozat. Here, given a larger parcel with less frontage along the square, Bullet and his son shifted it back again to form a more noble complement (Figs. 34 and 35). They molded a court of the standard shape, positioning it so that a range could be placed between court and garden. A small oval vestibule provided a grander entry into the court, and the main entrance and stair hall along the left wing opened onto a ceremonial suite along the garden.

The single-room *enfilade* at the end of the court was somewhat old-fashioned, but Bullet and his son used it to provide grand ceremonial rooms; the suites of Mme Pennautier on the first floor and of her husband below were nearly identical in plan.[54] Planning in the range along the square was entirely different. On the first floor, a large gallerylike *salon* enjoyed views from three of four windows, and the architects introduced a more "modern" distribution, with rooms of different sizes and shapes linked by a web of circulatory devices.

In August 1706, Pennautier sold his parcel to Crozat.[55] Bullet now confronted the problem of a residence for an important courtier, and it must have seemed imperative to closely approximate the noble type. He retained the basic disposition but modified it for a household quite different in stature (Figs. 36 to 37). In 1707, Crozat added two smaller lots to the north, along the rue Neuve-des-Capucines, permitting what no other Place Vendôme dwelling had yet been afforded – a secondary exit, through an immense stable and carriage court.[56] Bullet expanded the principal *corps-de-logis* to form a two-room deep pavilion, more closely approximating the noble dwellings then under construction in the Faubourg Saint-Germain (Fig. 14).

Bullet rethought the *porte cochère*, apparently turning for inspiration to an atypical noble dwelling along a major thoroughfare, Antoine Le Pautre's mid-seventeenth-century design for the Hôtel de Beauvais (Fig. 38). Bullet adopted a round porch akin to the one Le Pautre placed at the end of his entry passage,

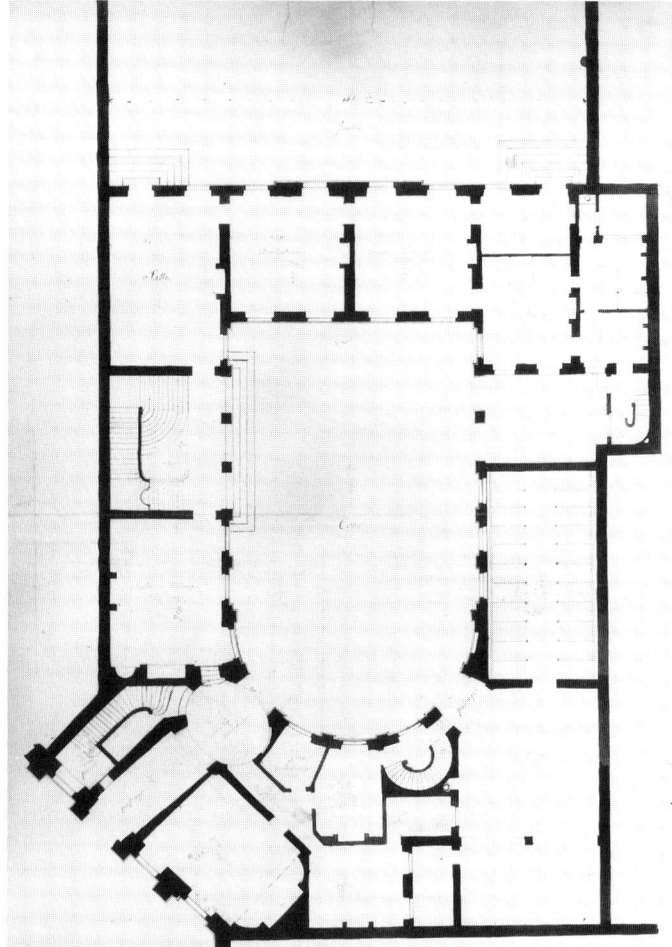

Figure 34
Pierre Bullet and Jean-Baptiste Bullet de Chamblain (drawing by
Chamblain), study for ground-floor plan, Maison Reich de Pennau-
tier, no. 19 Place Vendôme, c. 1705–6 [photo: Nationalmuseum,
Stockholm, THC 6225].

substituting coupled pilasters for freestanding columns, but labeling it "peristyle"; he called the room opening off it "*Suisse*" (its counterpart at Crozat's
house was labeled *portier*).

Across the court, Bullet built a real, open-air Doric peristyle (Figs. 37 and
39). The interior facade, with its colonnade and a first floor embellished by
Ionic pilasters, was one of the noblest anywhere in Paris at the turn of the
century.[57] The apartment, entered from the peristyle and stretching along the
garden, was probably for d'Évreux's use in the summer, since the principal
ceremonial rooms were on the first floor. Visitors mounted the grand stair to
the right (Fig. 40) and arrived in a first-floor vestibule in the form of a gallery,

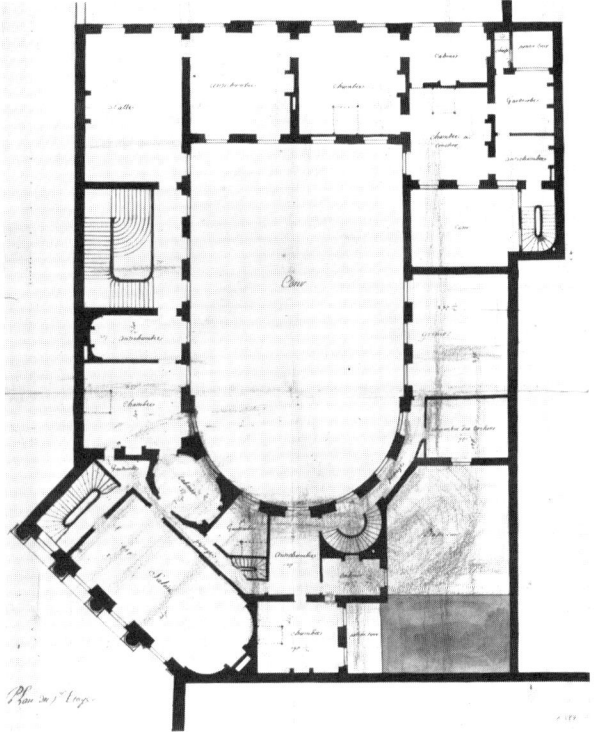

Figure 35
Pierre Bullet and Jean-Baptiste Bullet de Chamblain
(drawing by Chamblain), study for first-floor plan, Maison Reich de Pennautier, no. 19 Place Vendôme, c. 1705–
6 [photo: Nationalmuseum, Stockholm, THC 6244].

articulated nobly with a Corinthian pilaster order (Figs. 41 to 43).[58] Rounded
at either end, its doorways flanked by niches bearing statues, the gallery provided a magnificent prelude to the main *appartement de parade* along the
garden.

Bullet brought the dining room to the first floor and set it off the main
enfilade; the location allowed servants to prepare the room for a meal unseen,
congruent with noble ideology valuing invisibility of service (and keeping the
smell of food away from the public suite).[59] The unusually ample dining room
and the large *salle* that functioned as an anteroom along the garden were of a
scale starkly different from Crozat's small dining-anteroom (Fig. 32). With
one rounded end flanked by niches, echoing the niched ends of the galleries of
both Crozat houses, it was also exceptional in its nonrectilinear form. Variety
of room shape had been exploited during the seventeenth century, particularly
in the work of Le Vau and Le Pautre, but during the two decades or so
preceding the turn of the century such complexity had fallen out of favor;
Bullet reintroduced it at the Place Vendôme.

What is most remarkable about the pavilion set at the rear of the court is-

54

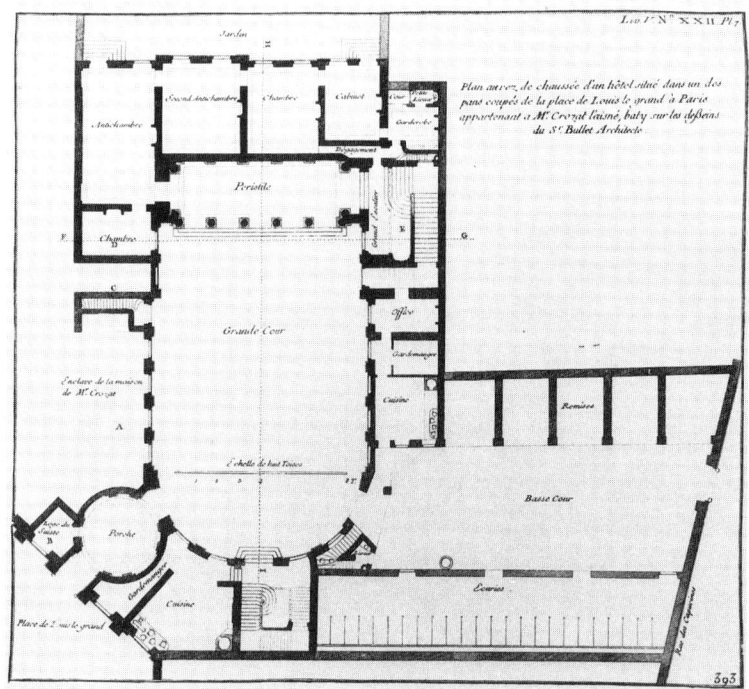

Figure 36

Pierre Bullet, ground-floor plan, Hôtel d'Évreux, no. 19 Place Vendôme, c. 1707, engraving in Jacques-François Blondel, *Architecture Française*, III (Paris, 1754) [photo: after reprint ed., Paris, 1904].

Figure 37

Pierre Bullet, court elevation and section, Hôtel d'Évreux, no. 19 Place Vendôme, c. 1707, engraving in Jacques-François Blondel, *Architecture Française*, III (Paris, 1754) [photo: after reprint ed., Paris, 1904].

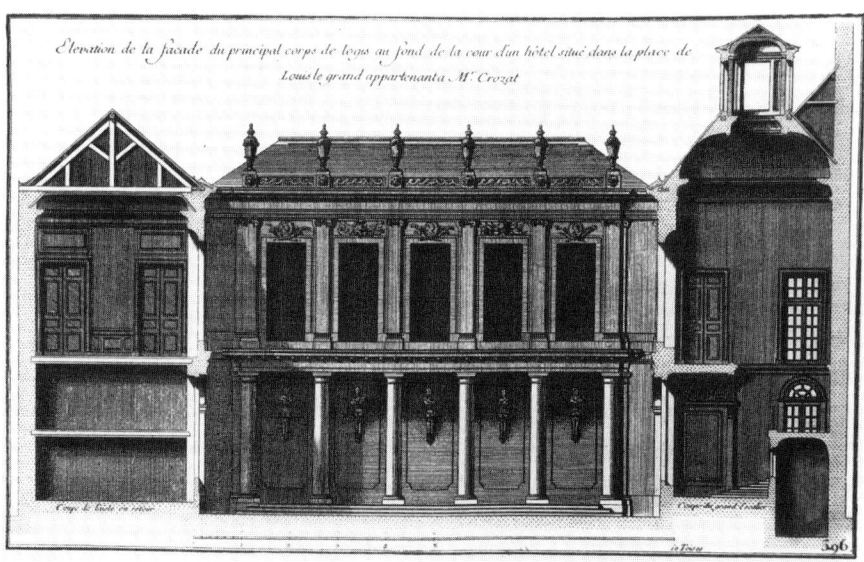

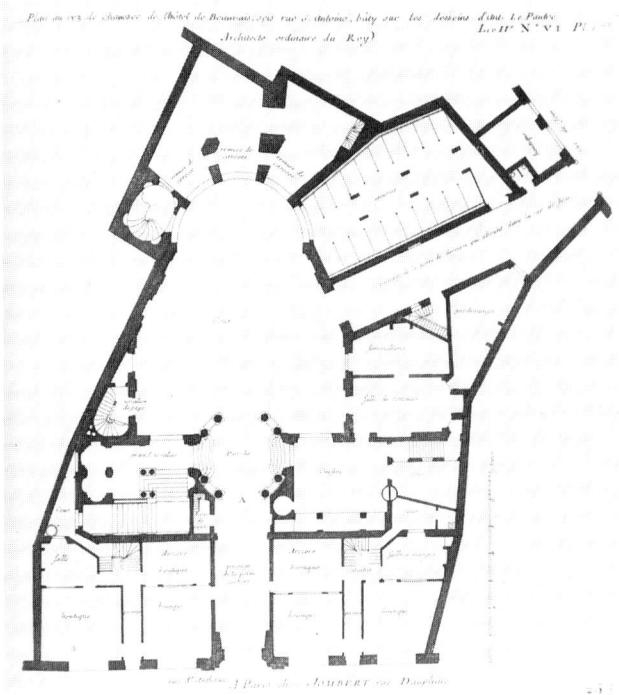

Figure 38

Antoine Le Pautre, ground-floor plan, Hôtel de Beauvais, rue Saint-Antoine, Paris, built c. 1657–60, engraving in Jacques-François Blondel, *Architecture Française*, II (Paris, 1752). Windows of a *grand salle* and *grand chambre* on first floor overlooked the rue Saint-Antoine for views of ceremonial processions; boutiques on ground floor [photo: after reprint ed., Paris, 1904].

that the entire range seems to have accommodated Crozat's son-in-law. In most noble dwellings, the husband and wife, normally about equal in rank, shared the ceremonial rooms along the garden, each with his or her own apartment for official reception. Nowhere are the vastly different social ranks of the comte d'Évreux and Marie-Anne Crozat clearer than in the placement of the ceremonial apartment of Crozat's daughter all the way across the court, with its windows along the square.[60] Crozat's daughter had her own separate entrance and a separate stair. Her life would have been quite detached from that of her husband, and many contemporaries noted d'Évreux's aloofness.[61] Thus, Bullet's plans provided the court nobleman with lodgings between court and garden and the financier's daughter with an apartment in the range along the public realm, in the bourgeois manner. The arrangements reflected distinctions in estate, but also differences of gender, as we shall see.

Crozat incorporated parts of the neighboring parcel into his house in a manner that suggests he was laying claim to the contiguous *hôtel*. The terrace

Figure 39
No. 19 Place Vendôme, court peristyle today [photo: author].

Figure 40
No. 19 Place Vendôme, detail of longitudinal section, engraving in Jacques-François Blondel, *Architecture Française*, III (Paris, 1754) [photo: after reprint ed., Paris, 1904].

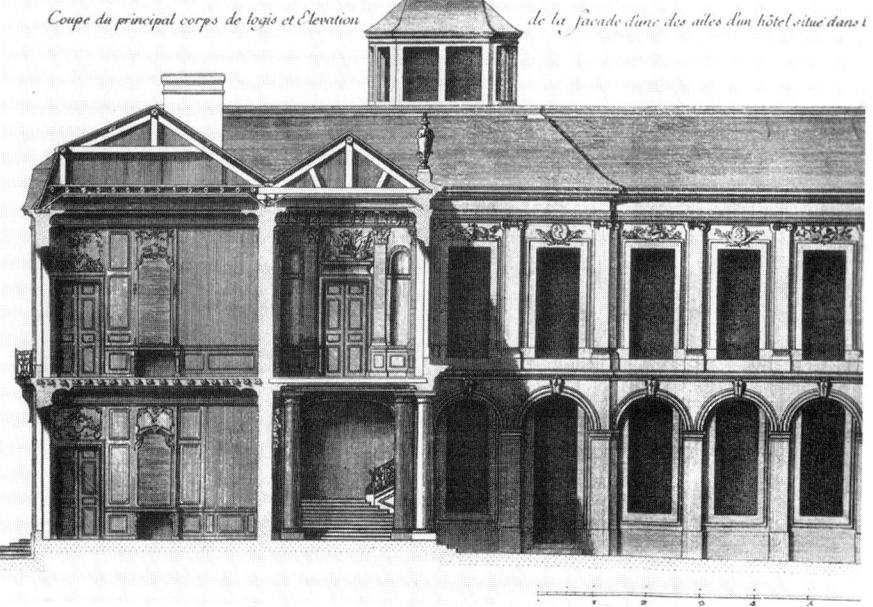

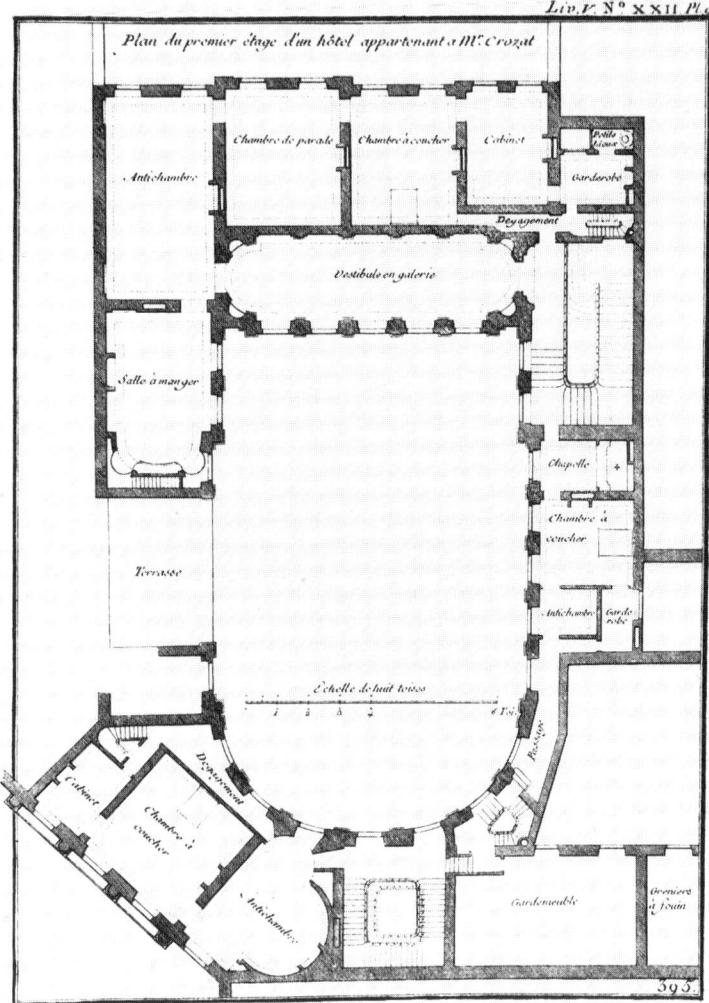

Figure 41
Pierre Bullet, first-floor plan, Hôtel d'Évreux, no. 19 Place Vendôme, c.
1707, engraving in Jacques-François Blondel, *Architecture Française*, III
(Paris, 1754) [photo: after reprint ed., Paris, 1904].

of the Maison Crozat intruded into the court of the neighboring *hôtel* (Figs.
32, 44, and 100), providing light for the vestibule, corridor, and secondary
stairs, but also establishing a proprietary relationship.[62] One project called for
the houses to be joined on the first floor by doors leading from Crozat's gallery
to both the *salle* and dining room of the Hôtel d'Évreux, with a continuous,
symmetrical garden facade incorporating the right wing of Crozat's house
(Fig. 45). D'Évreux may have vetoed that project, and Bullet built a party wall
separating the two gardens, leaving the Hôtel d'Évreux with an asymmetrical
facade (Fig. 46). And Crozat probably intended to share the stables so amply

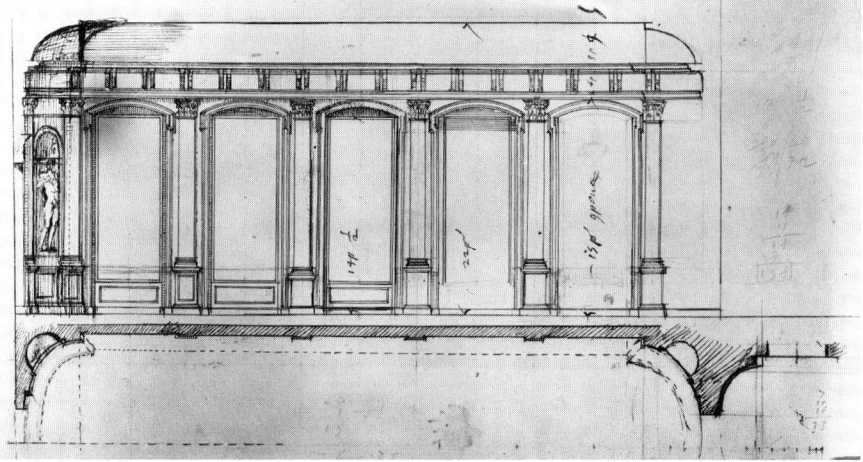

Figure 42
Pierre Bullet, study and plan, vestibule-gallery on first floor, Hôtel d'Évreux, no. 19
Place Vendôme, c. 1707 [photo: Nationalmuseum, Stockholm, THC 6788].

Figure 43
Pierre Bullet, study, view toward door of vestibule-gallery, Hôtel d'Évreux, no. 19 Place Vendôme, Bullet, c. 1707 [photo: Nationalmuseum,
Stockholm, THC 7064].

Figure 44
No. 19 Place Vendôme, court, with view of terrace of Maison Crozat [photo: author].

Figure 45
Pierre Bullet and Jean-Baptiste Bullet de Chamblain (drawing by Chamblain), study for first-floor plan of Hôtel d'Évreux with connections to north wing of Maison Crozat, 1706–7 [photo: Nationalmuseum, Stockholm, THC 6211].

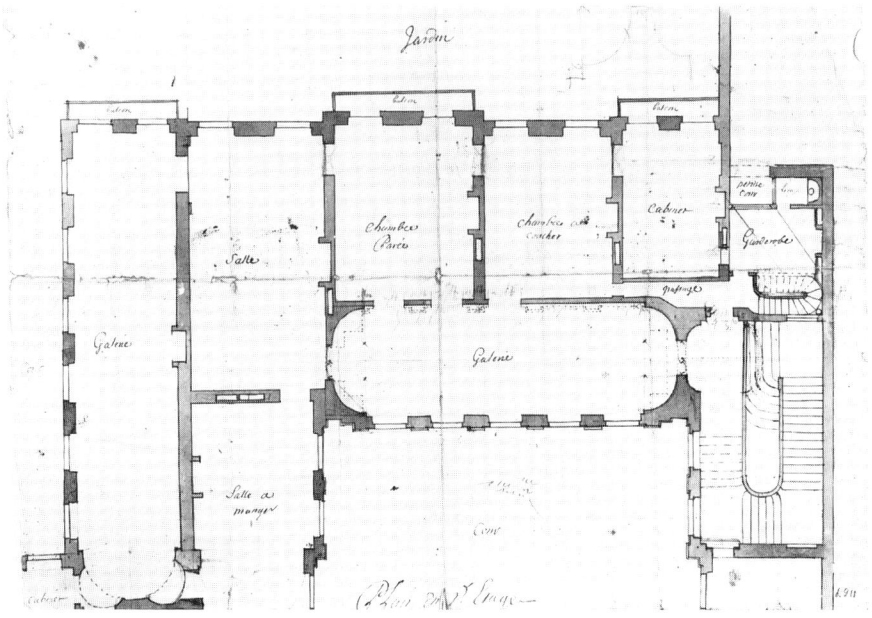

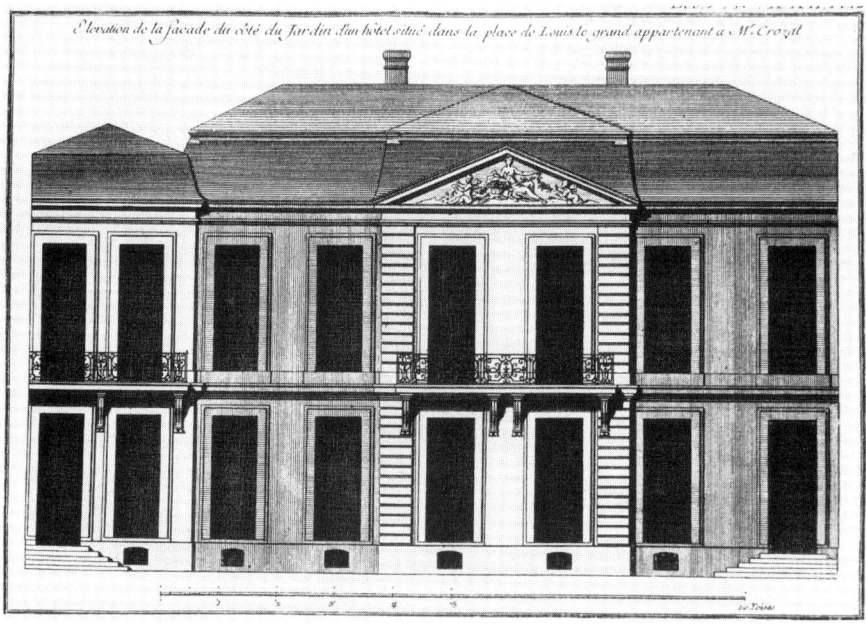

Figure 46
Pierre Bullet, garden facade, Hôtel d'Évreux, c. 1707, engraving in Jacques-François
Blondel, *Architecture Française*, III (Paris, 1754) [photo: after reprint ed., Paris, 1904].

provided for his son-in-law, since a passage initially linked the two grand
courts (Fig. 36).[63]

Lodgings for domestics extended along an *entresol* above the ground floor
in the right wing, continuing above the stables and carriage stalls of the subsidiary court (Fig. 47). They included a few small apartments for upper servants, many small rooms without fireplaces, and some larger rooms. Bullet
provided space for a much more extensive domestic staff than he had envi-
sioned at the Maison Crozat; he also, not surprisingly, better segregated it.

Crozat, rich and clever as he was, proved too eager to join the uppermost
ranks of the nobility. Insulting songs circulated about the "ignoble bottom"
now seated on a duchess's tabouret.[64] Members of d'Évreux's family publicly
called Crozat's daughter *le petit Lingot* (small piece of gold bullion).[65] According to Saint-Simon, who denounced the misalliance, Mme Crozat never approved of the marriage and never lost her good sense – which meant, of
course, her bourgeois identity.[66] In fact, the marriage did not last long, and
the couple occupied the house only briefly. D'Évreux abandoned his young
wife in 1712 and used her dowry to build a palatial residence set amid expansive gardens in the Faubourg Saint-Honoré – today the Palais de l'Élysée.

Gender and Planning at the Place Vendôme

Considerable differences in rank fundamentally shaped the "social geography"
of the Hôtel d'Évreux, but financiers also tended to remove their apartments

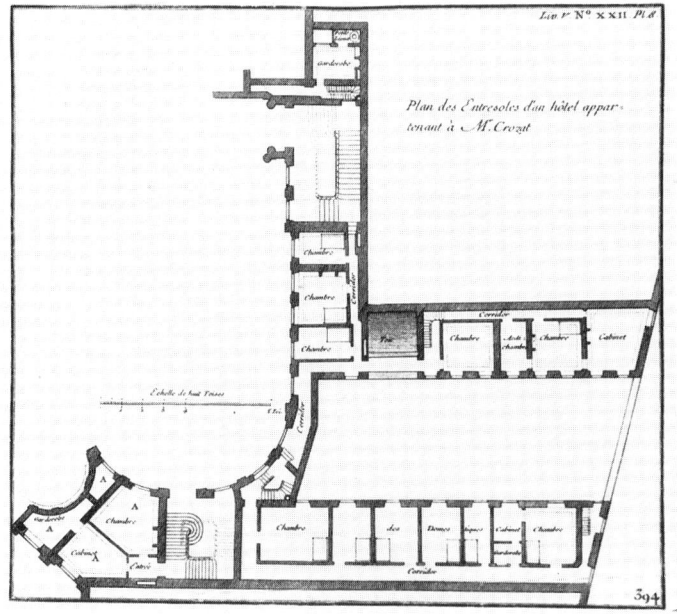

Figure 47
Pierre Bullet, *entresol* plan, Hôtel d'Évreux, no. 19 Place Vendôme,
c. 1707, engraving in Jacques-François Blondel, *Architecture Française*, III (Paris, 1754) [photo: after reprint ed., Paris, 1904].

from the public realm whenever possible. Bourvalais's suite occupied a range
between court and garden (Figs. 24 and 25), and even Crozat inhabited rooms
to the court side of the principal range, with his grandest ceremonial room
stretching along the right wing. So we must ask whether social rank was the
only factor, or even the key factor, in the distribution of space at the Hôtel
d'Évreux.

Both Mme Crozat and Mme Bourvalais seem to have retained more bourgeois identities than their husbands. Differences in self-perception and presentation are revealed in portraits of Crozat and his wife, executed some decades
after their Place Vendôme house was built (Figs. 48 and 49). These differences
do not seem to have been unique to the Crozat marriage; they appeared, as
well, in other unions where husband and wife emerged from fairly similar
financial milieux.

Men like Crozat and Bourvalais were extremely powerful, key figures in
royal finance. Both seem to have wanted, above all else, to be recognized as
noble. This seems clearly revealed in Crozat's portrait by Alexis-Simon Belle,
which focuses on his ceremonial costume and proudly displayed emblem of
the Order of the Holy Spirit. The wearing of the *cordon bleu* was a jealously
guarded privilege; it indicated membership in the most exclusive noble order,
normally open only to top military officers and royal ministers. Immediately
following the death of Louis XIV, Crozat and another Place Vendôme finan-

62

Figure 48
Alexis-Simon Belle, portrait of Antoine Crozat,
probably c. 1721–4, Versailles: Musée du Château
[photo: Réunion des Musées Nationaux].

cier, Le Bas de Montargis, were allowed to purchase offices in that order in
exchange for sizable loans to a nearly destitute government. Following the
Regency, the Crown instructed Crozat and Montargis to sell their offices and
relinquish the privilege of wearing the *cordon bleu* – an unprecedented revocation of the privilege, eventually reversed through bribes and the intervention
of powerful friends.

In contrast to the presentation of her husband, Mme Crozat appears in a
portrait by Jacques Aved in a domestic interior – the appropriate setting for a
bourgeois woman. Approximately two decades separate the portraits, but a
comparison is nonetheless instructive. Stopping work on her tapestry loom,
she removes glasses needed for her near-at-hand task with a reserved gesture
that seems a kind of synecdoche for a world relatively confined in comparison
with that of her husband. Her reserve, so different from the confident pose of
her husband, also diverges from the allegorical and sensual presentation prevalent in contemporary portraits of court noblewomen. Her lacy day cap con-
trasts markedly with her husband's *cordon bleu*.

Mme Crozat's world was rather circumscribed, vis-à-vis both her financier
husband and high-ranking women: physically, within her house, and morally.
Financiers might imitate the court nobility when it came to marital fidelity,
but among families perceived to be bourgeois, wives were normally expected

Figure 49
Jacques Aved, portrait of Madame Crozat (Marie-
Marguerite Legendre), 1741 [photo: Musée Fabre,
Montpellier].

to adhere to stricter codes of marital devotion than either their husbands or
women of the court.[67] Even if Mme Bourvalais and Mme Crozat retained more
bourgeois values than did their husbands, however, that alone does not fully
explain the placement of their suites; such differences did not prevail in all of
the households at the square, but the allotment of space reflected the norm.

The lives of financial wives were more open to public scrutiny than were
those of their husbands. During the day, while their husbands were at work,
tasks of official reception fell more heavily upon them. A financial wife at the
square almost always occupied the main ceremonial suite, the most important
room of which was the *chambre de parade* with its magnificent bed. At the
Place Vendôme, women's activities were on display, open to the gaze of society, in rooms set right along the public realm. That "patriarchal" gaze was, in
fact, *replicated* in the houses built for Crozat – by the placement of the terrace
of Crozat's house directly on axis with what was probably his daughter's
private bedroom (Figs. 44 and 100).[68]

The ideological paradigms governing the shaping of these domains emerged
from more complex constructions, in which gender and rank intersected. The
first high-ranking noblewomen at the Place Vendôme were widows, and they
also preferred to place their ceremonial rooms along the square, with private

suites facing the court. For those who spent their days receiving callers, watching the comings and goings of carriages was probably an enjoyable diversion, and the square provided a noble backdrop. When a financier's wife occupied the suite along the square, this was, in a sense, an adaptation of the noble custom according the mistress of the house the most distinguished locale.

At the Hôtel d'Évreux, however, ideological constructions of social estate, rank, and gender clearly intermingled in the presuppositions guiding Bullet's plan. Perhaps even more than their physical separation, it is the difference in the scale of accommodation provided for Marie-Anne Crozat and the comte d'Évreux that is so striking. In unraveling the social meanings guiding that allotment of space, the plan Bullet prepared for Pennautier, for the same site, assumes significance. At the Maison de Pennautier, husband and wife *shared* the range at the end of the court, each occupying an apartment of comparable extent. And when the last of Crozat's sons, the baron de Thiers, inherited no. 19 in 1743, he and his wife would also occupy it differently from the comte and comtesse d'Évreux. Thiers's wife, a member of the high-ranking Laval-Montmorency clan, *also shared* with her husband the noble pavilion set between court and garden.[69]

3

Typology at the Place Vendôme

FINANCIERS WHO CHOSE to reside at the Place Vendôme selected a setting that was in major respects fundamentally at odds with the noble *hôtel* type. Nonetheless, the first dwellings seem best understood as explorations in adjusting the aristocratic type to the contingencies of the square. In adapting that model, architects drew upon a whole arsenal of modern techniques – rooms with sizes and shapes that varied according to use, corridors, backstairs, and other circulatory devices – to fit compactly and elegantly the many rooms, spaces, and distinct realms their financial clientele needed. On that level, the houses of the Place Vendôme were among the most "modern" Parisian dwellings. The physical constraints of the square, however, meant choices often had to be made between traditional aristocratic modes of planning and use and others that were newly fashionable. Given those alternatives, the first generation at the Place Vendôme was generally slow to relinquish time-honored signs of nobility, even as the potency of those signs diminished.

A few types emerged that seemed compelling formulas given the spatial singularities of the setting. The irregular shapes of the parcels of the *pans coupés* were unique to the Place Vendôme (Fig. 9). Plans for those sites had no real precedents to draw upon, and perhaps for that reason they were among the most inventive. Conversely, an L-shaped type employed on narrower lots was akin to many dwellings at the Place Royale and others along main urban arteries. At the entries to the square, architects were faced with the most extreme limitations.

Two architectural clans that were deeply enmeshed in the development of the square dominated the formulation of these types. Investment partner Pierre Bullet and his son Jean-Baptiste built at least four dwellings and left numerous studies and unbuilt projects. Mansart's extended family invested heavily at the square and in its vicinity, and Mansart would exploit the dignity of the setting to enhance the stature of his clan.[1] With his wife Anne Bodin, daughter of a treasurer, he allied his children with leading financial families: Catherine-Henriette wed Claude Le Bas de Montargis in 1693; Catherine married Vincent Maynon, son of a general tax farmer, in 1699 (but died soon after); and son Jacques wed Samuel Bernard's daughter Madeleine in 1701.[2] During the first decade of the century, two of Mansart's children resided at one or the other of the royal squares he had designed in Paris – Jacques Mansart and his

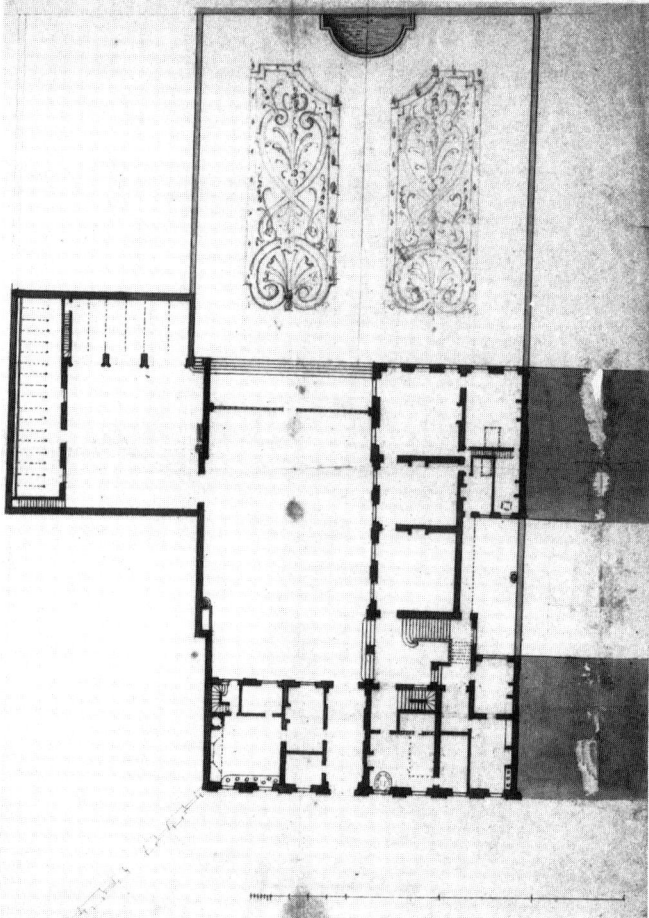

Figure 50
Jules Hardouin-Mansart (attrib.), unrealized study for ground-floor plan, drawing by draftsman affiliated with Mansart, nos. 9–11 Place Vendôme [photo: Bibliothèque Nationale, Est., Ha 18a t.III].

wife at the Place des Victoires, Catherine-Henriette and her husband Le Bas de Montargis at the Place Vendôme.[3]

Mansart's Unbuilt Projects (Nos. 9 to 11) and the Maison Le Bas de Montargis (No. 7)

Mansart was apparently responsible for at least three designs for houses at the square. Two were unexecuted projects for nos. 9 to 11, formerly Sauvion's parcel, which the king gave Mansart in 1703. Sauvion's purchase had left a single bay at the south end of the west range. Mansart purchased the

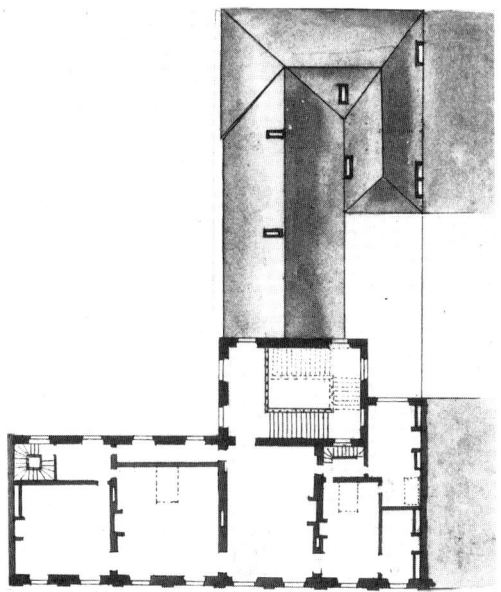

Figure 51

Jules Hardouin-Mansart (attrib.), unrealized study for first-floor plan, drawing by draftsman affiliated with Mansart, nos. 9–11 Place Vendôme [photo: Bibliothèque Nationale, Est., Ha 18a, t. III].

contiguous corner lot (no. 7) in early 1703, and then enlarged the parcel along the west range and shaped a smaller, more regular corner site (Figs. 9 and 26).[4]

Plans for the larger parcel reveal much about Mansart's ambitions in installing his daughter at the square. In one, Mansart explored a solution related to de Cotte's plan for no. 13, adding a small lot to the southwest for an ample stable court (Figs. 50 and 51). A second project, conceived in tandem with no. 7, extended along four sides of the parcel, like some of the larger *hôtels* of the Place Royale (Figs. 52 and 53).[5] An unusually impressive stair formed the prelude to the vast *salle* of a ceremonial apartment between court and garden. The scale of the stair and ceremonial rooms implied a proprietor of high rank, suggesting Mansart expected residents of a status akin to those at the Place Royale.

Those projects remained on paper, however, and had little impact on the formation of types at the square. The second was too grand and rather old-fashioned. Far more important for the development of the square was Mansart's design for a dwelling in the southwest *pan coupé*.

For Mansart, that house was a sign of the rising status of his clan. The strategic utility of the alliance with Montargis was clearly mutual, with Man-

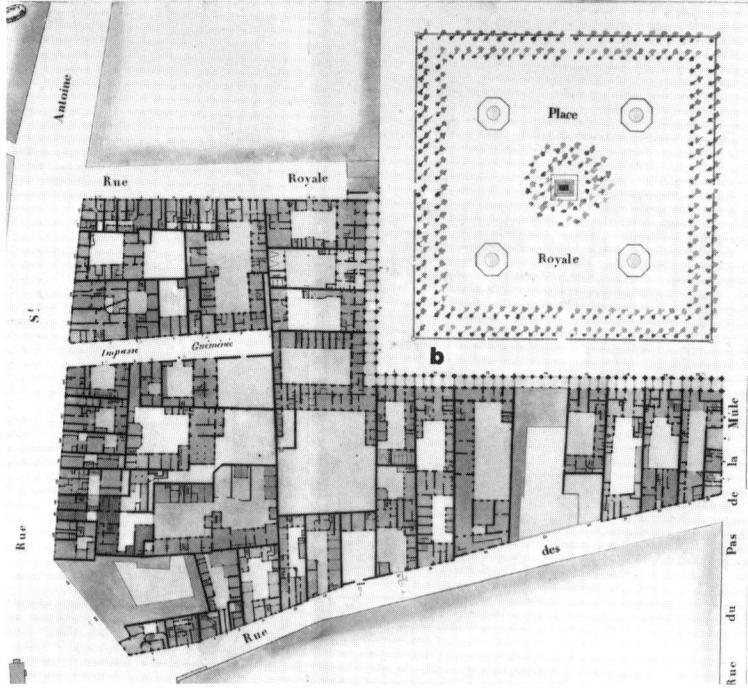

Figure 52

Place Royale (des Vosges), east and south ranges, cadastral plan, *Atlas Vasserot*, c. 1830–50; four-bay house labeled "b" occupied in 1745–58 by Blondel de Gagny [photo: Archives nationales, F³¹ 87 îlot 20 *bis*, document conserved at Centre historique des Archives nationales, Paris].

sart's influence at court furthering his son-in-law's career; Montargis soon became an Extraordinary Treasurer for War, then, in 1708, the Controller General of Finance named him Garde du Trésor Royal – among the most powerful fiscal officers.

The parcel was the smallest of the corner lots.[6] Mansart approached the challenges of the site in a manner analogous to that of Bullet at no. 19. He built the house around three sides of a rectangular court, shaping a compact pentagonal range along the square, joined by wings along the north and west party walls (Figs. 53 to 56). The disposition left no space for a garden, but it allowed for a range at the far end of the court. Mansart elegantly masked the odd angle of entry with a half-elliptical *porte cochère*, which shifted the axis and served as a vestibule for a second stair (Fig. 54). He placed stables off the *porte cochère*, the largest of them along the square.

On so limited a site, Mansart managed to introduce an apartment above the carriage stalls at the rear of the court (Fig. 55). Visitors entered it from the grand stair, set at the juncture of the main living quarters with the wing. It was an important apartment, probably the official and working suite of Montargis.

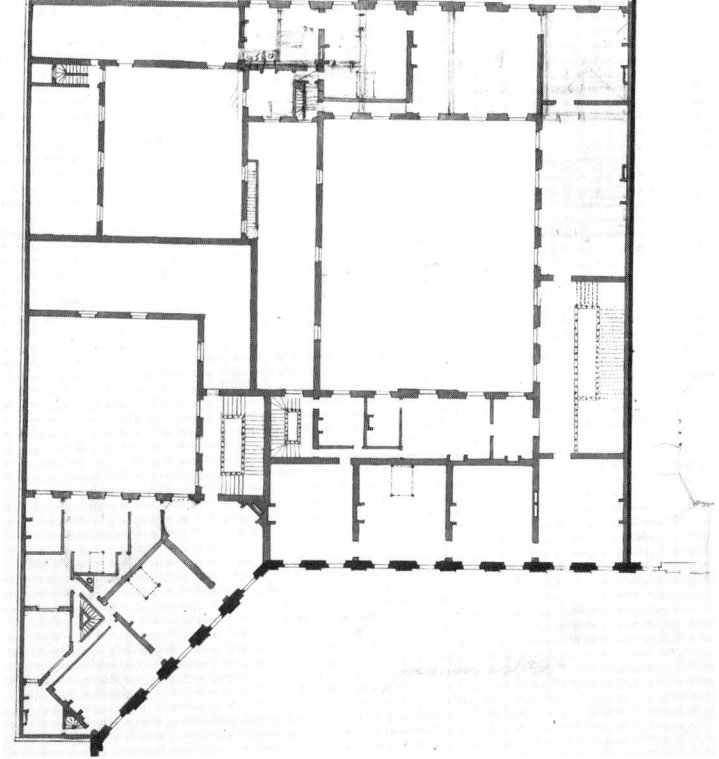

Figure 53
Jules Hardouin-Mansart, unrealized study for first-floor plan, drawing
by draftsman affiliated with Mansart, nos. 7–11 Place Vendôme, early
1703 [photo: Nationalmuseum, Stockholm, CC 2204].

Along the square, Mansart responded to the singular massing, molding
rooms of unusual variety and eccentric shape. In the *entresol*, a pentagonal
anteroom provided access to a square bedchamber along the square, which
opened onto a small dressing room with one rounded end and a triangular
water closet (Fig. 55); from the secondary stair, servants and select visitors
could enter the apartment through a diminutive hexagonal room.[7] On the first
floor (Fig. 53), an anteroom with canted corners served the ceremonial apartment along the square (presumably that of Mansart's daughter), as well as a
more modest suite along the court, and poorly lit residual spaces housed "invisible" functions: wardrobes and service stairs.[8]

Mansart's willingness to shape spaces in unconventional ways also appeared on the second floor, where Montargis's two daughters would most
likely have been lodged (Fig. 56). A corridor bisected the range, and each
apartment ended in an elegantly rounded *cabinet*.[9] Upper servants would have
slept in the smaller rooms, with more domestics in the mansard roof. What
most impressed Brice was that the "very irregular disposition of land" had

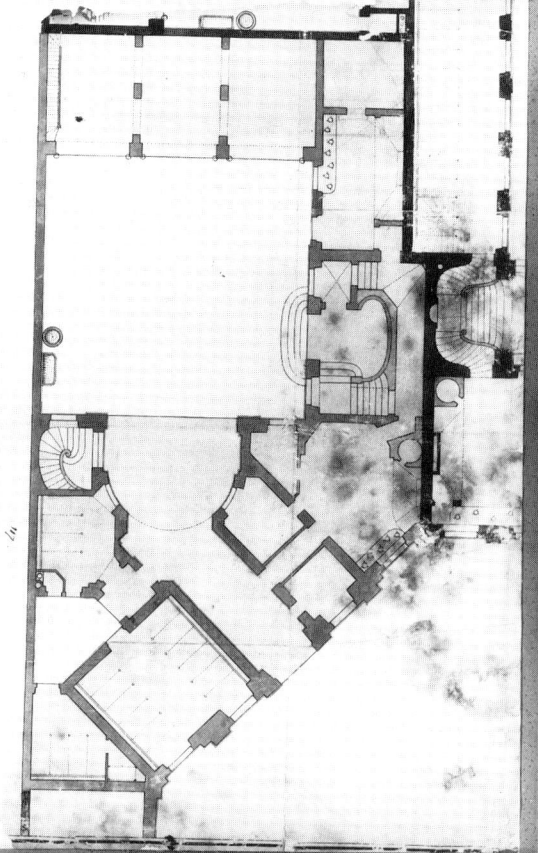

Figure 54
Jules Hardouin-Mansart, study for ground-floor plan,
Maison Le Bas de Montargis, drawing by draftsman
affiliated with Mansart, no. 7 Place Vendôme, with
bay (unrealized) of no. 9, early 1703 [photo: Nationalmuseum, Stockholm, THC 6327].

been "given . . . all the advantages it could have," perhaps meaning that the
ingenuity of Mansart's planning provided for an approximation of the noble
type on a restricted site.[10]

A few months after Mansart's death in 1708, Montargis sold the lifetime use
of the house to Anne-Charlotte Fare d'Aumont, the marquise de Créqui. Mme
de Créqui was the first widowed court noblewoman at the square, where the
scale of lodgings may have seemed appropriate to reduced needs, and the first
of a series of noble residents whose conduct was found shocking even by
relaxed court standards.

Mme de Créqui was a niece of Louvois, the minister who had initiated the
Place de Nos Conquêtes, and of his brother Charles-Maurice Le Tellier, arch-

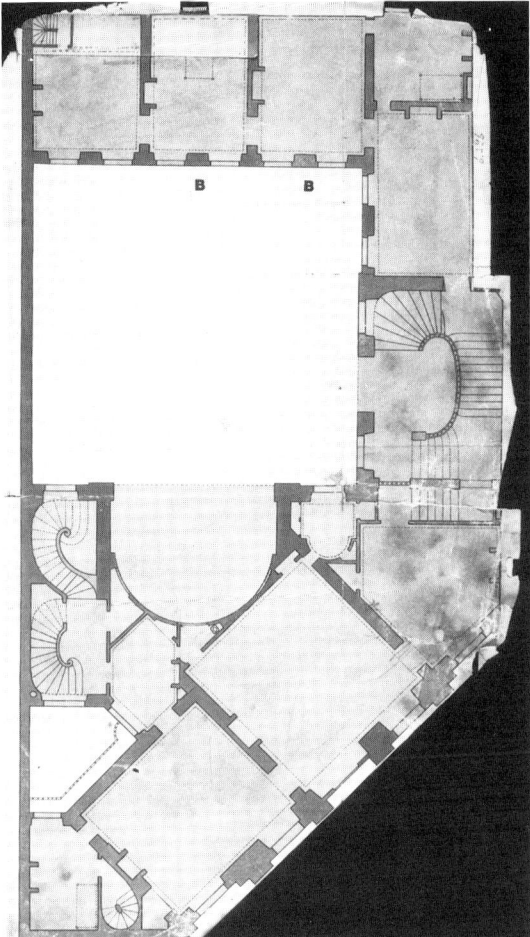

Figure 55
Jules Hardouin-Mansart, study for *entresol* plan,
Maison Le Bas de Montargis, drawing by draftsman
affiliated with Mansart, no. 7 Place Vendôme, early
1703 (with two rooms combined to form library
marked "B") [photo: Nationalmuseum, Stockholm,
THC 6326].

bishop of Rheims. She was the archbishop's favorite relation and his reputed
mistress. Le Tellier, who stayed with her when he was in Paris, provided
53,000 *livres* for her installation at the Place Vendôme.[11] He died suddenly in
1710, but Mme de Créqui continued to inhabit the house until early 1719,
when she renounced her opulent and notorious lifestyle.[12]

Possibly in connection with Mme de Créqui's occupancy, two rooms that
appear at the rear of the court in the *entresol* plan (Fig. 55) were combined to
form an exceptional *grand cabinet* functioning as a library (Fig. 57), perhaps
to accommodate a portion of Le Tellier's renowned library.[13] It is also possible

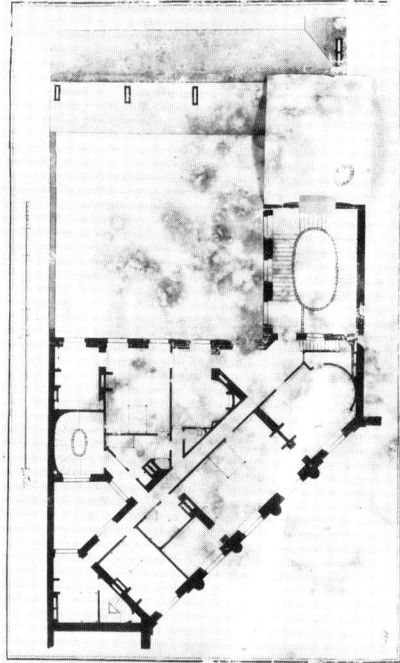

Figure 56

Jules Hardouin-Mansart, unrealized study for second-floor plan, Maison Le Bas de Montargis, drawing by draftsman affiliated with Mansart, no. 7 Place Vendôme, early 1703; as built, the grand stair did not extend above the first floor [photo: Nationalmuseum, Stockholm, THC 5993].

that the library was constructed for Montargis.[14] A relief portrait of Louis XIV presided over the ten-foot-tall oak book armoires that lined the entire west wall and adhered to parts of the walls to the north and south. Two curved corner panels have retained a light blue-green paint, which may have been the original color of the armoires.[15] Thin mirrored panels set between the four windows, plus a larger mirror above a fireplace on the south wall, enhanced the natural light.

Libraries were almost invariably attached to the male realm within the house; women rarely amassed extensive collections of books.[16] Bruno Pons proposed that the unusually ample bookcases were most likely constructed for Montargis's son-in-law, the président Hénault, when he and his wife moved into the house in about 1720;[17] Pons had also argued, however, that the prominent relief portrait of Louis XIV might suggest an earlier date.[18] In fact, when Mme Hénault died in 1728, her notary described a different "*cabinet* serving as a library," in the principal range on the first floor, which faced this library room across the court; *that cabinet* must have been the library of the président

Figure 57
Jules Degoullons (attrib.), sculptor, paneling from book armoires, carved oak, painted and gilded, h: 10 ft (305 cm), formerly installed in library at Maison Le Bas de Montargis, no. 7 Place Vendôme, c. 1705–15, reinstalled with modern cornice and modern cast of Louis XIV at the J. Paul Getty Museum, Los Angeles; originally, a fireplace was set into south wall, not beneath relief [photo: The J. Paul Getty Museum].

Hénault, admitted to the Académie française in 1723.[19] Mme Hénault's apartment, also located on the first floor, overlooked the square.[20]

Beginning in 1724, Hénault arranged for the rental of the *entresol* to his colleague at the Académie française, the abbé d'Alary, a former tutor of Louis XV. D'Alary had recently founded an important political club, conceived as an academy of politics.[21] Thereafter, the club assembled at d'Alary's *entresol* lodgings at the Place Vendôme every Saturday from five until eight in the evening, almost certainly in the ample library at the rear of the court.[22] In summer, after their meetings, the group strolled in the nearby Tuileries gardens.[23] Entirely male, composed largely, but not exclusively, of noblemen of the robe and sword – many of whom later had distinguished diplomatic careers – it was "a kind of English club," the marquis d'Argenson explained. Members called it the "club de l'Entresol." D'Argenson, later Secretary of State for Foreign Affairs, read aloud from foreign newspapers, and members discussed political, economic, and legal issues. Their meetings were so prestigious that in 1726, Horace Walpole, then an ambassador of England in France to negotiate a new alliance, asked to address the group.[24] Cardinal Fleury, effectively the chief minister of Louis XV, supported them until rumors circulated that the club actually governed France; in 1731, Fleury disbanded it.[25]

Eventually, all of the Montargis would return to this house designed by Mansart. Eldest daughter Anne-Charlotte – who had wed the high-ranking marquis d'Arapajon in 1715 and was shortly after named *dame d'honneur* of the duchesse de Berry – moved back, as did her parents, following her sister's death.[26] Hénault continued to reside with them for more than a decade.[27] Following the death of Montargis in 1741, his widow Catherine-Henriette arranged to retire to a convent. In the end, however, she remained in the house her father had built at the Place Vendôme.[28]

Other Dwellings in the *pans coupés* (Nos. 8 and 22)

Several studies by Bullet and his son for the two *pans coupés* of the east range were probably prepared for those assigned the parcels in 1705 (Fig. 58). Massing that coincided with these projects had already appeared in the drawing prepared for dissolving the partnership (Fig. 9). These projects illuminate more clearly several of the concerns with which architects and their clients grappled at the Place Vendôme.

Two projects for the southeast corner (no. 8) were likely prepared for Fontanieu, who had begun his career as Crozat's *commis* (Fig.9). In 1693, he wed Catherine-Geneviève Dodun, related to a future Controller General of Finance, and the following year he became Receiver General for La Rochelle.[29] Well-placed as Treasurer General of the Navy during the War of the Spanish Succession, Fontanieu was recognized as a man of "probity."[30]

In what is probably the earliest extant study (Fig. 59), Bullet used a semi-

Figure 58
Place Vendôme, view of east range (nos. 12–26) [photo: courtesy of Christopher Mead].

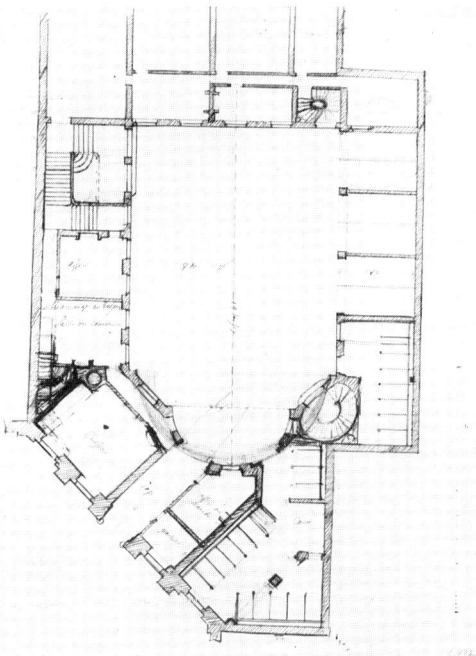

Figure 59
Pierre Bullet, unrealized study for ground-floor plan, no. 8 Place Vendôme (Maison "Fontanieu"), c. 1704–5 [photo: Nationalmuseum, Stockholm, THC 6997].

circular spatial joint to shift the entrance axis and provide a grander approach to the court and to a secondary stair adjacent to the range along the square. He managed the juncture more elegantly than Mansart had, apparently again drawing inspiration from Le Pautre's Hôtel de Beauvais (Fig. 38). Bullet oriented the principal rooms of the rear range toward the garden and provided secondary spaces along the court, permitting alternate access to the public suite. In each of two related plans, Bullet replaced the secondary rooms along the court with a grand entrance peristyle that functioned as an impressive entry to the public apartment; in each case, that suite was clearly intended for a male user (Figs. 60 and 61).[31]

Bullet's elegant plans remained unbuilt, but aspects appeared soon after at the Hôtel d'Évreux (Fig. 36) and later in the house built on this site (Figs. 62 and 63). In 1714, Fontanieu sold the lot to the Receiver General for Auvergne and general tax farmer Paul-Marie Delpech and his new wife Madeleine de Monchy. A generation younger than Crozat and Fontanieu, they had nonetheless forged a financial union typical of many of the first families at the square. Both were the progeny of general tax farmers long associated with Luillier, and they selected Pierre Le Maître the Younger as their architect.[32]

In Le Maître's design, which drew upon ideas earlier explored by Bullet and Mansart, a round vestibule provided a space for carriages to turn as they entered the court; there visitors disembarked at a grand portal in the left wing. Le Maître reverted to a single-room deep suite of *cabinets* for Delpech's use, set between court and garden.[33] Delpech's son-in-law, the marquis de Brehaut, later occupied an apartment directly above, on the first floor. Along the square, business callers could mount to Delpech's *bureaux* in the *entresol*, using one of two stairs opening off the vestibule; the other stair provided servants with alternate access to Mme Delpech's ceremonial and private apartments on the first floor. An appropriate use for the indirectly lit space at the center of the first-floor range perplexed Le Maître. In one study, he inserted a circular joint connecting a small room along the court with two of three ceremonial rooms along the square;[34] in another, he merged the small room and the joint to form an elongated anteroom (Fig. 63).[35] Thus, Le Maître, too, experimented with variety of room contour and inventive circulatory spaces in the range along the square, albeit with less daring and finesse than Mansart or Bullet.[36]

For the northeast *pan coupé* assigned to Luillier (Fig. 58), Bullet and his son prepared two unexecuted projects corresponding with revisions on the 1704 drawing (Fig. 9). An advantage of the parcel was its direct access to the cul-de-sac de la Corderie as a secondary exit. The starting point for one project was the garden, ample and regular in its perimeter, complemented by a private garden that could be entered from the *cabinet* of a ground-floor suite in the wing (Fig. 64). In the second project, they focused on providing traditional, noble apartments between court and garden, on both the ground and first floors (Figs. 65 and 66).[37] On the first floor, a dining room that opened off the main stair would have doubled as an anteroom to two apartments in the range along the square, each entered from a small oval "*salon*." A paved terrace above the carriage stalls linked the *grand cabinet* in that range with a *cabinet* in the suite to the rear of the court. Once again, Bullet provided an elegant but unbuilt project, and the parcel was still empty in 1718 when Luillier's grandson sold it to John Law.

Figure 60

facing page top) Pierre Bullet, unrealized study for ground-floor plan, no. 8 Place Vendôme (Maison "Fontanieu"), c. 1704–5. Rooms along the garden, *right to left: cabinet, Grand Cabinet, chambre, serre papier* [photo: Nationalmuseum, Stockholm, THC 6973].

Figure 61

(*facing page bottom*) Pierre Bullet (or after Bullet), unrealized study for ground-floor plan, no. 8 Place Vendôme (Maison "Fontanieu"), c. 1704–5 [photo: Bibliothèque Nationale, Est., Ha 18a II].

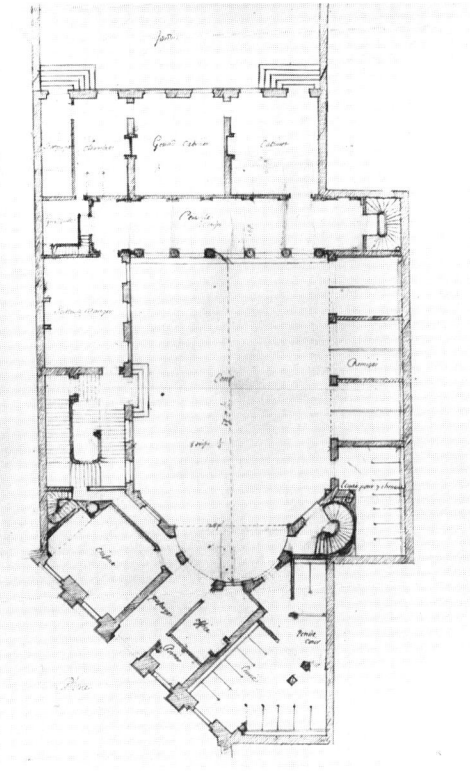

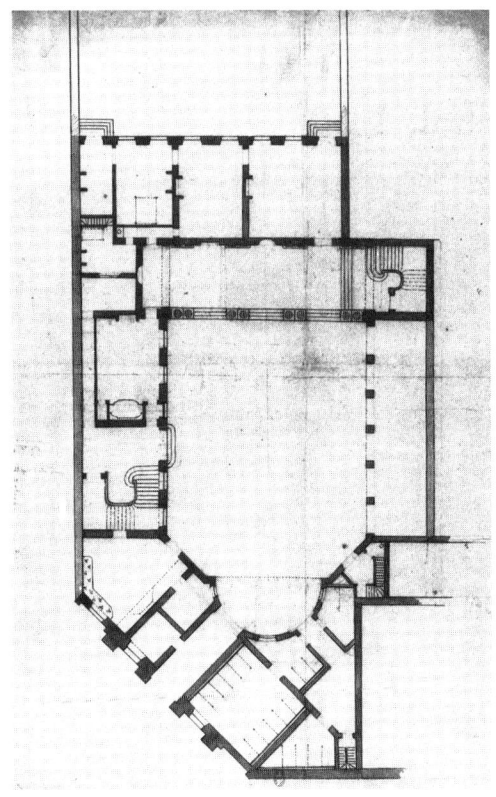

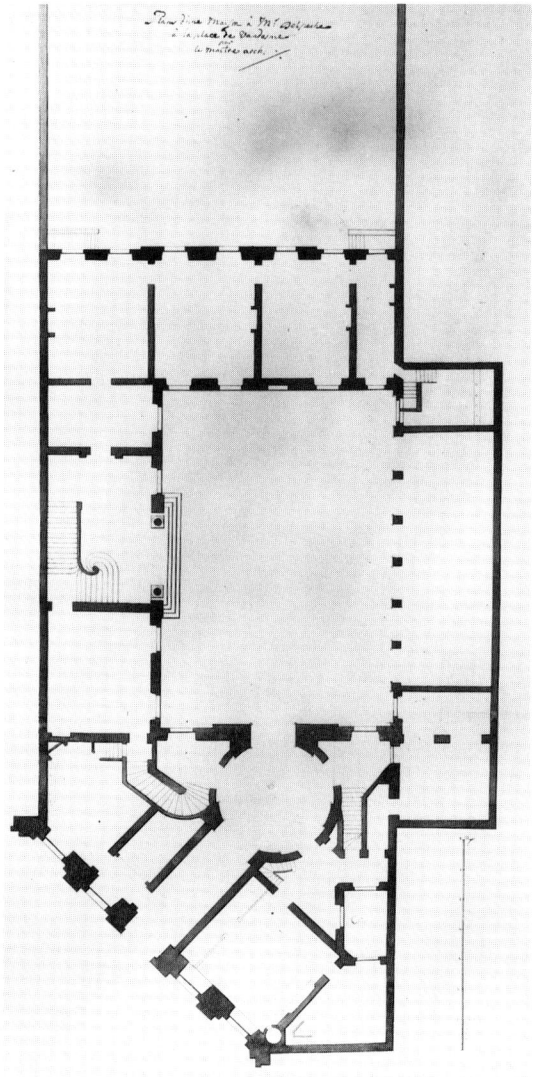

Figure 62
Pierre Le Maître the Younger, ground-floor plan, Maison Delpech, no. 8 Place Vendôme, 1714 (redrawn, perhaps by Carl Hårleman) [photo: Nationalmuseum, Stockholm, THC 6421].

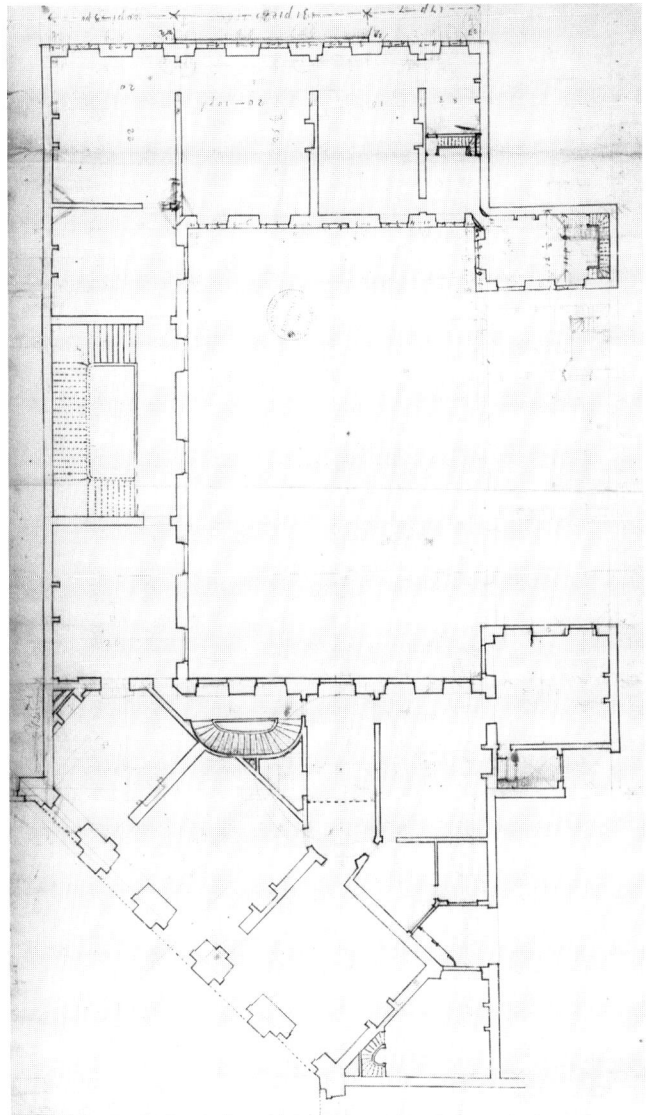

Figure 63
Pierre Le Maître the Younger, first-floor plan, Maison Delpech, no. 8 Place Vendôme, 1714, Bibliothèque de l'Institut de France, Ms. 1308, f°27 [photo: Jean-Loup Charmet].

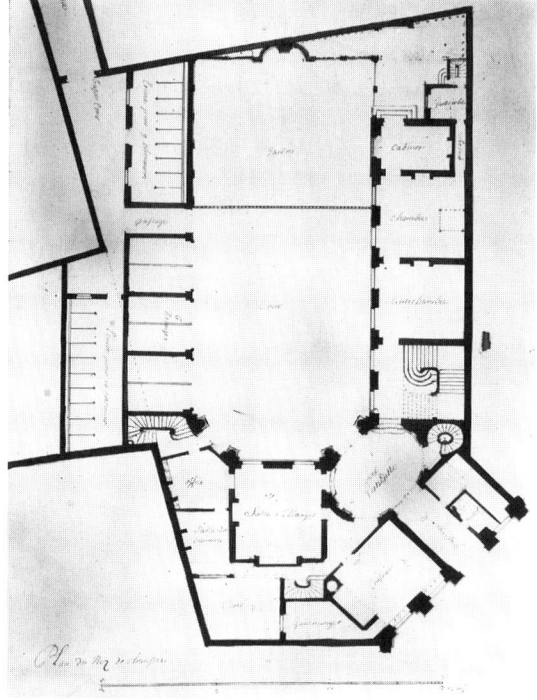

Figure 64

Pierre Bullet and Jean-Baptiste Bullet de Chamblain
(drawing by Chamblain), unrealized study for
ground-floor plan, no. 22 Place Vendôme, c. 1705
[photo: Nationalmuseum, Stockholm, THC 6913].

Figure 65

(*facing page top*) Pierre Bullet and Jean-Baptiste Bullet de Chamblain (drawing by
Chamblain), unrealized study for ground-floor plan, no. 22 Place Vendôme, c. 1705
[photo: Nationalmuseum, Stockholm, THC 6281].

Figure 66

(*facing page bottom*) Pierre Bullet and Jean-Baptiste Bullet de Chamblain, unrealized
study for first-floor plan (drawing by Bullet), no. 22 Place Vendôme, c. 1705 [photo:
Nationalmuseum, Stockholm, THC 7039].

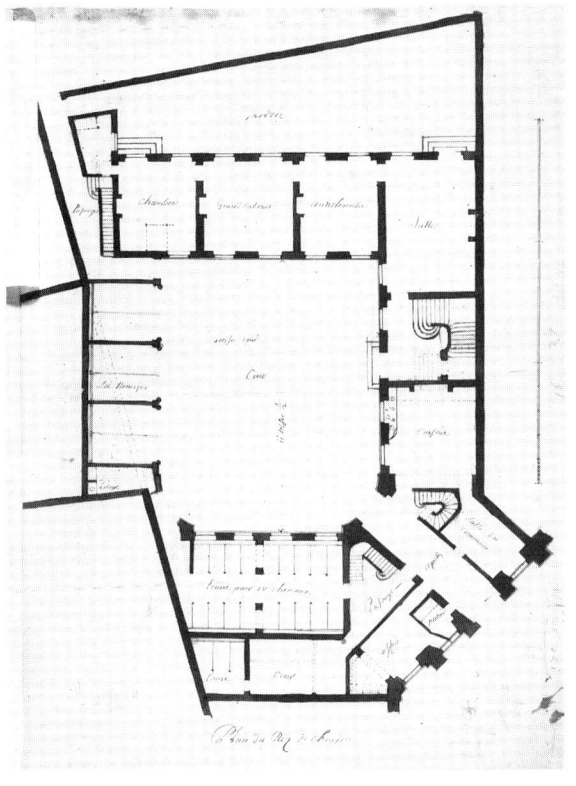

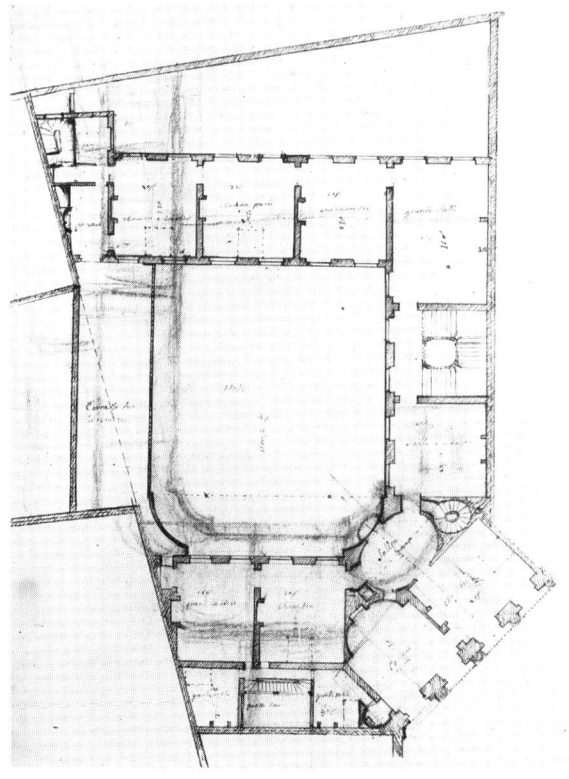

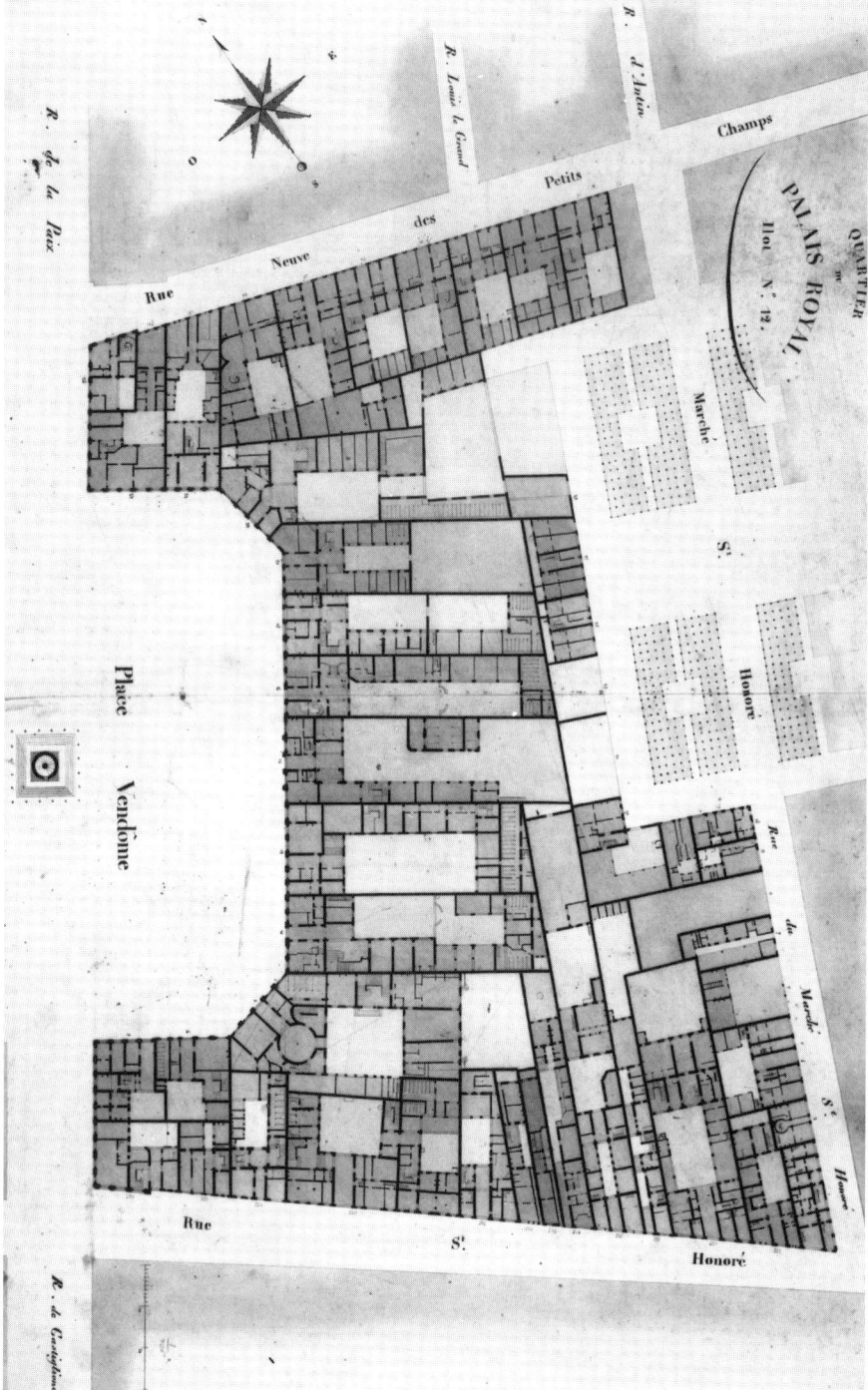

Figure 67

Place Vendôme, east range, cadastral plan, *Atlas Vasserot*, c. 1830–50. Note enlarged gardens and stables at rear of parcels; second wing added along north wall at no. 20; for numbers of houses today, see Fig. 9 [photo: Archives nationales, F³¹ 74 îlot 12, document conserved at Centre historique des Archives nationales, Paris].

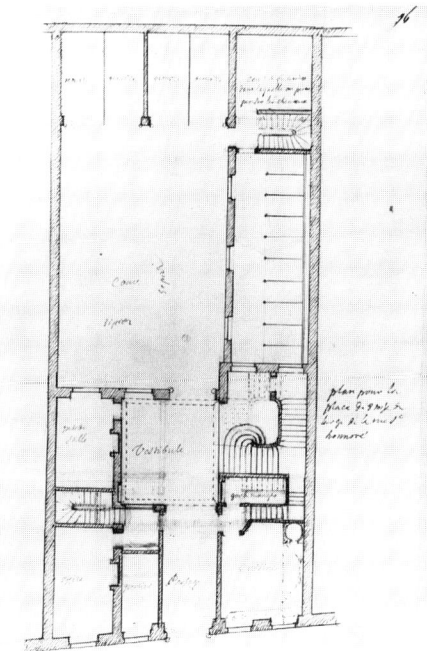

Figure 68
Pierre Bullet, unrealized study for ground-floor plan, house of L-type ("*hôtel-sur-rue*"), rue Saint-Honoré, c. 1705 [photo: Nationalmuseum, Stockholm, THC 6306].

The L-Shaped Type

Along the east and west ranges, the most common solution was an L-shaped type, with the main living quarters overlooking the square joined to a narrower wing along the court (Fig. 67). It was akin to a type that appeared frequently at the Place Royale (Fig. 52) and along important urban streets, where the *corps-de-logis* might be set above ground-floor boutiques (Figs. 19 and 20). Bullet and his son employed it, too, in plans for dwellings along the rue Saint-Honoré and other streets in the quarter (Figs. 68 to 69); in one project for the rue Saint-Honoré, however, Chamblain managed to remove the main *corps-de-logis* from the street (Fig. 70).[38]

It was so prevalent at the Place Vendôme in part because many sale contracts restricted building heights along one party wall so that adequate light and air would reach the courts of compressed sites; this resulted in coupled courtyards for longer parcels and grouped courts at the entrances to the square. Houses on elongated lots had gardens, but they were modest along the east range, where most proprietors eventually extended them to the walls of the Jacobin monastery (Figs. 9 and 67).

This standard massing resulted in formulas of planning, and studies by

Bullet and his son reveal many of their conventions (Figs. 71 to 74). Except along the entries to the square, the principal range was two rooms deep, with the main ceremonial apartment along the square and a more modest suite behind it; the narrower wing stretched along a party wall. Architects generally set the grand stair at the intersection of the wings; in one atypical variant, Bullet placed it in the main range at the corner opposite the wing, to enhance the magnificence of the approach to a gallery, reached following a procession through the ceremonial suite along the square (Fig. 71).[39]

In 1709, Chamblain designed one of the most elegant houses of the type (no. 9) for Jean Bonaventure Le Lay de Villemaré (1660–1743) (Figs. 26, 75 to 78). Of an old robe family attached to the Parlement of Rennes, Villemaré was also a close associate of his neighbor Bourvalais. He bought the parcel from Montargis in December 1708; for more than three decades, he resided at the square with members of his extended clan.[40]

Among the extant plans for the house are two studies for the *entresol* zone. In an early project, an entrance passage rose only as high as that zone (Figs. 75 to 76). In the *entresol*, directly off the main stair, Chamblain placed an anteroom with a curved wall; the anteroom had one door opening onto a corridor, another to an *office*, a third to a chamber with two beds, a fourth to a wardrobe, and a fifth opening onto a dining room. The complexly shaped dining room, set along the square, had a niche for a *buffet* flanked by two apses for fountains. Revisions drawn over the ground-floor passage (perhaps by the elder Bullet) suggest the grander entrance vestibule that was actually built (Figs. 75, 77, and 78). The realized vestibule rose a full story in height, extending up through a simplified *entresol*; windows along its upper zone lit the anteroom, corridor, and two small private rooms. Chamblain offered two alternatives for a reshaped anteroom (one octagonal, another with rounded corners) and reconceived the dining room, enlarging and regularizing it to avoid what Jean Courtonne would criticize as a trend resulting in "the appearance of a cut-up *parterre*."[41]

In two unusual plans of this type, architects introduced impressive ground-floor apartments. One study, in Chamblain's hand (Figs. 72 and 73), is quite close in massing to the dwelling built on parcel no. 15 for the duchesse de Gramont in 1713; she leased it upon completion to John Law.[42] More daring was a design for no. 24, prepared at about the same time by Boffrand, for

Figure 69

(*facing page top*) Jean-Baptiste Bullet de Chamblain, study for first-floor plan, house of L-type ("*hôtel-sur-rue*"), c. 1705 [photo: Nationalmuseum, Stockholm, THC 6271].

Figure 70

(*facing page bottom*) Jean-Baptiste Bullet de Chamblain, unrealized study for ground-floor plan, house along rue Saint-Honoré, with principal ranges oriented toward garden, c. 1705 [photo: Nationalmuseum, Stockholm, THC 7031].

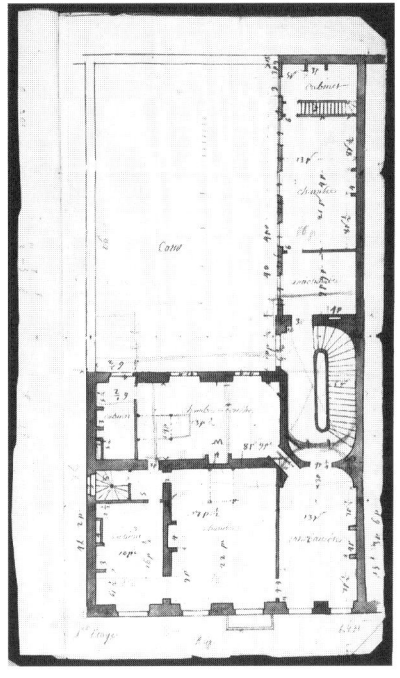

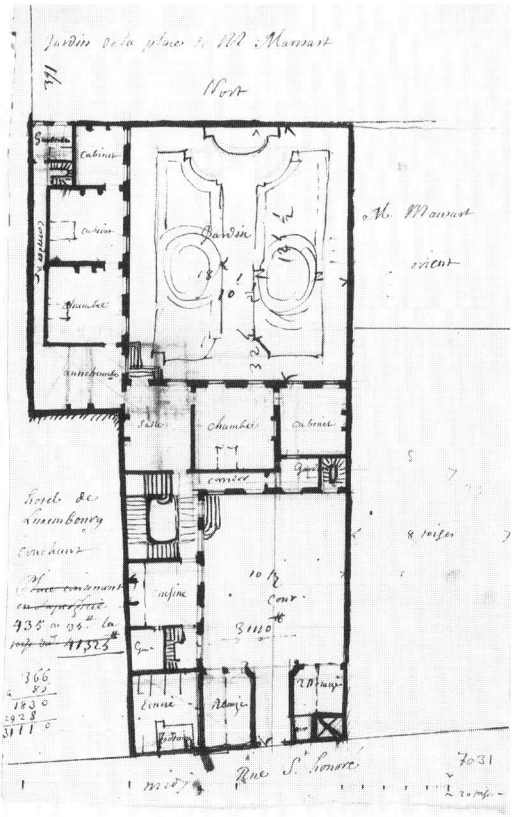

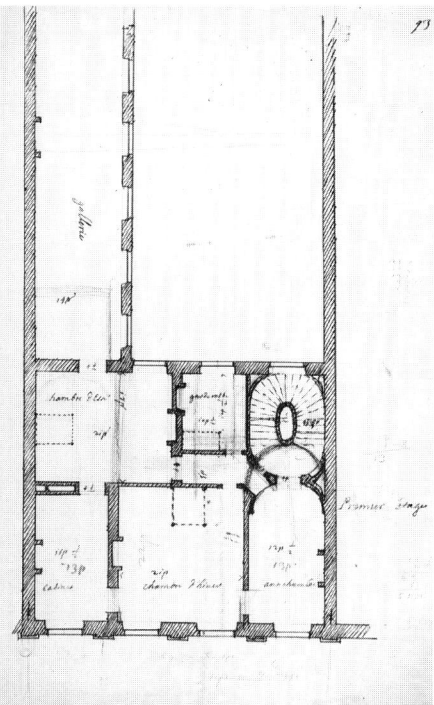

Figure 71
Pierre Bullet, unrealized study for first-floor
plan, house of L-type, Place Vendôme (perhaps no. 16), c. 1700–10 [photo: Nationalmuseum, Stockholm, THC 6303].

Catherine-Thérèse Blondot, daughter of a *commissaire de la marine* and wife
of Séraphin Rioult de Curzay.[43] Boffrand took advantage of the site, which
extended to the rue Neuve-des-Petits-Champs, by placing the entry and mundane functions along the street (Figs. 9 and 67).[44] Exploiting the representational grandness of the square more fully than other architects had done, while
adhering to the noble model, Boffrand managed to provide a unique apartment just behind the Place Vendôme facade on the ground floor (Fig. 58). He
probably conceived the unusual suite for Rioult.[45]

The Smaller Houses

Finally, there were the smaller dwellings, built on compact lots along the
entries to the square. It was Bullet, presumably, who laid out the basic type in
the partition drawing (Fig. 9). The partners assigned Bullet two of the smaller
lots along the south range (nos. 3 and 5), and among his unrealized plans,
several survive for very modest dwellings. One of Bullet's projects, for a house
of two bays, specified its location "along the entrance to the Place de Vendôme" (Fig. 79);[46] with his son, he also prepared studies for houses of three
bays.[47]

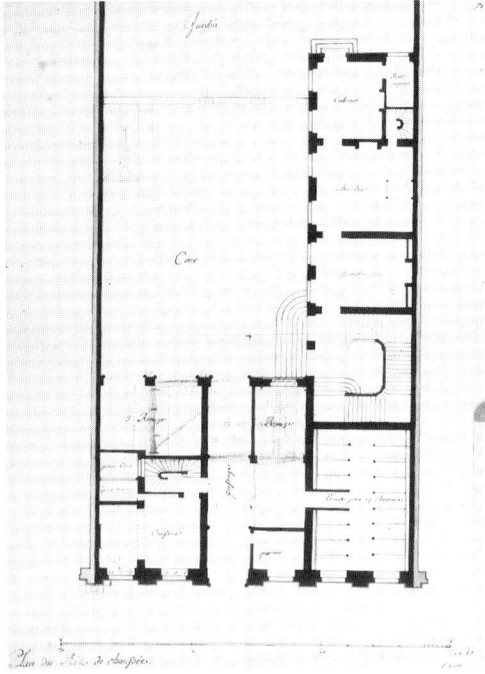

Figure 72
Jean-Baptiste Bullet de Chamblain, study for ground-floor plan, house of L-type, Place Vendôme (probably no. 15), c. 1700–10 [photo: Nationalmuseum, Stockholm, THC 6280].

These houses were closest in type to the smaller *hôtels* of the Place des Victoires (Fig. 21). The planning was, of necessity, tight, with a just a single range along the square. Bullet's primary concern seems to have been the provision of one ample ceremonial room – a *chambre de parade* or *grand cabinet* – that enjoyed a view of the square. Paradoxically, some of the smaller lots were initially among the most expensive, since buyers covered the cost of building facades along the square, and dwellings on corner lots had two. In fact, most of the lots along the north and south ranges were among the last to be sold.[48]

Architects and investors first began to build houses along the southern entry following the liquidation of Sauvion's assets in 1707. A group including investment partner Herlaut, the architect de Cotte, and his associate Noël Beaudet de Morlet acquired three of Sauvion's lots: no. 2 (which went to Beaudet), no. 6 (retained by de Cotte), and no. 25 (added to Herlaut's extensive holdings).[49] Two years later, Luillier sold parcel no. 4 to Heuzé de Vologer, Treasurer of France in Alençon, who built the first house along the entries to the square.

In December 1712, de Cotte sold no. 6 and his design for a house to be built on it to Charles Ycart, a *secrétaire du roi* and lawyer involved in finance.[50] The plan was a compact version of the L-shaped type, with a small court and no garden (Fig. 80). By foregoing a two-room deep distribution on the first floor (Fig. 81), de Cotte was able to place a large anteroom, a grand ceremonial bedchamber and a smaller *cabinet* along the square, with a corridor behind and a private apartment in the wing. In the *entresol*, de Cotte provided a nearly identical suite along the square and accommodated dining in the wing.[51]

Many of the plans and projects for houses at the Place Vendôme were innovative, but use tended to be more conservative. At the beginning of the century, the *salon* largely dislodged the vast *salle* in noble dwellings, yet relatively few Place Vendôme dwellings incorporated *salons*.[52] Instead, the most important room of the ceremonial apartment was usually the *chambre de parade*. Theoretically, bourgeois families had no need for ceremonial bedchambers, which only added to the representational value of such rooms among the socially ambitious. When spatial constraints forced a choice between the newly fashionable *salon* and the venerable *chambre de parade*, financiers chose the latter.[53]

The Place Vendôme appealed to powerful financiers at the turn of the eigh-

Figure 73

(*bottom left*) Jean-Baptiste Bullet de Chamblain, study for *entresol* plan, house of L-type, Place Vendôme (probably no. 15) c. 1700–10 [photo: Nationalmuseum, Stockholm, THC 6280].

Figure 74

(*bottom right*) Jean-Baptiste Bullet de Chamblain, unrealized study for *entresol* plan, house of L-type, Place Vendôme, c. 1700–10 [photo: Nationalmuseum, Stockholm, THC 6993].

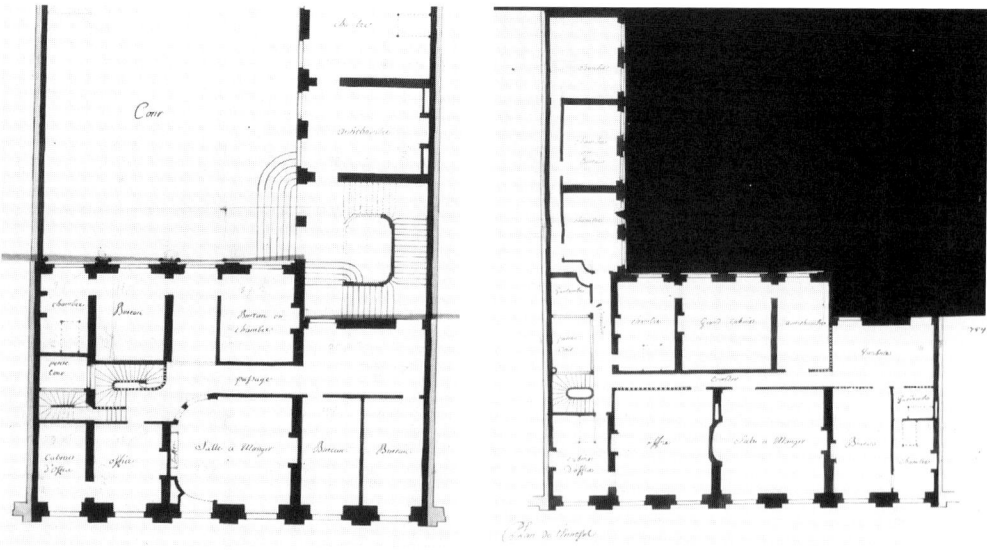

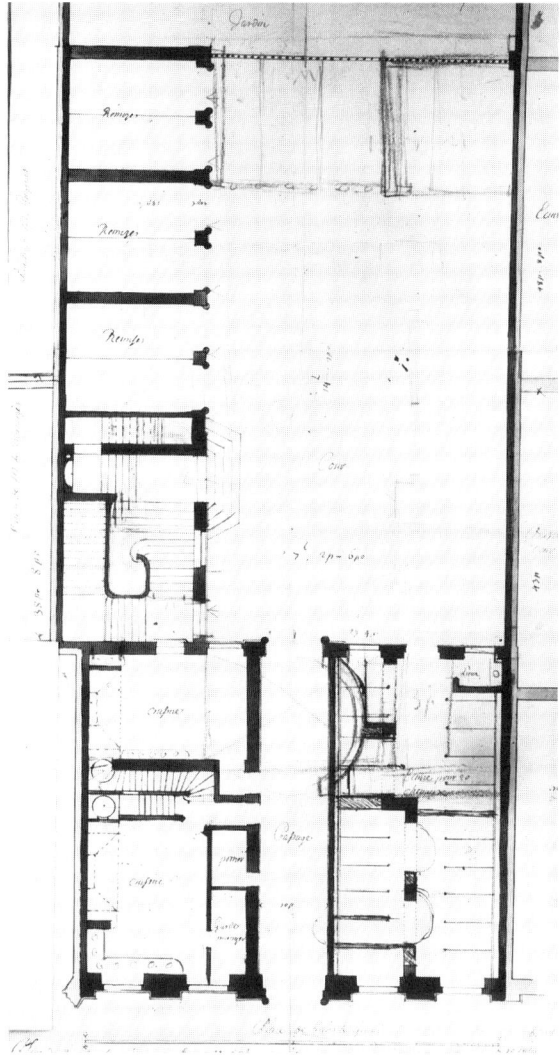

Figure 75
Jean-Baptiste Bullet de Chamblain, unrealized study for
ground-floor plan, Maison Le Lay de Villemaré, no. 9
Place Vendôme, 1709 [photo: Nationalmuseum, Stockholm, THC 6314].

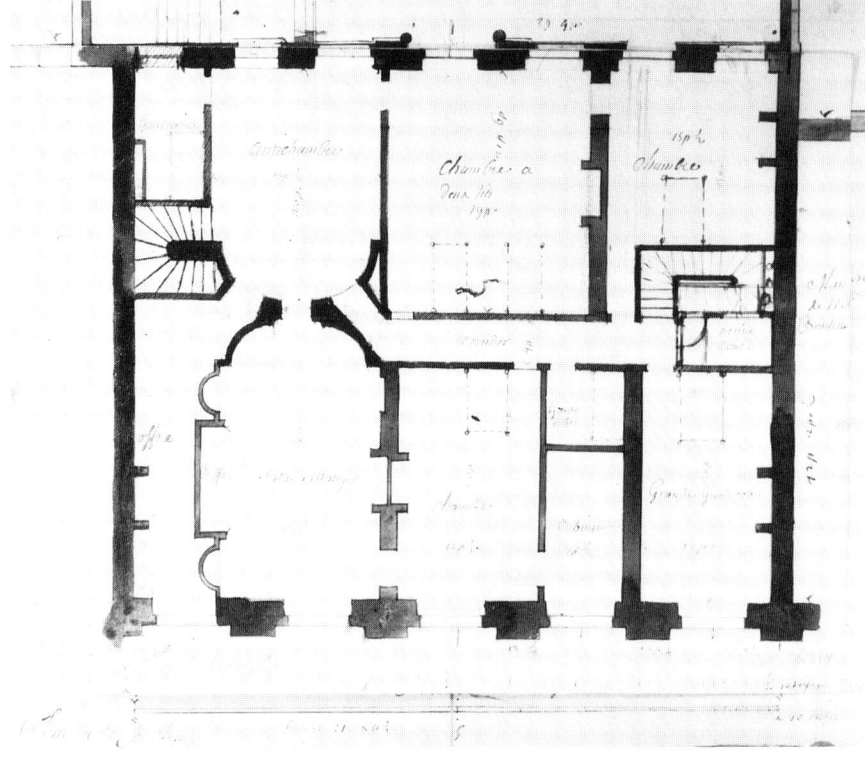

Figure 76
Jean-Baptiste Bullet de Chamblain, unrealized study for *entresol* plan, Maison Le Lay de Villemaré, no. 9 Place Vendôme, 1709 [photo: Nationalmuseum, Stockholm, THC 6314].

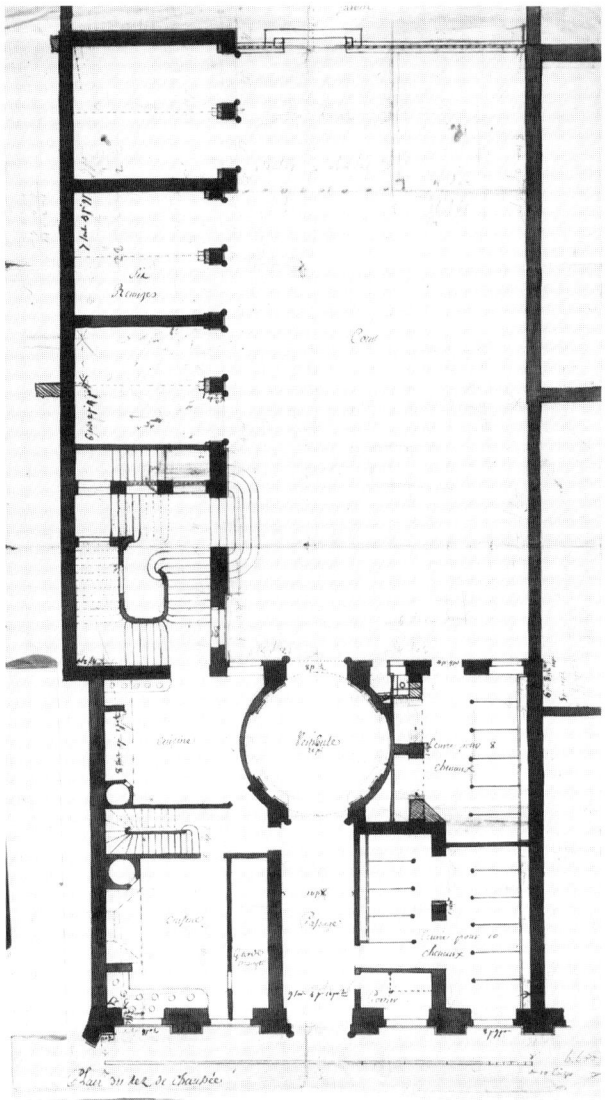

Figure 77
Jean-Baptiste Bullet de Chamblain, ground-floor plan, Maison Le Lay de Villemaré, no. 9 Place Vendôme, 1709 [photo: Nationalmuseum, Stockholm, THC 6685].

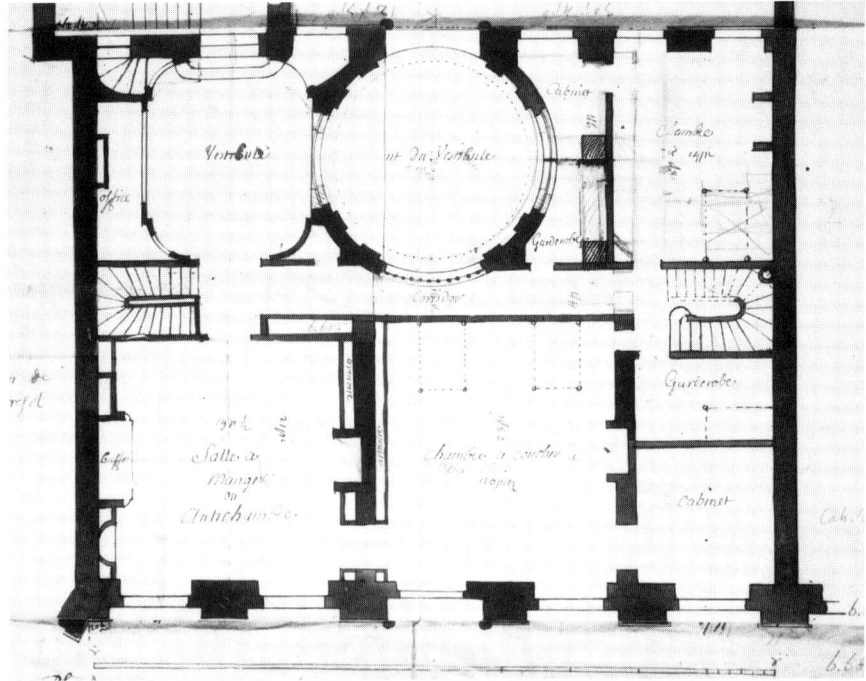

Figure 78
Jean-Baptiste Bullet de Chamblain, *entresol* plan, Maison Le Lay de Villemaré, no. 9
Place Vendôme, 1709 [photo: Nationalmuseum, Stockholm, THC 6685].

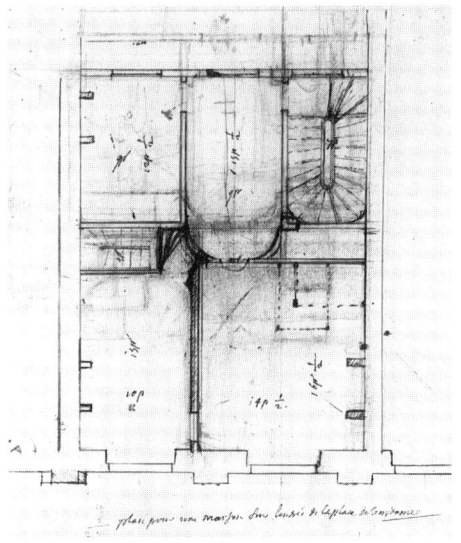

Figure 79
Pierre Bullet, unrealized study for first-floor
plan, house of two bays "at the entrance to
Place Vendôme," c. 1700–5, [photo: Nationalmuseum, Stockholm, THC 6994].

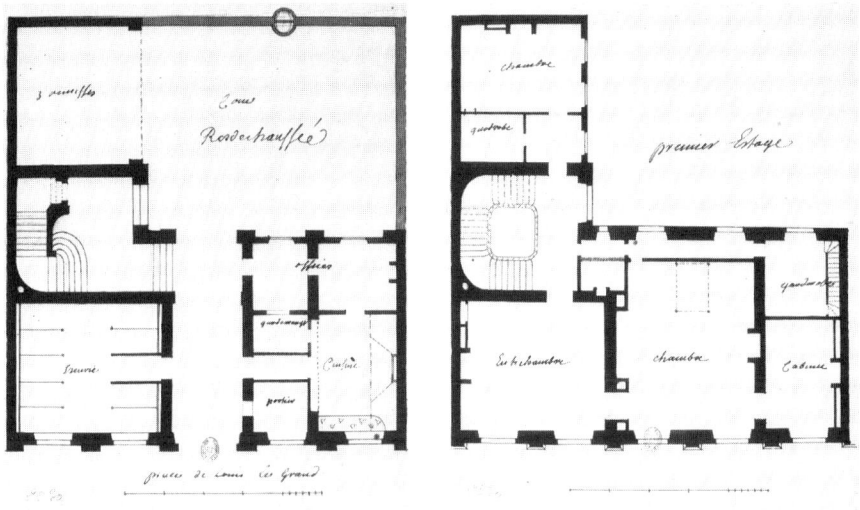

Figure 80

(*top left*) Robert de Cotte, ground-floor plan, drawing by draftsman affiliated with de Cotte, Maison Ycart, no. 6 Place Vendôme, 1712 [photo: Bibliothèque Nationale, Est., Ha 18a III].

Figure 81

(*top right*) Robert de Cotte, first-floor plan, drawing by draftsman affiliated with de Cotte, Maison Ycart, no. 6 Place Vendôme, 1712 [photo: Bibliothèque Nationale, Est., Ha 18a III].

teenth century, but the venture was not a resounding success. When Louis XIV died in September 1715, there were still empty lots behind the facades along the south and north entries, in the northeast *pan coupé*, and behind eight bays of the east range. Of twenty-eight parcels, houses had been built on just seventeen. The facades in front of empty parcels were still unfinished, since the proprietors undertook the sculptural enrichment including keystone masks, corbels above the first-floor windows, and even pilaster capitals.

Even in its incomplete state, however, the Place Vendôme was a highly prestigious place of residence for financial families. But Brice was not alone in suggesting that the nobility of the setting was inappropriate to "bourgeois" men of finance. During the Regency, the families of the Place Vendôme would find that their concentration at this royal square attracted resentment across a range of French society.

4

The Regency and Its Aftermath

The 9th [of March], they conducted to the Bastille sieur Bourvalais, famous financier (*maltôtier*), sieur Myot and three other of their associates. Sieur Myot was found in his granary, where he was hidden amidst the hay.[1]

Louis XIV's death in September 1715 cast Place Vendôme financiers into the most vulnerable positions of their careers. Rancorous social critique proved only one of the risks associated with their residence at the square. In establishing so conspicuous a presence in the capital and so openly displaying their wealth and pretensions, they left themselves exposed to more severe forms of public vengeance. In 1716, the new Regency government began a tribunal, a Chambre de Justice, to "tax" the profits of all those who had advanced funds to the Crown during the last two wars.

While the country faced bankruptcy and the tribunal fined and, in some cases, jailed financiers, the exuberant and sumptuous new domestic style of the Rococo flowered among the court aristocracy. Like the tribunal, it pointed to a more general abandonment of values and standards established during the previous reign. With Louis's death and the forming of a new government, financiers lost their protectors at court. Profits garnered during Louis's wars were now condemned as exorbitant.

Courtiers, fully freed from the demands of residence at Versailles, now focused their attention on their Paris dwellings to a degree unprecedented since the middle of the seventeenth century. Continuing a mode that began in the last years of Louis's reign, they focused on those realms that framed activities contrasting most keenly with the very public lives they had led at Versailles. They turned their attention first to private apartments and soon after to new semipublic suites of rooms, which came to be called apartments of *société* or *compagnie*. These spheres were conceived spatially and decoratively in a new style, the Rococo. Not simply different from the classical style of Versailles associated with Louis XIV during the height of his power, the Rococo was in many respects its antithesis – even if it had begun to emerge two decades or so before Louis's death and affected Versailles itself. Those seeds would blossom among members of the court aristocracy during the Regency, fueled in part by funds disgorged by financiers and profits from speculation. John Law and members of the Regent's circle used some of those funds to complete the square that bore the former king's name. Somewhat ironically, the Regent's circle adopted the Place Vendôme as a satellite of the Palais Royal, and, in doing so, they fundamentally altered its character.

The Chambre de Justice, 1716–1717

Luxury [among financiers] has absolutely fallen and a simplicity, noble but modest, has taken its place. . . . Financiers . . . [are paying for] all the embezzlement, extortion, tormenting abuses of power, bribery and other crimes they have committed . . . [January 4, 1717].[2]

Periodically during the *ancien régime*, generally following a period of war when financiers had been particularly critical in raising funds, the Crown would attempt to lessen its debt through a tribunal known as a Chambre de Justice. The last and largest of the seventeenth century began in November 1661, when the Crown tried Superintendent of Finance Nicolas Fouquet for misuse of royal funds. Along with Fouquet, many financiers were tried and fined; some were imprisoned, others bankrupted. If Fouquet's extravagant *château* and gardens at Vaux-le-Vicomte were probably not, in themselves, the cause of his arrest and punishment, such conspicuous display clearly contributed to his fall.

By the time Louis XIV died in late 1715, massive debt had accumulated from the almost relentless wars of the end of the reign. The new Regency government acted exactly as Louis had at the beginning of his personal reign. It moved to reduce the debt by attacking the Crown's creditors, particularly those who were politically weakest. Fifty-four years had passed since the last Chambre de Justice, and many financiers may have believed that it was by then an archaic institution. Such tribunals were not to be taken lightly. Sentences could include steep fines, seizure of property, imprisonment, even execution. In its rather ruthless mode of procedure, a Chambre de Justice was conducted, in the words of J. F. Bosher, "like a witch-hunt."[3]

Among the first to be scrutinized in 1716 was the financier who had adopted the highest profile at the Place Vendôme. Two days before the tribunal officially began, agents of the Chambre arrested Poisson de Bourvalais at his house at Champs, near Paris. They seized and sealed Bourvalais's *maison de plaisance* and his dwelling at the Place Vendôme, the largest at the square, set behind one of the representationally grandest portions of the facade (Figs. 6 and 8). Within a week, judges ordered the sale of Bourvalais's prized stable of Spanish and English horses to pay for the proceedings against him; by the end of the month, they had confiscated six cart loads of precious furnishings.[4]

Soon after Bourvalais's incarceration, officers of the Chambre arrested his neighbor and associate Villemaré, seizing and sealing his house (no. 9), and they imprisoned Ordinary Treasurer of War Claude-François Paparel, who resided at no. 14, which extended behind the grand central pavilion of the east range (Figs. 7 and 58).[5] They arrested Aubert, among the first residents at the square (no. 12), closely allied with former Controller General of Finance

Pontchartrain.[6] Herlaut, an original investment partner and early resident (no. 20), died suddenly two months after the Chambre began – possibly one of the suicides that accompanied the tribunal.[7]

Financiers of the Place Vendôme suffered some of the harshest judgments, despite the Regent's attempt to exempt the Crozat brothers, Montargis, and court banker Samuel Bernard.[8] The tribunal convicted Paparel of embezzlement and sentenced him to death, and it fined Bourvalais 4,466,000 *livres*. The Regent, however, moderated those sentences. Just days before his scheduled execution, Paparel was sentenced to life imprisonment plus appropriation of his property; Bourvalais's fine was limited to seizure of his lands in Brie, his country house at Champs, and his dwelling at the Place Vendôme.[9] The Chambre fined Antoine Crozat 6,600,000 *livres* – the largest "tax."[10] Aubert sold one of his Place Vendôme houses (no. 10), with sale proceeds paid directly to the Chambre.[11] The tribunal broke Paparel and Bourvalais. Bourvalais, who "could not restrain his tears each time he entered the Chambre to submit to interrogation," died in early 1719 at the house to which his family retreated at the Place des Victoires.[12]

Fines and harsher treatment were cast as "taxes" and punishments for hiding assets, but retribution for too opulent a display of wealth clearly figured in the assessment. At the opening of the tribunal, Chancellor Voysin charged that financiers, "by their luxury and the ostentation of their riches, have insulted the public that they have impoverished."[13] Ridiculing pamphlets and broadsheets circulated, several condemning Bourvalais, among them "Dialogue or Interview of Bourvalais and the Devil of Money Locked in his Cashbox," which specifically lampooned his "magnificent Hôtel."[14] A high profile contributed to the vulnerability of financiers, and the most conspicuous address was apparently the Place Vendôme.[15]

Financiers were certainly not the only group to inhabit magnificent dwellings. Many court nobles had opulent *hôtels* in the Faubourg Saint-Germain, built and furnished since 1689 – the period under scrutiny. Some had married daughters of financiers, receiving substantial cash dowries used to build those houses. Often a dwelling was part of the bargain, paid for with funds now regarded as suspect. The judges considered, but refused to either examine or tax those sources of noble wealth. "This would trouble a great number of families," a memorandum explained, ". . . [and] cause the ruin of several persons of condition, for whom need alone pushed [them] to contract unworthy alliances, and who, having sacrificed the honor of their Houses to repair the debris of their fortunes, seem to be owed, at least, the tranquil enjoyment of that which they have bought so dearly."[16]

The papers of the Chambre offer insights into households at the square, especially that of Bourvalais.[17] Testimony disclosed that the *grand cabinet* opening onto the garden (Fig. 24) was indeed the center of Bourvalais's financial operations. Among the first informers (encouraged by the promise of a reward) was a water carrier who had helped build, below Bourvalais's *cabinet*, a spe-

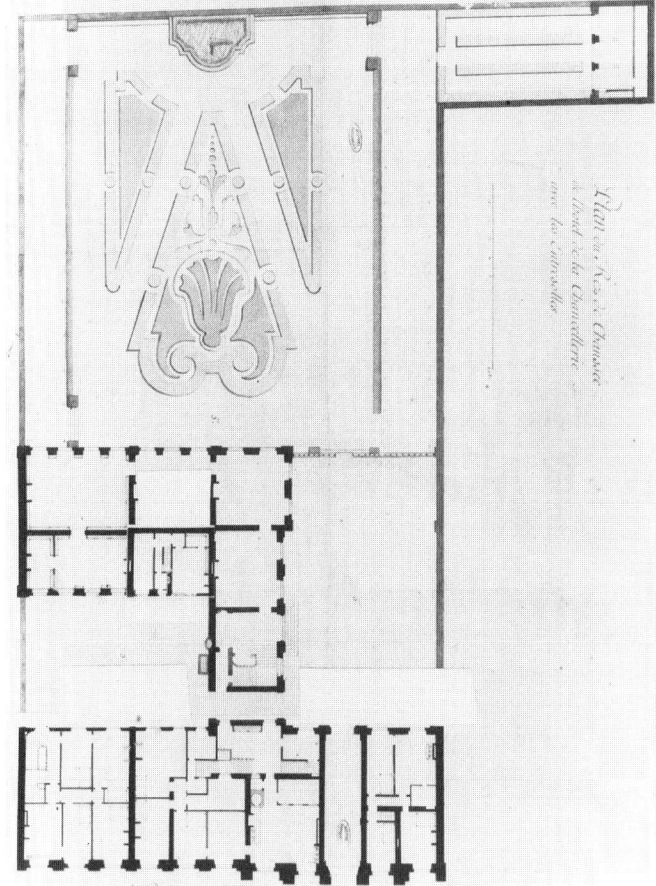

Figure 82

Robert de Cotte, study for ground-floor plan, with *entresol* rooms along square and in three bays facing court in rear range, drawing by draftsman in the Bâtiments du roi, Chancellerie, nos. 11–13 Place Vendôme, 1717 [photo: N III Seine 1208/2, document conserved at Centre historique des Archives nationales, Paris].

cial brick chamber paved with stone; he claimed Bourvalais used it to hide cash. Bourvalais protested that it was a latrine facility, but a footman described large sums of money he had carried into the *cabinet*.[18]

Bourvalais's confiscated dwelling was not sold to reduce the state's debt. The maréchale d'Estrées, already renting the former Hôtel d'Évreux, and the duchesse d'Albret (wife of d'Évreux's eldest brother) each coveted the house and lobbied for it.[19] The Regent gave it to the duc and duchesse d'Albret-Bouillon, who briefly resided there, but the gift was soon rescinded and it became the Chancellerie – the official residence of the newly appointed Chancellor, Henri-François d'Aguesseau (Fig. 82).[20]

D'Aguesseau brought to the Place Vendôme a presence quite unlike that of Bourvalais. As the chief legal official, the Chancellor was considered the first

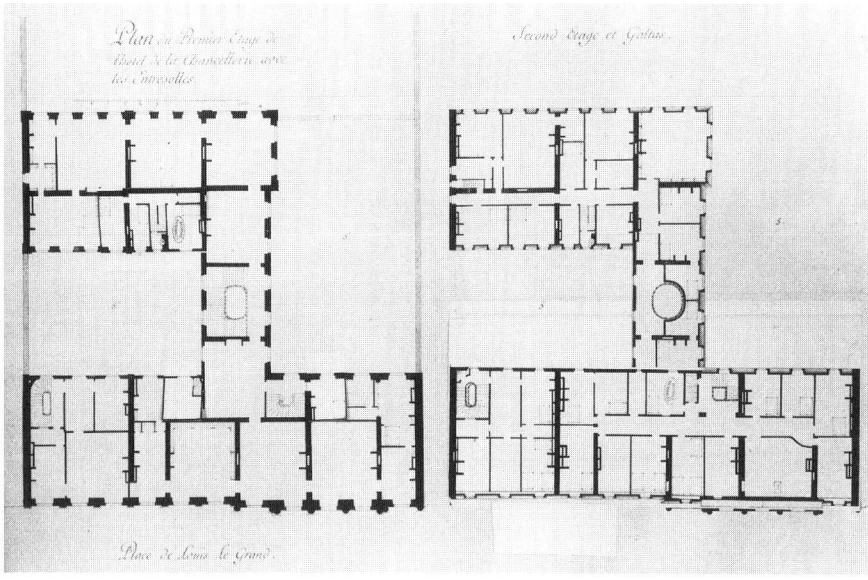

Figure 83

Robert de Cotte, studies for first- and second-floor plans, drawings by draftsman in the Bâtiments du roi, Chancellerie, nos. 11–13 Place Vendôme, 1717; three-bay *grand cabinet* is at left end of the first-floor suite along garden [photo: N III Seine 1208/3, document conserved at Centre historique des Archives nationales, Paris].

among the Crown's great officers, and d'Aguesseau was widely respected for his intellect, integrity, piety, and modesty; even Saint-Simon found him "gentle, good, human, and easily and agreeably approached . . . noble without the slightest avarice."[21] His wife was Anne-Françoise Le Fèvre d'Ormesson, of another leading robe clan, and they shared devotion to their children, to each other, and to their family life. Of twelve children, six apparently resided at the Place Vendôme, no doubt occupying rooms off the corridors that now extended the entire length and breadth of the second floor (Fig. 83); when Mme d'Aguesseau died in late 1735, all four adult sons, plus two daughters-in-law, still lived at the Chancellerie.[22]

The Chancellor, "who worries about the noise of carriages and who has much work to do, is building an apartment for himself at the rear of the house, and he does it at his own expense."[23] Bourvalais had already used the suite along the garden as a working apartment, but the Chancellor needed additional reception rooms and a library. De Cotte, designer of the original dwelling and now First Architect of the King, supervised its conversion into the Chancellerie. Most significantly, de Cotte appropriated stable space to enlarge the noble range between court and garden, accommodating new public rooms for the Chancellor on both the ground and first floors (Figs. 82 and 83).

One impressive first-floor ceremonial room along the garden, a *grand cabinet*, remains largely intact from that conversion (Figs. 84 and 85). De Cotte punctuated the cornice with reliefs of Justice (bearing her scales and sword) and flanked the mirrored bay of the fireplace with a pair of Corinthian pilasters, enhancing representational grandeur of the room.[24] The new ceremonial rooms, especially Mme d'Aguesseau's state bedchamber overlooking the garden on the first floor, glittered as opulently as those court families enjoyed at the time, but d'Aguesseau furnished several official rooms rather "soberly" in the estimation of biographer Isabelle Storez; when the Chancellor died in 1751, many of the armchairs in the reception rooms were upholstered rather conservatively in black (and sometimes red) leather.[25]

Among the casualties of the Chambre was Herlaut, the largest landholder at the square, who died so suddenly in May 1716. He must have had exceptionally close relations with Chamillart, Controller General of Finance from 1699 to 1708. In a highly unusual bequest, Herlaut left his Place Vendôme house to Chamillart's wife and the balance of his still empty lots (nos. 1, 16 to 18, and 23 to 25) to Chamillart's son. Chamillart, who had named Herlaut Treasurer General of the French and Swiss Guards in 1702, had been critical in building Herlaut's fortune.[26]

The parcel Herlaut selected in 1701 for his own house (no. 20) was oddly

Figure 84
Robert de Cotte, architect, *grand cabinet* (*in situ*), with nineteenth-century overdoor portraits, Chancellerie, nos. 11–13 Place Vendôme, c. 1718, [photo: after Jules Vacquier, *La place Vendôme, dite aussi de Louis le Grand ou des Conquêtes* (Paris: F. Contet, 1913)].

Figure 85
Robert de Cotte, architect, "Justice," detail of cornice, *grand cabi-net*, Chancellerie, nos. 11–13 Place Vendôme, 1717 [photo: after Jules Vacquier, *La place Vendôme* (Paris: F. Contet, 1913)].

configured, fronted by three bays along the east range and one in the *pan coupé*, akin in shape to Crozat's parcel, but two bays narrower and only half as deep (Fig. 9). Herlaut's architect, possibly Pierre Le Maître the Younger, had employed the standard L-shaped type.[27] To enlarge the lot of 223 square *toises*, Herlaut added a narrow strip of land that extended behind the parcel to the cul-de-sac, permitting a more extensive garden, with a *parterre* and an oblique *allée* of chestnut trees, plus a service entry. At the point where the garden met the cul-de-sac, Herlaut built a small inhabitable pavilion.

For his private apartment, Herlaut had chosen the relatively modest second story. At most Place Vendôme houses, second-floor rooms were treated simply, generally lacking expensive mirrors, elaborately sculpted paneling and cornices, painted overdoors, marble fireplace mantels, and parquet floors. Proprietors most often chose first-floor rooms overlooking the court for their private suites, leaving the second floor to children, relations and important members of the household staff. Herlaut's private rooms extended along the wing of the second floor, with the room at the intersection of the wing with the main *corps-de-logis* serving as his bedroom. The bedroom had a jib door in the paneling that led to a hidden stair descending to a small first-floor anteroom; the anteroom opened onto a ceremonial bedroom along the court and a *cabinet* along the square.

Herlaut was a widower, and it may be significant that his ceremonial bedroom faced the court; in virtually every other dwelling, the principal *chambre de parade*, normally occupied by the woman of the house, overlooked the Place Vendôme, and here his ward Magdeleine Baunier had a second-floor suite facing the square. Herlaut's dwelling, "less magnificent" than those of Crozat, d'Évreux and Bourvalais, according to Brice, still had "all the *commoditez*" and "*ajustemens*" required among those "*les plus à la mode*."[28] It was elegant enough to attract the interest of the Regent's mistress, the comtesse de Parabère.

A Satellite of the Palais Royal

Once the Regency began, the Place Vendôme held a new appeal for the court. It was convenient to the Regent's residence, the Palais Royal, directly linked along the rue Saint-Honoré and the rue Neuve-des-Petits-Champs (Fig. 1). It held a new dignity from its association with the former monarch. Some of those attached to the Orléans household had begun to move to the square a few years earlier, among them the abbé de Thésut, *secrétaire des commandements* of the future Regent; in 1713, he purchased, with the maréchal des Fourneaux, lifetime use of a dwelling they were to build on parcel no. 2 at the south entry (Figs. 9 and 67).[29] The Regent's principal mistress, Mme de Parabère (Fig. 86), and her friend Charles de Nocé – the two most notorious influence peddlers during the Chambre de Justice – acquired houses at the square following the 1716–17 tribunal, perhaps using the very funds they had extracted from some of their neighbors.[30]

Among the first to arrive were the maréchal Victor-Marie d'Estrées and his wife, Lucie-Félicité de Noailles; they leased the former Hôtel d'Évreux before the end of 1715. The Regent soon appointed d'Estrées to his new advisory councils on war, commerce, and the navy; through these councils, court noblemen, ousted from traditional advisory roles by Louis XIV, sought to reclaim their power.[31] An amateur chemist and honorary member of the French Academy, d'Estrées brought part of his celebrated fifty-two thousand rare books, as well as his prize collections of medals, rare and precious textiles, porcelain, jewels, and "all sorts of *curiosités*," and installed the abbé Goullé, a student at the Academy of Inscriptions and Medals, to serve as his librarian. His example may have had an impact on Crozat, who would also assemble an impressive library and install a librarian, and on his son Tugny, who later became a book collector and amateur chemist. Evidence has not emerged to indicate which apartments the maréchal and his wife inhabited, but their relationship was utterly different from that of the comte d'Évreux and Crozat's young daughter, and they almost certainly would have shared the range between court and garden.[32]

Their marriage was an aristocratic union of independent equals. Mme d'Estrées was notorious for extramarital liaisons and gossip linked her with, among others, the président Hénault, her neighbor at the square. She kept her friends amused by pretending to be the lover of d'Aguesseau, a close friend of her family widely respected for moral rectitude, publicly calling him "my wanton one."[33] Her public flaunting of real and fictive affairs, unthinkable for a wife or daughter of a financier, entertained fellow courtiers.[34] "He always

Figure 86
J.-B. Santerre, portrait of the duc d'Orléans
and the comtesse de Parabère, Versailles:
Musée du Château [photo: Réunion des
Musées Nationaux].

lived very well with his wife," said Saint-Simon of d'Estrées, "[and] she with
him, each according to his [or her] own ways."[35]

John Law, who would provide accommodation for several members of the
Regent's circle at the Place Vendôme, was also the man who most threatened
the livelihoods of financiers during the Regency. Familiar with the Bank of
England and banks in Scotland and Amsterdam, Law had moved to Paris –
and to the Place Vendôme – at the end of Louis XIV's reign, to renew his
proposal for a state bank.[36] The Regent proved more sympathetic than Louis
XIV, and in May 1716, he allowed Law to begin with a private bank. Two
years later, it evolved into a state bank using paper currency that financiers
were forced to accept (even when it was not worth its face value). With the
Regent's support, Law soon formed the vast Compagnie des Indes, merged it
with the bank, and sold shares of the combined enterprise to the public. During 1718–19, the Crown removed administration of direct taxes from the
Recette générale and assigned it to Law's company, which also outbid general
tax farmers to win collection of indirect taxes. Within less than six years, Law
ousted financiers from many of their most profitable sources of income.[37]

Law, perhaps encouraged by the Regent, undertook the completion of the

Place Vendôme. In 1718, Law purchased several empty parcels, nos. 3, 5, 21, 22, and 28 (Fig. 9), and Jacques V Gabriel, then Contrôleur at Versailles, designed houses for the lots.[38] Members of the Regent's circle purchased or rented most of the new dwellings, commissioning fashionable, sumptuously gilded interiors.[39] They clearly did not take the former Chancellor Voysin's charge that "luxury" and "ostentation" had "insulted the public" to refer to themselves.

As early as 1717, Chamillart's wife "donated" the house she had inherited from Herlaut (no. 20) to the Regent's principal mistress, Mme de Parabère.[40] Parabère may have begun renovation, but she soon coveted a contiguous dwelling, newly built by Gabriel for Law, on the larger site in the northeast corner (Figs. 7, 9 and 58).[41] In early 1720, she acquired no. 22 and leased no. 20 to her friend Nocé.[42]

A later plan reveals that Gabriel broke completely with the *pan coupé* type (including unrealized projects for this site) in designing no. 22 (Figs. 9 and 67). Gabriel chose an L-shaped disposition, probably conceived from the outset for Mme de Parabère. The house turned its back to lots along the rue Neuve-des-Petits-Champs and opened south toward no. 20; the two gardens were separated only by a low party wall, with doors providing access.[43] At the entry to the dwelling, Gabriel rounded one end of an impressive vestibule, which shifted the axis.

Mme de Parabère, not one to shrink from public display, claimed the first-floor rooms overlooking the square for her ceremonial apartment. When the Regent visited her, his presence was occasionally quite visible in illuminated rooms along the Place Vendôme.[44] After purchasing the house, Parabère commissioned interior decoration from Gabriel, and among the rooms he conceived for her was a small, opulent *cabinet* overlooking the square, revealing aspects of the new focus among court nobles on the more private spaces of their dwellings.

The *cabinet*, entered from Mme de Parabère's *chambre de parade*, was the most exclusive room of the ceremonial apartment (Figs. 87 and 88).[45] Gabriel enhanced its intimacy by canting the corners of the fireplace wall facing the window, and he lined the room with delicately carved and gilded wood paneling. Above a thin cornice, lunettes framed roundels painted with birds, accompanied by a monkey and some small animals. Elegant, bare-breasted sphinxes in the sculpted frames colluded with this menagerie, part of the new libertine vocabulary adopted by a court nobles distancing themselves from the allegorical and historical lexicon associated with Versailles.[46] The Regent's circle called Parabère "the little raven," and the many painted birds may have been a pointed and playful conceit (her fictive "aviary"), to be enjoyed by intimate friends. A passage from the small *cabinet* led to Mme de Parabère's private apartment along the court, consisting of a bedroom, two wardrobes, a small *cabinet de toilette* and a *cabinet* for a *chaise percée*.[47] Mme de Parabère enjoyed her opulent dwelling until 1732, but extravagant spending had already brought financial difficulties by the mid-twenties. In 1732, Parabère sold her *hôtel* to Nicolas-Alexandre de Ségur, *président à mortier* at the Parlement of Bordeaux, and his wife Charlotte-Emilie Lefevre de Caumartin, and she returned to no. 20.[48]

The other houses designed by Gabriel were modest in size, for the smallest parcels: nos. 3, 5, 21, and probably 28.[49] His clientele called upon him to devise elegant dwellings despite the constraints of the sites. The most impressive was no. 21, leased for life in 1719 to Louis-Augustin Angran de Fonspertuis, a friend of the Regent and his *capitaine des chasses*, who, like many of the intimates of the Regent, profited handsomely from speculation in Law's bank (Figs. 7 to 9). Gabriel supervised the creation of an opulent decor, and one of its foci was, once again, the small *cabinet* of the ceremonial suite on the first floor, overlooking the square (Figs. 89 to 91).

Fonspertuis claimed that apartment, taking the largest room along the square as his ceremonial bedchamber, and thereby structuring his house differently from most financial dwellings. A great gulf in social status separated Fonspertuis, of an old robe and military clan, from his wife Rose de Châteauvieux, a *fille d'Opéra* whom he wed in 1705; she "lived marvelously with him," according to Luynes, and here she occupied a more modest suite in the *entresol*. Their son, accorded a large second-floor apartment, became a *conseiller au Parlement*, but was known less for judicial wisdom than for squandering his father's wealth.[50]

For this intimate of the Regent, Gabriel conceived of a *cabinet* (still *in situ*) as luxuriant as that of Mme de Parabère. Both had a precious quality that derived from diminutive size, extensive gilding, and elegant and playful ornamental vocabularies. Gabriel shaped an alcove, where Fonspertuis apparently installed his desk, and he set into it a large mirrored panel facing the window overlooking the square.[51] Fonspertuis commissioned separately the ceiling by Claude III Audran, where weightless arabesques and medallions encasing am-

Figure 87

(*facing page top*) Jacques V Gabriel, architect; Jules Degoullons, André Legoupil, Pierre Taupin, sculptors; first-floor *cabinet*, Hôtel de Parabère (1720–3), no. 22 Place Vendôme, photographed *in situ* before paneling was removed [photo: after Bruno Pons, *De Paris à Versailles 1699–1736: Les sculpteurs ornemanistes parisiens et l'art décoratif des Bâtiments du roi* (Strasbourg, 1986); permission: Presses Universitaires de Strasbourg].

Figure 88

(*facing page bottom*) Jacques V Gabriel, architect; Jules Degoullons, André Legoupil, Pierre Taupin, sculptors; detail of paneling formerly installed in first-floor *cabinet* of Hôtel de Parabère (1720–3), no. 22 Place Vendôme, now reinstalled in private house [photo: after Bruno Pons, *De Paris à Versailles 1699–1736: Les sculpteurs ornemanistes parisiens et l'art décoratif des Bâtiments du roi* (Strasbourg, 1986); permission: Presses Universitaires de Strasbourg].

Figure 89
Jacques V Gabriel, architect; Louis Herpin and Charles Loysel or
Charles-Louis Maurisan, sculptors; east wall of first-floor *cabinet
(in situ)*, Hôtel Angran de Fonspertuis, no. 21 Place Vendôme
(1719); oval relief is a later insertion [photo: Art Resource/Girau-
don].

orous couplings of the gods were accompanied by birds and small animals – a
lexicon akin to that of Mme de Parabere's *cabinet*.

Fonspertuis's *cabinet* was entered from his *chambre de parade*, the largest
room of the ceremonial suite overlooking the square, where he displayed
paintings, many of them Dutch and Flemish.[52] Opening off the stair along the
wing was a spacious dining room; like the one at the neighboring Hôtel
d'Évreux, it was unusual at this time in its prominent location on the first
floor. Beyond the dining room was a large *cabinet*, lined with six panels, each
approximately seven-feet high, of framed *papier des Indes*. For Fonspertuis, a

Figure 90
Jacques V Gabriel, architect; Louis Herpin and Charles Loysel or
Charles-Louis Maurisan, sculptors; niche along north wall of
first-floor *cabinet (in situ)*, Hôtel Angran de Fonspertuis, no. 21
Place Vendôme (1719) [photo: Art Resource/Giraudon].

director of the Compagnie des Indes, it was a kind of exotic, but not overly
serious, "attribute" (perhaps like the birds of Parabère's *cabinet*) and he called
the room his *cabinet des Indes*. Along the court, Gabriel placed a library
embellished by wood panels painted "in cameo," crowned with another ceiling of delicate arabesques painted by Audran. Next to it, Gabriel installed a
small *cabinet* for a *chaise percée*, its walls similarly lined with panels painted
with animals "in cameo," and a private bedroom, the latter later converted
into a *cabinet de porcelaine* for Fonspertuis's celebrated antique Japanese and
Chinese pieces.[53]
When the inflated prices of Law's bank shares collapsed in 1720, Law

Figure 91
Claude III Audran, painted ceiling, first-floor *cabinet (in situ)*, Hôtel Angran de Fonspertuis, no. 21 Place Vendôme (1723) [photo: Art Resource/Giraudon].

briefly transferred the trading of the shares to the Place Vendôme, which contemporaries considered a display of power to silence his more troublesome critics – including leading financiers, the Chancellor, and some among the Regent's *roués*.[54] The frenetic trading disrupted the square for about two months; Law transferred it again, and then purchased the remaining empty parcels. By December, however, he had to flee France, and his "system" would be dismantled by some of his most powerful critics – Antoine Crozat, Samuel Bernard and the Pâris frères.[55]

Following the reestablishment of the court at Versailles and the Regent's death in 1723, the character of the Place Vendôme changed again. Law's holdings at the square were liquidated, and soon after the new proprietors – mostly members of the building trades formerly associated with Law and among his creditors – constructed houses on the last empty parcels, which they leased or sold to financiers and *secrétaires du roi*. A predominantly financial character reemerged.[56]

The grandest of the last houses was no. 23, designed by Gabriel for Abraham Peyrenc de Moras in 1723–4; the parcel had been acquired through two intermediaries (including Gabriel), perhaps reflecting caution about too open a display of speculative profits. Of a formerly Protestant family from Languedoc, Peyrenc was the son of a "surgeon-barber" involved in tax collection, a heritage relentlessly lampooned. To explain his rise, charges abounded that Peyrenc had abducted Marie-Anne Fargès, daughter of a major munitions dealer, so that her father would agree to an alliance with his lowly clerk. Whatever the circumstances of their marriage, Peyrenc's rise was not so precipitous; he was active in extraordinary finance before he wed and was heavily taxed by the Chambre de Justice. But his unusually successful speculation in shares of Law's bank rendered his assets and personal history suspect.[57]

Peyrenc had purchased nos. 23 and 25, about equal in size, but reapportioned them to enlarge the dwelling he intended to occupy, no. 23, which had facades along the northern entry street and the square (Figs. 9 and 111). Gabriel adopted a massing similar to the house built for Nocé at no. 26 (Fig. 67). He supplemented the L-shaped range immediately behind the Place Vendôme facades with a narrow wing for stables along the west party wall, providing a secondary entry on the rue Neuve-des-Capucines. Peyrenc compensated for a constricted site with an elaborate program of interior decor.[58]

Apartments of the *entresol* and first floor were similar, with public rooms set along the square and a semiprivate suite overlooking the entry street. Gabriel set a large anteroom and dining room facing the square in the *entresol*.[59] At the corner, he placed a *cabinet* that opened onto Peyrenc's more private rooms, which included a bedchamber, a library, and two small wardrobes. On the *noble étage*, the *grande chambre* overlooking the square preceded a *cabinet* in the corner; the *cabinet* was linked to Mme Peyrenc's bedchamber and a *grand cabinet* along the entry street (served by two wardrobes lit along the court). In the richly decorated suite on each floor, the small *cabinet* linking the public and semiprivate apartments became a focus for embellishment.

Gabriel conceived the corner *cabinets* as diminutive light-filled rooms. Although modest in size, each had three windows, one overlooking the square, two facing the entry street. In Peyrenc's *entresol cabinet*, tall mirrors lined three walls, and Audran, who had quite recently worked for Peyrenc's neighbor Fonspertuis at no. 21, covered the ceiling with arabesques. Since it opened off the dining room, it was probably an intimate space to retire to after meals.[60] The library extended the full width of the range along the entry street; Gabriel illuminated it along the street and court and lined its walls with tall mirrors that enhanced the natural light.

Mme Peyrenc's *cabinet* was apparently the most lavishly decorated room of the house (Fig. 92). On five tall panels that Audran provided with arabesques and gazebolike garden stages, his associate Nicolas Lancret painted large theatrical figures: an "actress," a clown, a "Turk" (Fig. 93), a woman strolling with a parasol, and a female pilgrim. Amorous allusions predomi-

Figure 92
Jacques V Gabriel, architect; Nicolas Lancret and Claude III Audran, painters; Jules Degoullons, André and Mathieu Legoupil, sculptors; first-floor "*cabinet* in the corner" (before dismantled), Maison Peyrenc de Moras, no. 23 Place Vendôme (1724), from E. Féral, *Notice sur un très beau salon décoré par Lancret dont la vente aura lieu à Paris . . . le Mercredi 27 Mai 1896* (Paris, 1896) [photo: New York Public Library].

Figure 93
Nicolas Lancret and Claude III Audran, painters, detail of paneling (1724), formerly in first-floor "*cabinet* in the corner," Maison Peyrenc de Moras, no. 23 Place Vendôme, Musée des Arts Décoratifs, Paris [photo: Musée des Arts Décoratifs].

112

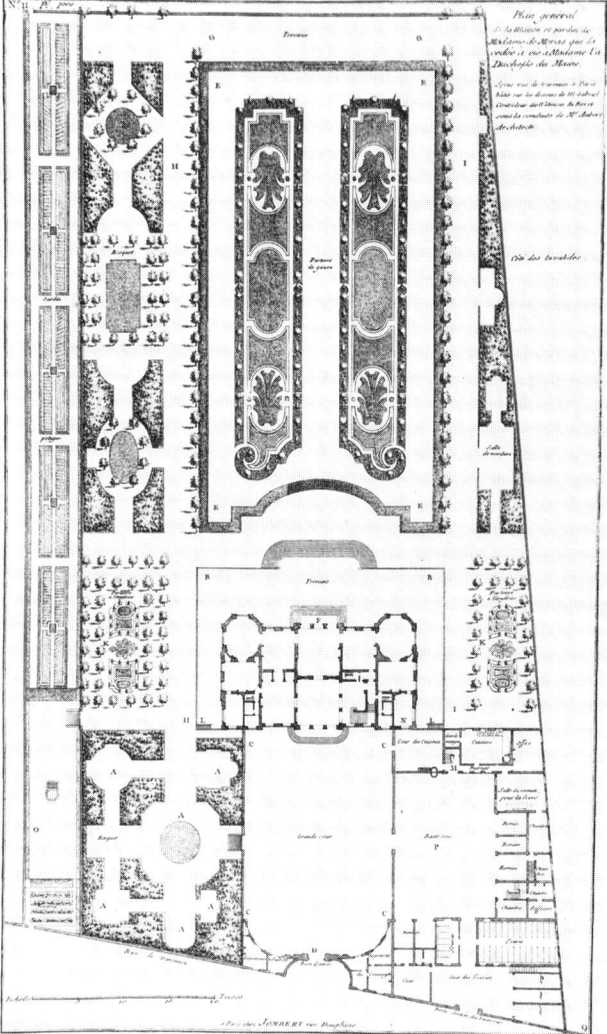

Figure 94
Jean Aubert, general plan, Maison Peyrenc de Moras, rue de
Varenne, Faubourg Saint-Germain, 1728–31, engraving in
Jacques-François Blondel, *Architecture Française*, I (Paris,
1752) [photo: after reprint ed., Paris, 1904].

nated in smaller roundels of couples in rustic settings, painted by Lancret and
inserted into sculpted "mosaic" fields above the painted doors and above the
fireplace: One pair frolicked with a swing; another peered into a birdcage; a
young shepherd stumbled across a sleeping shepherdess; and a man played the
bagpipes for a reclining companion. Hovering above, on the coved ceiling,
were more arabesques by Audran.

There was an overladen quality about Mme Peyrenc's gilded *cabinet* that
certainly revealed its expense and perhaps suggested to some contemporaries

the conspicuous display routinely attributed to *nouveaux riches*. But Gabriel and Audran and their teams of sculptors and painters worked for the court, and part of their appeal would have been their complete familiarity with the sorts of decorative ensembles installed for courtiers. For Peyrenc, this opulent house was, in fact, just a stepping stone. Having sought as recently as 1723 to obscure his purchase of parcels at the Place Vendôme, he had the assurance by 1728 to build a dwelling of the noble type on a large parcel in the Faubourg Saint-Germain, today the Musée Rodin (Fig. 94).[61]

> The only fruit of the Chambre de Justice . . . was to open the door to thousands of denunciations, true or false. Panic and dismay penetrated all finance and those allied to it; money was hidden and its circulation totally interrupted. A few financiers were sacrificed to the rage of the people. . . . [62]

Following the humiliations of the Chambre de Justice and the menace of Law and his system, financiers began to forge corporate structures to augment their security. The receivers general were first, beginning as early as 1716. They were followed by the *secrétaires du roi*, periodically forced to augment fees already paid for their offices. During the 1720s, the secrétaires du roi again came under attack, when the Crown extended from twenty to sixty years the period of service required to obtain hereditary nobility in provincial offices. They responded with a new corporate organization, arguing that it enhanced their ability to lend funds; that structure helped to protect its members, limiting individual liability.[63]

General tax farmers emerged strongest from the financial chaos of the Regency. In 1726, Cardinal Fleury established a more permanent body of forty general tax farmers, each of whom advanced a sizable bond (which might remain in the tax farm for more than one generation), replacing the groups that had bid on new contracts every few years. Fleury enhanced the dignity of their posts, and he called them the "forty columns of the state."[64]

"Not at all Monsieur Jourdain . . ."

He was not at all Monsieur Jourdain, not at all Tucaret, he was nothing of that which has been played at the comedy, because there was nothing foolish in his manner: he had an extravagant pride which, in a certain way, ennobled him. . . . [1]

The portrait left by the président Hénault of one of the leading financiers of the early eighteenth century – Samuel Bernard – could as easily depict Bernard's chief rival, Antoine Crozat.[2] Crozat and Bernard vied for the popular title of the richest man in France. Their deaths in 1738 and 1739 marked the end of an era – even if power had shifted after the Regency to a younger generation.[3]

During the 1720s, Crozat restructured his dwelling to accommodate and represent his upwardly mobile clan. A consideration of his household – in its broadest sense, including even the domestic staff – reveals more clearly the familial and representational strategies of financiers residing at the Place Vendôme. In this chapter, I examine at greater length Crozat's goals and his manipulation of social signs in the domestic realm, and to better situate Crozat, I offer a series of comparisons with three other financiers – Samuel Bernard (who reigned from the Place des Victoires) and the general tax farmers Jean-Remy Hénault (father of our portraitist) and Louis-Auguste Duché (who resided at no. 18 Place Vendôme).

The Maison Crozat in the 1720s

Crozat, having recovered from the Chambre de Justice, soon began expanding his presence at the square. In 1719, he purchased part of the grounds of the former Hôtel de Luxembourg, extending his own garden to the newly projected rue Neuve-du-Luxembourg.[4] For Crozat (and, in the 1740s, the Chancellor), this permitted two noble amenities, extensive gardens and a court of honor freed from the sight and smell of stables (Figs. 9 and 95).[5] Crozat expelled his horses to a more distant structure with a separate entry.[6]

Spaces once encumbered by carriages and stables could now be reclaimed to bring a newly impressive dynasty under Crozat's roof. Despite the disastrous marriage of his daughter, Crozat arranged remarkable alliances for his sons. In 1722, the eldest, Louis-François, wed Marie-Thérèse Gouffier, grand-

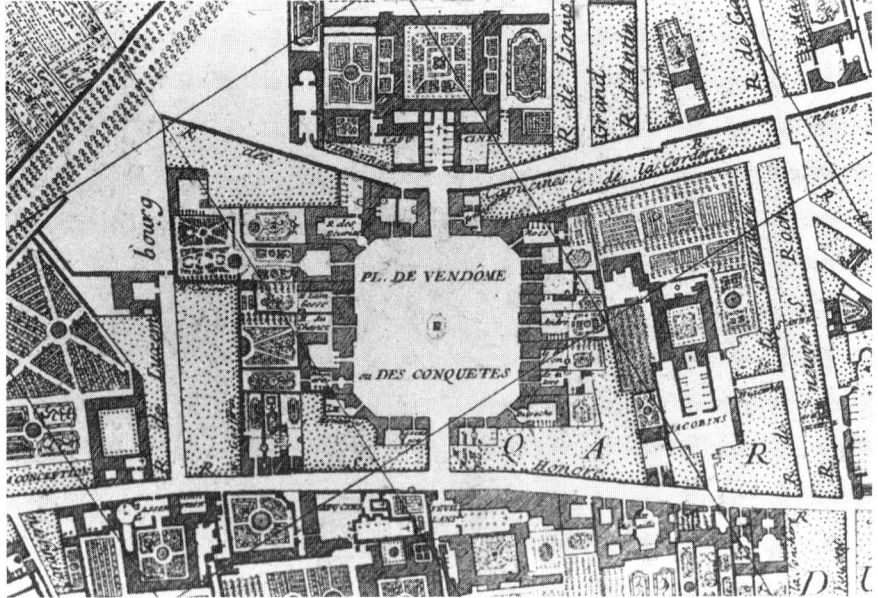

Figure 95

Delagrive plan of Paris, 1720s, detail of Place Vendôme and vicinity; Maison Geoffrin indicated along the north side of rue Saint-Honoré, west of Place Vendôme, and Maison La Live de Pailly on west side of rue (Neuve) du Luxembourg [photo: after *Atlas des anciens plans de Paris*, eds. A. Alphand, L. Michaux, and L.-M. Tisserand (Paris, 1880)].

daughter of the duc de Luynes. Three years later, his middle son, Joseph-Antoine, *conseiller au Parlement* and *maître des requêtes*, married a daughter of the prominent Amelot de Gournay robe clan; that allied Crozat with Le Peletier des Forts, soon after named Controller General of Finance. In 1726, he wed his third son, Louis-Antoine, to Marie-Louise-Augustine de Laval-Montmorency, of one of the foremost court families. Upon each marriage, Crozat relinquished at least one seigneurie, each son adding that name to his own: The eldest became the marquis du Châtel, the middle son the président de Tugny, and the youngest the baron de Thiers.

Beginning about 1724, Crozat, then sixty-nine, called upon architect Victor-Thierry Dailly to renovate his house to accommodate his married (and soon-to-be-married) sons and their wives. According to Blondel, Crozat's house "was almost completely changed."[7] By early 1726, Dailly had transformed the ground floors of both wings into fashionable apartments (Fig. 96).[8] He rebuilt the entrance passage, introducing to each side a short flight leading to an impressive vestibule adorned with a Doric order. Crozat lodged his eldest son's wife, Mme (Gouffier) du Châtel, in the apartment off the grand stair hall to the left and provided his daughter, the now separated comtesse d'Évreux, with a suite to the right.[9] Ceiling heights in each suite were more intimate than the full ground story, but grander than the *entresol*, and each

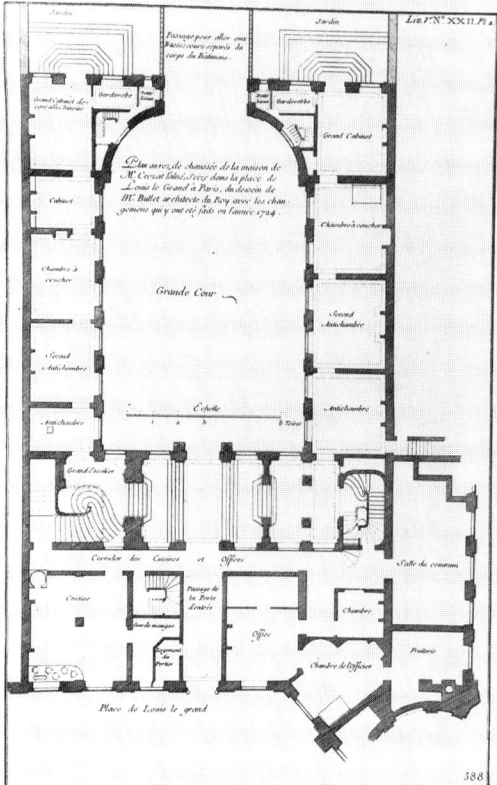

Figure 96

Victor-Thierry Dailly, ground-floor plan, Maison Crozat, no. 17 Place Vendôme, c. 1724, engraving in Jacques-François Blondel, *Architecture Française*, III (Paris, 1754) [photo: after reprint ed., Paris, 1904].

apartment included two anterooms, a large bedchamber and a *grand cabinet* that opened onto stairs descending to a small private garden. Mme du Châtel's suite had a second *cabinet* as well, and in both wings, wardrobes, rebuilt water closets, and service stairs to an *entresol* (above the smaller rooms) were all tucked behind the curved walls that terminated the court.

Dailly decorated Mme du Châtel's *grand cabinet* "à la Chinoise," with large panels of black Chinese lacquer (each over six-feet high, apparently removed from a screen) set into sculpted Rococo *boiserie* (Fig. 97). This fashionable "improvement" of a Chinese artifact by remounting it in a French frame was akin to the setting of antique Chinese and Japanese porcelain into gilded French mounts, which appeared in abundance in the house of Fonspertuis (no. 21).[10] Crowning each panel, as well as four mirrored bays, were gilded Chinese figures seated beneath canopies, flanked by parasol-bearing attendants and exotic animals (Fig. 98). Above the window and a French door, Dailly

Figure 97

Paneling originally installed in *cabinet Chinois*, at end of apartment of south wing, Maison Crozat, no. 17 Place Vendôme c. 1724–8; reinstalled at Atelier Jansen, Paris, before sale [photo: Atelier Jansen, Paris].

installed more reliefs "in the taste of China."[11] It was an opulent *cabinet chinois* that could compete with any installed in a noble dwelling during the 1720s.[12]

The first-floor apartment above that of Mme du Châtel was remodeled, too, so that it now ended in a *cabinet* enjoying a view of the garden, over-

Figure 98
Detail of paneling originally installed in *cabinet Chinois* of Maison Crozat, Place Vendôme, reinstalled in private house [photo: A. C. Cooper, Ltd., London].

looking a terrace paved atop the suite below (Figs. 32 and 99). Du Châtel, his brothers, and their wives were initially also lodged at no. 17, but Crozat later reopened connections to no. 19 and may have provided some accommodation in the adjoining dwelling (Fig. 100).[13]

Daughters of financiers and their new husbands might be given separate *hôtels* as part of the marriage bargain, but sons and their wives were more likely to be provided for in the financier's own dwelling, forming large dynastic households that were often more extensive and complex than those of the court nobility.[14] Financiers often promised accommodation for the new couple in the marriage contract.[15] By the 1720s, Crozat's extended clan spilled be-

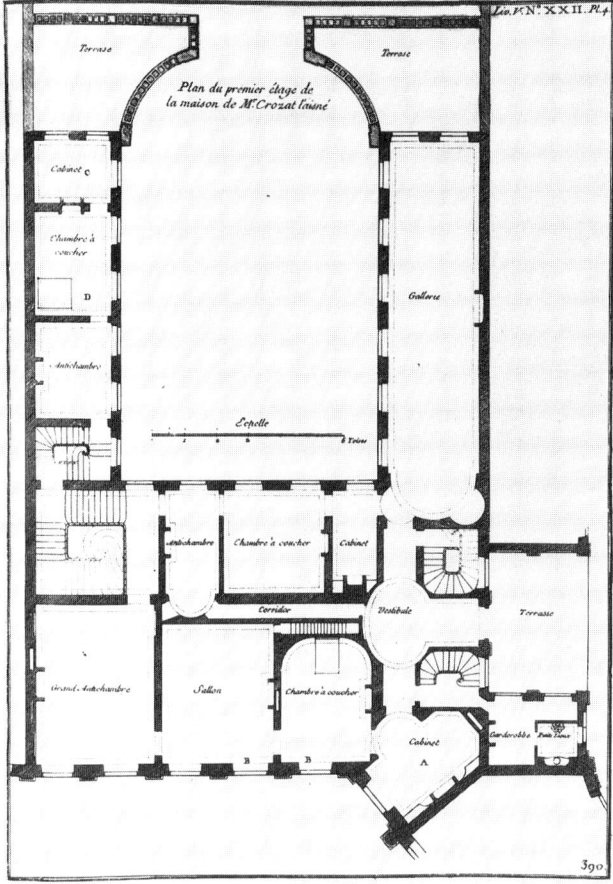

Figure 99
Victor-Thierry Dailly, first-floor plan, Maison Crozat, no. 17
Place Vendôme, c. 1724, engraving in Jacques-François Blondel, *Architecture Française*, III (Paris, 1754) [photo: after reprint ed., Paris, 1904].

yond the bounds of the square to the rue Neuve-des-Capucines immediately
northwest of it, where his brother-in-law and associate in the royal trading
companies, Joseph Legendre d'Arminy, lived in a house built for him by de
Cotte in 1713 (Fig. 95);[16] in 1726, Louis-Philippe Desvieux, a director of the
Compagnie des Indes and general tax farmer (related by marriage to the Legendre clan), had Michel Tannevot build a dwelling that shared a party wall
with no. 19 (Fig. 111).[17] In addition, Crozat kept his house at the Place des
Victoires, where he lodged his wife's widowed mother, who resided there with
a staff of just four.[18] The relative modesty of her household is striking, but it
was typical of elite widows (especially those of financial and robe families),
who tended to live unpretentiously, frequently retiring to lay lodgings attached

120

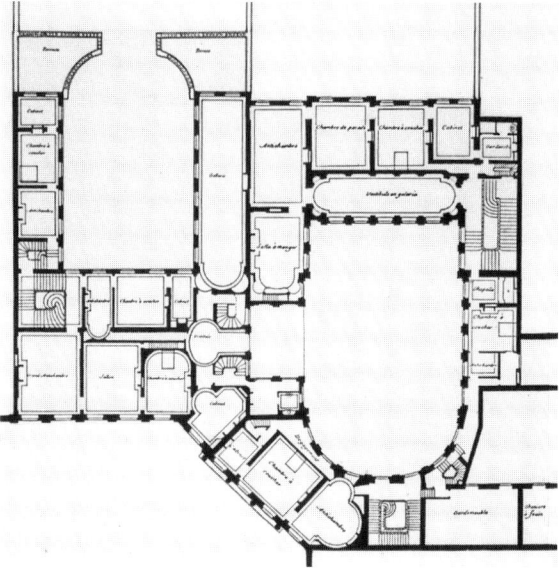

Figure 100
Michael Dennis after Jacques-François Blondel, *Architecture Française*, III (Paris, 1754), first-floor plans of Maison Crozat and Hôtel d'Évreux, nos. 17–19 Place Vendôme, c. 1724 [photo: University of Missouri – Kansas City].

to convents. Several widows among the court aristocracy, it is of interest to note, retired to the Place Vendôme.

Crozat, Bernard, and Duché each lived for a period at a royal square built in honor of Louis XIV; J.-R. Hénault may have as well.[19] The Place des Victoires was the first site to attract them and Crozat, who resided in Pennautier's house from 1687 to 1690, rented the modest no. 6 shortly after he wed in 1690 (Fig. 21); eight years later, he bought the largest house at that square, today no. 3.[20] Within two years, however, Crozat cast his eye on the new, grander Place de Louis-le-Grand. By 1702 or 1703, Bernard, too, leased a Place des Victoires dwelling, perhaps already the large Hôtel de Bauyn (no. 5) that he rented later, situated between Crozat's house and one owned by Hénault.[21] By 1720, when his son moved to the Place Vendôme, Hénault had installed his household on the rue de Richelieu, facing Law's bank.[22] Bernard, too, built a far more ample dwelling on a larger site nearby, along the rue Notre-Dame-des-Victoires, but he maintained a residence at the Place des Victoires.[23] Duché, in keeping with the robe identity of his clan, had lived at the Place Royale during the early twenties, but he moved to this financial quarter a few years later; he leased no. 18 Place Vendôme in 1731, then purchased it in 1733 (Figs. 67 and 101).[24]

With the exception of Bernard, each had been raised in a provincial financial milieu, to a family that had already achieved a modest level of nobility.[25]

Figure 101
Armand-Claude Mollet, architect (attrib. Bruno Pons); Jacques Gaultier, sculptor; paneling installed in first-floor *grand cabinet*, later *chambre de parade* (1725), no. 18 Place Vendôme (Maison Duché during thirties), h: 13 ft; reinstalled, with modern cornice, at the J. Paul Getty Museum, Los Angeles [photo: The J. Paul Getty Museum].

Bernard was born in Paris in 1651, to a still practicing Protestant clan outside the realm of finance, whereas the Duché, and apparently the Crozat, were *nouveaux convertis*. The rise of Bernard, son of a royal painter, was most meteoric, fed by the revocation of the Edict of Nantes in 1685. During the War of the Spanish Succession, the Crown found Bernard – the last among them to convert – best positioned to draw upon vast reserves of Protestant capital, and it named him court banker.[26]

Crozat, Bernard, and Hénault wed within their milieux.[27] All three purchased robe offices for their sons (three of four as *présidents* in the Parlement of Paris), but Crozat underwrote military careers for du Châtel and Thiers.[28] Bernard's sons married into the *noblesse d'épée* and Crozat forged alliances with the court and high robe; only Hénault arranged an alliance (to Montargis's daughter) intended to extend his family's web of financial relations.

Daughters with large dowries may have enjoyed greater social mobility, but often at immense personal cost. Bernard made as disastrous an alliance for his first daughter as Crozat had, albeit to someone close to her own milieu – to Mansart's son.[29] Bernard forged a happier (but satirized) alliance for a daughter from his second marriage, who wed Mathieu-François Molé, *président à mortier* in the Parlement of Paris, in 1733.[30] Bernard, Crozat, and Hénault had mistresses, and Bernard openly acknowledged three daughters borne by Mme Fontaine.[31] Bernard wed the youngest to Claude Dupin, a provincial financier chosen for his character rather than rank. In the late thirties, Mme Dupin and her husband, whom Bernard positioned in the general tax farm, rented no. 12 Place Vendôme;[32] she may have already begun to assemble what became in the forties a celebrated *salon*.[33]

Among their sons, the président Hénault achieved the highest renown – as a member of the Académie française, the author of a history of France, and an habitué of *salon* society.[34] Crozat's sons did not achieve that level of distinction, but du Châtel was a respected military commander and man of intellect; Tugny an amateur chemist; and Thiers, who also had a distinguished military career, frequented the *salon* of his aunt Mme (Legendre) Doublet.[35] Bernard's sons (like his son-in-law Jacques Mansart) were best known for profligacy; both had declared bankruptcy by 1731.

The four financial families lived somewhat differently in their Paris dwellings. J.-R. Hénault and his wife resided modestly, in a more bourgeois manner, in a house "as closed as a convent, by their taste for economy," according to their son, who contrasted it with "the house of Bernard . . . a house of games and good cheer and the meeting place of the best company."[36] Bernard was infamous for his gambling, a prime noble avocation – effectively signaling disdain for bourgeois "economy" – and his expenditure on his "table" was legendary.[37] Saint-Simon, hardly an unbiased observer, found Crozat's *compagnie* "very mediocre."[38]

Crozat and Bernard worked especially long hours, which alone set them apart from nobles of the court.[39] Bernard's household could easily accommodate both work and a door open to *compagnie* because he kept his *bureau* at the Place des Victoires and entertained in the house on the rue Notre-Dame-des-Victoires. Bernard's separation of his work from his family's dwelling was unusual during this period, although general tax farmers had already converted some houses throughout Paris into *bureaux* for meetings and general business, supplementing those members maintained in their own residences.[40] Most financiers managed, like Crozat, to separate work from *compagnie* and official reception through circulatory strategies that kept the realms largely separate. Bernard maintained lodgings in both residences, including a magnificently furnished ceremonial bedroom in the dwelling on the rue Notre-Dame-des-Victoires, but he seems to have resided more regularly in the house where he worked.[41] Bernard accommodated his sons and their spouses in the house on the rue Notre-Dame-des-Victoires, but his daughter and the président Molé were lodged in the noble Faubourg Saint-Germain.[42] Hénault's and Duché's households were smaller. Still, even after the death of his daughter, Hénault's son-in-law and granddaughter resided with him; Duché, who was childless, lodged the separated wife of "Mr. Duché, *avocat général* of the Cour des Aides of Montpellier," on the second and third stories of no. 18 Place Vendôme.

Figure 102
Hyacinthe Rigaud, portrait of Samuel Bernard,
1727 drawing after 1726 painting (also by Rigaud) [photo: Nelson-Atkins Museum of Art,
Kansas City, Missouri (Purchase: Nelson Trust)].

Among the four financiers, only Crozat and his rival Bernard attempted to
incorporate a gallery into their houses. Each equipped that room opulently.
Crozat displayed Japanese porcelain on gilded pedestals, a clock in a Boulle
marquetry case, an expensive harpsichord, a variety of chairs, tables, and
other objects, including a tricktrack game (which suggests that the room
served as a kind of *salon*); the contents of his gallery were appraised at more
than all of the furnishings in the entire ceremonial apartment of either Duché
or Hénault.[43] Bernard installed his gallery in the house on the rue Notre-
Dame-des-Victoires, and in 1727, he turned his attention to a new decorative
program.

   Presiding over the gallery was a 1726 portrait by Rigaud (the epitomal
court painter), in which Bernard was seated at a desk, flanked by a globe and
a fleet of ships, attributes of his power as a primary director of the royal
trading companies (Fig. 102).[44] Jean-François de Troy provided four paintings
of legendary subjects from Roman history, which, it has been argued, may
refer to Bernard's role as patriarch of a well-placed clan.[45] Three of four of
these subjects had appeared in the reinstalled gallery of the Hôtel de Toulouse,
immediately south of the Place des Victoires. Bernard, at age seventy-six, was
quite likely emulating one of the grandest of the *grands seigneurs*.[46]

Significantly, it was Bernard's own portrait that he displayed so prominently in his gallery. Crozat had installed a large portrait of himself with his family, probably one painted for him by Matteis in 1703, in his *cabinet*.[47] Nobles of the blood, proud of their lineage, often hung portraits of their forbears in their ceremonial apartments. Satirists would insist that financiers must have had faceless ancestors, since they never displayed portraits of their predecessors.[48]

Hénault and Duché focused opulent display in a room or two of their ceremonial suites. Hénault concentrated on a *salle* and *cabinet*;[49] Duché selected the *chambre de parade* on the first floor overlooking the Place Vendôme, which he himself occupied (Fig. 101). The single most magnificent object of Duché's ceremonial *chambre* was his bed, and draped from its imperial crown were curtains of an unusual white wool embroidered with "roses and fruits of the Indies"; the same fabric lined the walls around the bed and reappeared in door and window curtains and in seat coverings.[50] Since Duché's brother and a cousin were active in the Compagnie des Indes, the fabric may have functioned as a kind of familial "attribute," rather like the large pieces of *papier des Indes* that Fonspertuis installed in a *cabinet*. Here, given the context and expense, the reference probably bore greater representational weight. Duché's claiming of the principal ceremonial suite overlooking the square was atypical among financial families. Fonspertuis had done the same thing; here, as at the Hôtel de Fonspertuis, the apportionment of space may have emerged from a higher stature enjoyed by the family of the master of the house relative to that of his wife; Mme Duché had a modest suite in the *entresol*, with a fairly unassuming bedchamber. Her chamber opened onto rooms associated with entertaining friends rather than official reception, a realm newly called that of *compagnie*.[51]

When it came to the chapel, it was, once again, only Crozat and Bernard who incorporated this noble sign – Bernard at the Place des Victoires house, Crozat in the apartment built for the comtesse d'Évreux. Significantly, Bullet had not originally provided a chapel at the Maison Crozat, but he planned one from the outset for the Hôtel d'Évreux. It was a sign – as Bernard, Crozat, and their visitors were well aware – of a "great house."[52]

Emulating longstanding practices among nobles of the sword and robe, each financier displayed in his house at least one work of art that represented the source of his clan's status – the Crown – some, perhaps, royal gifts honoring service to the state. Bernard presented the effigies most prominently, displaying an equestrian statue of Louis XIV on a marble pedestal in a ground-floor anteroom of his house on the rue Notre-Dame-des-Victoires and a portrait of the Regent in his ceremonial bedroom at the Place des Victoires; Crozat may have owned a bronze copy of the equestrian statue of the Place Vendôme, in addition to the large painting of Louis XIV that hung in his *château* at Tugny at the time of his death.[53] Hénault displayed a portrait of Louis XIV with the royal family in his *cabinet*, and Duché, who also owned a small equestrian statue of Louis XIV, hung portrait prints of Louis XIV, Louis XV, and Fleury (plus one of Samuel Bernard) in an *arrière cabinet*.[54] Such display was common among financiers, but for Crozat, Bernard, and Duché, it also reiterated the imagery of the colossal statue always visible from the ceremonial rooms of their dwellings.[55]

Crozat's *Maison*

Supporting the opulent lives of elite families were battalions of domestics, themselves effective signs of nobility. Those wearing the distinctive household livery were striking elements of display, and their masters deployed them in strategic places. Liveried servants represented the *maison* on the streets of Paris, and their importance in the realm of social representation is attested to by sumptuary laws that periodically limited the opulence of materials that might be employed in their costumes.[56]

The world of domestics was hierarchically organized, with distinct foci centering on the most important sites of representational display. "Everyone wants to surpass his neighbor by the luxury of his carriages, his table, his *toilette*," wrote the princesse de Palatine in 1719, pointing to the most critical arenas of display.[57] Each required domestic labor and defined a center of the world of servants: the stables, the department of *cuisine*, and the realm of wardrobes and *cabinets de toilette*.

The gender of members of the domestic staff was itself a social sign. In noble dwellings, there were *femmes de chambre* attending to the mistress and perhaps a governess for young children, but servants were otherwise male, and a largely male retinue was itself a sign of nobility. The presence of a male chef, for example, indicated a noble household, whereas a female cook signaled a bourgeois family. Crozat employed a male chef.

Brice remarked upon Crozat's "very large number of domestics."[58] Crozat's extended *maison* resembled the household of a nobleman of the blood, but it was also distinct in several respects. Most obviously, it was enlarged by a variety of financial assistants who worked in Crozat's *bureaux* during the day and at least one, his cashier, who slept there at night.

At the top of the hierarchy of a noble household were members of the domestic staff who provided service that we would today call professional: those who oversaw the management of the proprietor's financial and other affairs (intendants and secretaries), doctors, and chaplains. Among the more important indicators of status was the location of a domestic's bedroom (or, in some cases, apartment). The value of the mobile objects provided by the proprietor (especially the bed) and certain types of furnishings – mirrors, desks, fireplace accessories, individual *chaises de commodité*, and, occasionally, prints and paintings from the proprietor's collection – operated as signs of rank. Crozat had an intendant, an officer common in important noble households but rare among those of financial families, and Crozat lodged him in 1738 in a well furnished apartment on the second floor along the square.[59]

More modestly lodged on that floor was the abbé Capperonnier, a professor at the Collège Royal who had served as tutor to Crozat's sons, and later, it seems, as Crozat's librarian (Crozat apparently adopting a noble practice introduced by the maréchal d'Estrées).[60] Crozat's doctor resided on the same floor, in a room along the square. Mme Crozat's secretary had two rooms on the *entresol*.

Below them in rank was the *maître d'hôtel*, in charge of daily household purchases and expenses, and he presided over the *valets* and *femmes de chambre*, who provided the most personal and intimate service.[61] The first *femme de chambre* had two rooms in the *entresol*, embellished with tapestries and small paintings, adjoining Mme Crozat's private apartment; a second had two rooms on the second story and a third had single room in the mansard roof.[62] On the ground floor, for surveillance purposes, the porter slept off the entry and the *officier* next to the *office*. Crozat provided twenty-four additional domestics – ranging from the male chef and other members of the kitchen staff to a *valet de chambre*, coachmen, and a *frotteur* (who took care of parquet floors) – with rooms in the mansard roof, partly in barracklike arrangements with several beds to a room.[63]

Crozat may not have spent as much on his "table" as Bernard had, but he enlarged the space devoted to dining and transferred it in the twenties to the *entresol*, overlooking the square. To support the display of "the table," Crozat expanded his kitchen, so that it became a complex department occupying much of the ground floor and extending into partly subterranean rooms beneath the Mme du Châtel's apartment. It was believed that bourgeois women should, properly, oversee the kitchen staff, but in noble dwellings the master and mistress wanted that department out of sight (and, preferably, out of auditory and olifactory range), so that dishes miraculously appeared at mealtimes – the most important of them served by those dressed in the household livery.[64] The principal kitchen at the Maison Crozat, still set along the square, would have been the hearth of the servant's realm. A staff of at least four or five spent their days in the kitchens, taking their own meals in the ground-floor *salle de commun*, below Crozat's terrace. During the day, the whole ground floor must have bustled with the activities of domestics, generally expected to perform their tasks "invisibly" and "noiselessly" in other parts of the house.

Adequate provision for carriages and horses was as important as the table as a sign of nobility, but Crozat had to wait until the twenties to build extensive stables at a remove from his main living rooms. Crozat's seven coachmen and grooms slept close to the site where they worked, in an *entresol* above the stables that Crozat built at the far end of the garden (Fig. 95). For a stable hand, Crozat provided a simple bed, one or two chairs, and perhaps a table or two.

Bernard's domestic staff was also extensive, but those of Hénault and Duché were a good deal more modest. Duché's servants numbered just ten: a *maître d'hôtel*, a chef, a porter, a *valet*, a chambermaid, two lackeys, and three "domestiques." He provided rooms for most on a "fourth floor" and even on a "fifth floor," so the tall mansard roof must have been twice subdivided in height. The chambermaid apparently had a room in the *entresol* next to Mme Duché's bedroom, and Duché lodged his *valet* there as well.

Crozat's *maison* was quite large compared with Duché's, but how closely did it approximate that of a *grand seigneur*? We might compare Crozat's staff with that of his former tenant d'Estrées, who had been elevated to the rank of duke; he died in the Faubourg Saint-Germain, just a few months after Crozat. There were, in fact, posts a high-ranking nobleman maintained that even the wealthiest financiers did not attempt to emulate. Among them were young male pages, vestiges from large medieval households, and d'Estrées had four. When it came to *cuisine*, he employed a more specialized staff, including a *rotisseur* for meats, a *patissier* for baking, and a *garçon de buffet*. D'Estrées and his wife maintained a larger fleet of carriages and vehicles (at least one requiring *porteurs de chaise*); to oversee their stables, they maintained separate *écuyers*, important officers in noble households.[65]

Crozat's neighbor d'Aguesseau, the highest robe official, maintained a staff that more closely resembled that of the duc d'Estrées, despite the Chancellor's reputation for relative modesty. Following sizable retrenchments after his wife's death in 1735 and his own retirement in 1750, d'Aguesseau still employed an ample staff that included an intendant, several secretaries, a librarian, a chaplain, a doctor, a chef, a pastry cook, a *rotisseur*, a wine steward, two valets, a chambermaid-concierge, a *Suisse*, a coachman, a groom, four postilions, two lackeys, and two other male servants.[66] Next door, at no. 15, the widowed duchesse de Boufflers maintained a smaller staff of eleven in 1739, rather small when compared with that of Crozat or even that of d'Aguesseau in retirement, but larger than the Duché's and more than twice that of Crozat's widowed mother-in-law.[67]

Thus, Brice's charge that financiers at the Place Vendôme had lodged themselves as *grands seigneurs* was not entirely accurate, whatever the pretensions they adopted. Their sons, not surprisingly, more closely approximated the *train de vie* of noblemen of the court and high robe. In the next chapter, I turn to Crozat's sons Tugny and Thiers, who inherited this dynastic complex in 1743. They largely rebuilt their dwellings, with representational aims quite different from those of their father.

6

Mobility, Adaptation, and Reconstruction

THE PROFILE OF THE SQUARE had changed by the thirties and forties, largely because of the mobility of its financial clans. High-ranking nobles periodically leased houses there, too, including the prince de Léon and the maréchal de Coigny during the thirties (at nos. 12 and 15); the duc de La Vallière and the widowed duchesse d'Antin in the forties (the latter at no. 9); and the comte de La Marck and the comte de Saint-Florentin in the fifties (at nos. 6 and 7). The robe formed a more sizable presence, an outcome of the careers and alliances of many sons of financiers.[1]

Among the most successful clans was the one formed by Peyrenc's sons, who forged alliances with the high robe and returned to the square briefly, just before 1750. During the thirties and forties, their relation, magistrate Moreau de Nassigny, had already installed an extended family; his brother Moreau de Séchelles (father-in-law of François-Marie Peyrenc de Moras) soon after leased no. 5.[2] Peyrenc de Saint-Priest, *conseiller au parlement*, returned with his father-in-law, royal intendant Barberie de Courteille. During the mid-fifties, Séchelles, then Peyrenc de Moras, each briefly served as Controller General of Finance. "These are called rapid fortunes," Barbier opined, "not only in wealth but in elevation."[3]

These families, along with the Chancellor d'Aguesseau and his sons, constituted a high-robe presence. By the thirties and forties, the social profile of the Place Vendôme resembled more closely that of the Place Royale, but it was still predominantly financial. New residents transformed their dwellings to accommodate changed identities, in renovations best illuminated, once again, at the houses of the Crozat family. When the président de Tugny and the baron de Thiers inherited nos. 17 and 19 in 1743, each embraced modifications in use and decor akin to those introduced by high-ranking nobles in and near the capital during the thirties and early forties. For them, Pierre Contant d'Ivry shaped refined private suites and a fashionable new sphere called *compagnie*.

It was the court nobility that had conceived the new apartment of *compagnie* or *société* as a public realm distinct from the magnificently decorated ceremonial suite; it was a less formal sphere, where friends assembled for dining, conversation, reading aloud, musical concerts, and games of various sorts. Rooms conceived and decorated for official reception seemed ill suited to more casual assemblies; courtiers increasingly preferred more intimate, fashionably decorated spaces, as congenial settings for sociability.

At least one room essential to the new realm had appeared in elite houses much earlier: a separate dining room that was more than a simple anteroom set up with a table and chairs at mealtimes. But such rooms only became common in urban *hôtels* at the turn of the eighteenth century, and in many of the first houses at the square – including the Maison Crozat – an anteroom doubled as a dining room (Fig. 32). During the thirties and forties, the stature of the dining room grew, in tandem with the *salle de compagnie*, "where *compagnie* retires after a meal," a less formal room than the *salon*.[4]

The mode of use that eventually required a new sphere within the house was certainly aristocratic, but court etiquette did not provide the model. The prototype seems to have been the less rigidly ceremonial, more "bourgeois" mode of living associated with the Regent and his circle at the Palais Royal.[5] In the architectural lexicon of the thirties and forties, the realm associated with *compagnie* had two meanings: the single sort of public sphere serving the needs of a bourgeois household and a secondary public suite in a noble one.[6] The appeal of the new realm grew during the period following the reestablishment of the court at Versailles, when courtiers built relatively few new *hôtels* in Paris. Instead, many renovated their houses, shaping new apartments of *compagnie*. These suites may have first appeared in suburban dwellings near the capital, intended for relaxation and escape from the ceremonial of court life. For those houses, courtiers adopted the term for bourgeois houses and linked it to their expected enjoyment, calling them *maisons de plaisance*.[7]

It became critical to distinguish between a *salon* and a *salle de compagnie* only, it would seem, when courtiers began to incorporate two sorts of public suites in their dwellings. In an urban context, the domains of *parade* and *compagnie* were often not as physically distinct as J.-F. Blondel suggested, except in very large *hôtels*; quite often, the *salle de compagnie was* the *salon* – refashioned, redecorated, and renamed in accord with a new mode of use.

When court aristocrats introduced this less formal public sphere into their *hôtels* and country houses during the late twenties, thirties, and forties, financial and robe families followed suit. At the Place Vendôme, renovation of the Crozat houses reveals how two sons of a prominent financier incorporated this new semipublic sphere, as well as the representational dilemmas this fashionable, more "bourgeois" domain may have posed for financial clans. The social identities of Crozat's sons were still in transition, despite impressive careers and alliances.

The Maison Crozat de Tugny During the 1740s

Following the deaths of Antoine Crozat in 1738, his brother Pierre in 1740, and Mme Crozat in 1742, the marquis du Châtel inherited his uncle's house on the rue de Richelieu (with Pierre Crozat's collection of paintings and sculpture), the président de Tugny received the Maison Crozat and the baron de Thiers acquired the former Hôtel d'Évreux. Tugny and Thiers so transformed their Place Vendôme dwellings that Blondel noted, when he published in the fifties engravings after plans of c. 1724 (Figs. 96, 99, and 100), "these . . . almost do not at all resemble the distribution of today. . . ."[8]

The rebuilding campaigns reveal Contant's considerable talents as a shaper of smaller and more complexly interwoven rooms, which he treated with a newly nuanced decorative vocabulary. Contant exploited the classical orders and variety of color to endow each new public and private room with a representational character congruent with its use and with the strategic aims of his clients.

When Contant reshaped the former Maison Crozat, he converted it from the dwelling that had housed a financial dynasty into one serving a much smaller robe household (Figs. 103 and 104).[9] His interventions began at the entrance passage, which he made loftier, lifting its vault to the height of the first floor.[10] The grand stair now rose in a straight flight followed by two curved, "suspended" flights to the first floor, a "singular composition" that impressed Blondel (Fig. 104).[11] Contant enveloped the cage with a fictive "architecture" of painted and plaster doors, windows, and arcades.[12] To the right of the entry passage, beyond the vestibule serving the right wing, the stair to Crozat's *bureaux* was no longer needed. Contant demolished it and used the space for an additional wardrobe.

At the summit of the grand stair, Contant introduced a vestibule illusionistically painted with an order of marble columns with bronze bases and capitals, an imposing prelude to the reconceived public apartments. He refashioned and reversed the circuit of the ceremonial rooms overlooking the square, and he devoted the entire left wing to dining, one of the foci of the new realm of *compagnie*. The original dining room at the Maison Crozat had been modest, doubling as an anteroom to the first-floor apartment along the court (Fig. 32); in the twenties, Crozat moved it to a larger space in the *entresol*, a typical location. Now, in the forties, Contant provided more amply for dining on the *noble étage*, a prominence in keeping with other renovations to elite dwellings during the thirties and forties.[13]

The new significance of the dining room meant it could be "decorated . . . with some magnificence," Blondel counseled.[14] In one project (Fig. 103), the landing of the grand stair opened directly onto a buffet in the wing, which guests would have traversed before entering a large dining room. Contant revised that plan, sacrificing some of the extent of the dining room to remove the buffet from the public circuit (Fig. 104). The removal of the bedecked buffet was a meaningful social sign, since it had come to be associated with ostentatious display in bourgeois houses.[15] In the dining room, Contant set large mirrors directly across from the three windows along the north wall and had grisaille "architecture" (perhaps a pilaster order) painted on the panels between the mirrors.[16] Eight grisaille paintings of "amours" presided over the

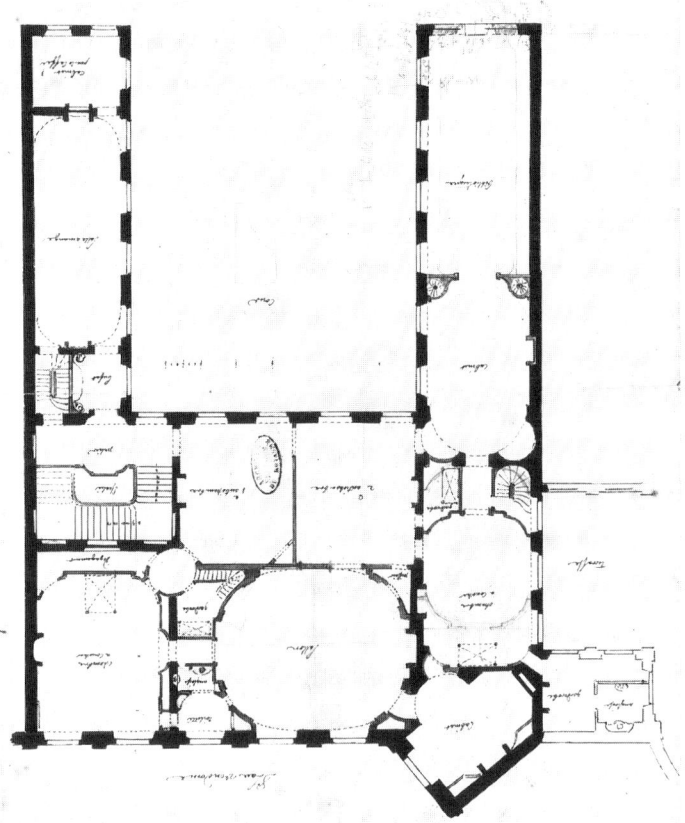

Figure 103

Pierre Contant d'Ivry, project (penultimate?) for reconstruction of first floor, Maison Crozat de Tugny, no. 17 Place Vendôme, c. 1743 [photo: Archives nationales, T 188¹, document conserved at Centre historique des Archives nationales, Paris].

meal, and sounds of water splashing from two marble fountains accompanied the convivial talk at the table. After dining, guests could retire to a *cabinet* "for the taking of coffee"; pale yellow, built-in corner armoires, painted with flowers and plants of China and the Indies, made the space octagonal and perhaps presented the conceit of an exotic "garden" room.[17] Opening off it was a shallow belvedere, flanked by two Ionic columns connected by a curved cornice, overlooking the real garden.

The *grand appartement* occupied the main range along the square. Contant eliminated Crozat's suite along the court and the corridor that had segregated business from social realms, replacing these with two ample anterooms. He lined the first in paneling treated to resemble colored marble and embellished it with grisaille overdoors by Riscouet and Dumont le Romain.[18] In the ample yellow and green second anteroom, Contant introduced a richer decor, with

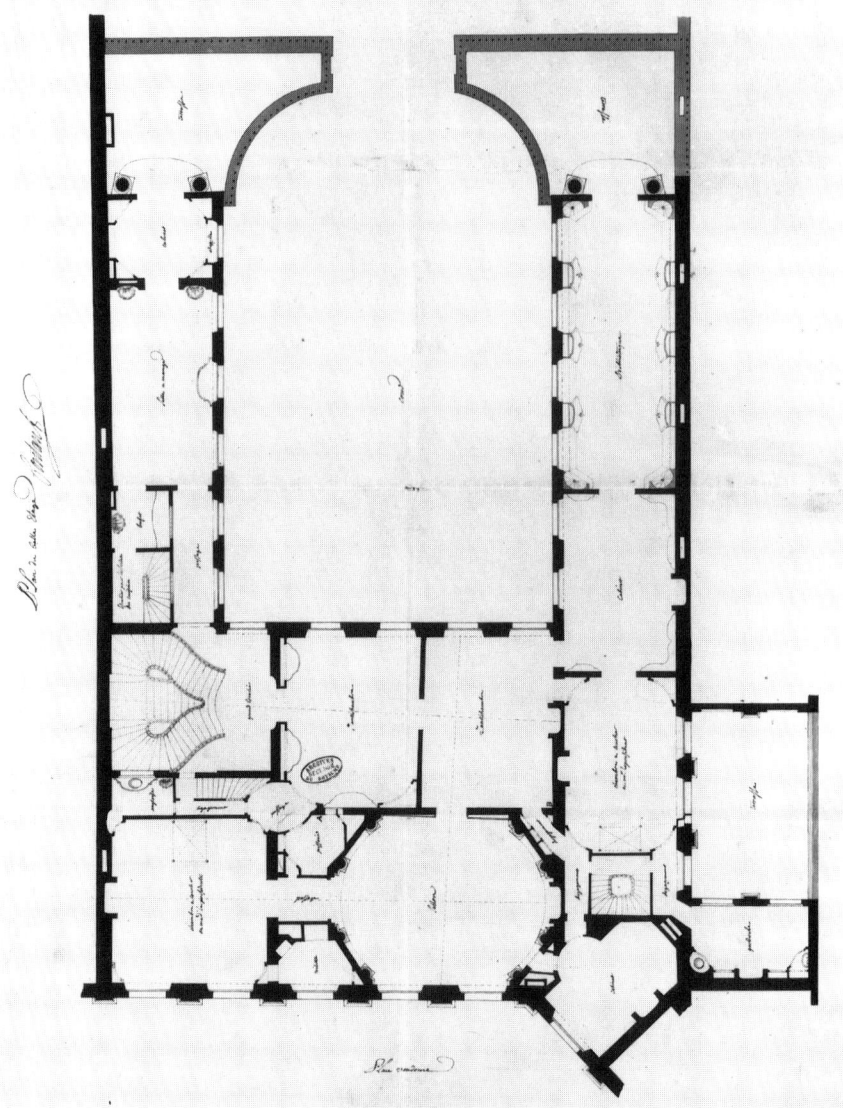

Figure 104
Pierre Contant d'Ivry (signed), final plan, reconstruction of first floor, Maison Crozat de Tugny, no. 17 Place Vendôme, c. 1743–4 [photo: Archives nationales, T 188[1], document conserved at Centre historique des Archives nationales, Paris].

carved paneling and overdoors of "the four elements," painted by Dumont le Romain in pale green on pale yellow grounds, "in the form of medallions."[19]

From the second anteroom visitors entered the elongated octagonal *grand salon*, enveloped in paneling painted to imitate lilac marble and illuminated by two windows along the square. Contant encircled the room with eight engaged Ionic columns, set in pairs framing the mirrors in each of the canted corners. He installed more mirrors above the fireplace, on the doors to Mme

Tugny's ceremonial bedroom, and between the windows, dematerializing the walls to enhance the effect of a peristyle of fluted columns bearing ornate capitals.[20] Flanking the doors from the second anteroom were "paintings . . . of antique figures carried on pedestals"; along the same wall, beneath a frieze of putti frolicking against a pale blue ground, hung two twelve-foot-high paintings by Dumont le Romain.[21] The mirrors especially impressed Blondel, who found that "in reflecting objects, [they] procure more grandeur to this *salon*, and form a surprising effect that merits the greatest admiration."[22]

Contemporaries who described this room called it a *salon* or *grand salon* rather than a *salle de compagnie*.[23] The nearly freestanding Ionic order introduced a ceremonial character. As courtiers embraced more relaxed semipublic suites within their dwellings, some among those with less social confidence, including financiers and sons of financiers, may have preferred a more formal mode. The rococo style was still very much in vogue, and such prominent use of a classical order may have been intended to counter any lingering associations with a "bourgeois" mode of living that still adhered to the *salle de compagnie*.

Contant placed Mme de Tugny's ceremonial bedchamber along the square, in the space that formerly served as an anteroom, and connected it by a passage with the *salon*. In residual spaces flanking the passageway, Contant shaped a polygonal *aisance* and a pentagonal *cabinet de toilette* that overlooked the square; he placed Mme de Tugny's private water closet (*angloise*) off one corner of the chamber. Contant encased the *cabinet de toilette* with pale yellow paneling and installed large mirrors above the marble mantel of the fireplace, set into one canted corner, and above a shelf of the same pale violet marble (which may have served as the dressing table), inserted into the other. Grisaille paintings of *jeux des enfants* presided above the door from the bedchamber and a fictive door that faced it. Mme Tugny furnished the room with two small sofas and a small desk. Given the opulent fittings and prominent setting, her *cabinet de toilette* seems quite akin to what would soon more regularly be called a *boudoir*.[24]

For Tugny, Contant focused on a series of rooms serving his intellectual interests, aligned along the right wing (Figs. 103 and 104). To develop that suite, Tugny sacrificed his father's prized sign of nobility, the gallery, replacing it with a *cabinet des tableaux* – filled with Dutch, Flemish, and French works (plus a few notable Italian paintings) – and a large library.[25]

In providing so prominent a site for his library, Tugny was acting as did many men of the robe. Like the président Hénault, Tugny had retired relatively early (by age 45), and in 1743, he bore the title of "honorary *président*." As a retired magistrate, he avoided the sort of sarcasm often directed at financiers who amassed large libraries – they bought books for display, it was said, but never actually read them.[26] Tugny's father and his uncles had already, in fact, assembled extensive libraries, and Antoine Crozat left his books to Tugny.[27]

Tugny's collection of books was one of several prominent libraries at the square during the 1740s. These included one installed by Fontanieu's son Gaspard-Moïse, "so famous for his love of history," at no. 26 and another assembled by Nicolas-Alexandre de Ségur, honorary *président à mortier* at the Parlement of Bordeaux, in an *entresol* suite at no. 22.[28] The most renowned was that of d'Aguesseau; it was said his successor Lamoignon allowed d'Aguesseau to continue to occupy the Chancellerie after his retirement, specifically so he would not have to move his considerable library.[29]

For the président de Tugny, Contant reshaped the remainder of the gallery, inserting small round stairs into canted corners. This permitted access to two levels of pale green bookcases, punctuated by cartouches of ancient authors, as well as trophies and medallions representing the arts and their protectrices. Contant preserved and reinstalled Matteis's ceiling painting of Aurora with Twilight, Night, and the Hours of the Day, he provided a diversion from reading with French doors that opened onto another belvedere overlooking the garden.[30]

The interest in science among cultivated amateurs, which grew during the century, was in evidence by the fifties at several houses of the Place Vendôme, including that of Tugny. Just as the maréchal d'Estrées had done during the Regency, Tugny installed a laboratory, reached by a small stair from Tugny's apartment to the second floor; his brother Thiers set up a *cabinet de physique* at no. 19.[31]

Blondel found the new interior decor exemplary, writing a few years later that "the paneling of these apartments should excite the interest of connoisseurs, by the choice and the richness of ornaments that one sees there, an aspect of architecture that Mr. Contant understands exceptionally well."[32] Variety of color was presumably an aspect of what Blondel meant by choice. Earlier in the century, public rooms had been most often lined in paneling painted white and highlighted with gilding, which would become the norm again later, especially in ceremonial rooms. Color had been introduced through textiles, in the form of wall hangings, curtains, and upholstery; crimson (associated with nobility) and green long predominated, although blue (associated with the Bourbons) increasingly appeared.[33] As the *appartement de compagnie* emerged, architects began to employ a greater range of color, incorporating pastel tones, in painted paneling as well as textiles; that expanded palette helped to define the individual character of each new space.[34]

Beyond color, Contant made significant choices in his decorative vocabulary, most significantly in deploying a classical order in the *salon*. The central role accorded to the orders marked a new departure, even if Contant remained attached to certain rococo elements.[35]

Tugny's household was very different from that of his father, and Contant's pastel-colored rooms comprised only about half of the dwelling. Like his uncle Pierre, who had invited the painters La Fosse and Watteau to reside with him, Tugny lodged Dumont Le Romain and his wife from 1745 to 1750.[36] Although Tugny and his wife were childless, when he died in early 1751, those composing their *maison* numbered at least an additional twenty-five. Among them were Tugny's close friend Jean-Louis Saladin, son of the Swiss banker Jacques-André Saladin (formerly engaged in business with Antoine and Pierre Crozat). Jean-Louis, who became Minister of the Republic of Switzerland in France and, from 1745 to 1749, consultant to the French Compagnie des Indes, occupied the suite built for the comtesse d'Évreux.[37] Residing in the apartment in the opposite wing in 1750, also apparently as a family friend, was the comte de Fontenay.[38] The other twenty-three were domestics serving just Tugny and his wife, fewer than those comprising the *maison* of Antoine Crozat, but vast nonetheless.[39]

The Hôtel de Thiers (No. 19)

When the baron de Thiers and his wife renovated the contiguous dwelling during the same years, subtle differences emerged. These may indicate strategic distinctions in the ways the two Crozat brothers sought to represent themselves, as well as, perhaps, disparities in self-perception. Once again, Contant offered alternatives requiring significantly different amounts of demolition and reconstruction.[40]

On the ground floor in each of his projects, Contant reversed the circuit. It now proceeded counterclockwise from the peristyle through two anterooms, a *salon* and Thiers's ceremonial bedchamber – all facing the garden (Figs. 36 and 105). The compressed route freed space to the left of the peristyle. There Contant shaped an expanded and densely planned private suite, incorporating rooms of unusual form and calibrated size, knit by an elegant system of circulation: a *cabinet*, a pentagonal *salle des bains* (along the party wall), a rounded *angloise* (lit along the court), and a bedchamber with canted corners and a private alcove – clustered around a diminutive circulatory hub. Beyond Thiers's private suite, Contant installed a large *cabinet et bibliothèque* (in space formerly appropriated by Antoine Crozat), and he provided it with direct entry from the round "peristyle" along the square.

Mme de Thiers claimed the ceremonial and private apartments on the first floor, directly above those of her husband. In a project dated 1744, closest to the executed renovations, Contant reconceived the stair, which rose in two curved flights within a semicircular cage, "decorated with architectural members, partly real, partly false, executed by M. Pietre, a painter of some reputation for these works," Blondel explained (Figs. 106 and 107); it was "faintly illuminated" but "otherwise of a very ingenious composition."[41] Beyond two nearly freestanding Ionic columns that flanked the landing at the top of the stair (Fig. 108), Contant again reversed and condensed the ceremonial promenade.

The landing provided access to the garden *enfilade* and to a new suite devoted to *compagnie* along the court. Along the garden, Contant fashioned a polygonal anteroom, setting the fireplace into an apse at one end of the *enfilade* vista, which now extended through centrally placed doors (as did that of the ground floor). Contant reclaimed the former doorway of the anteroom,

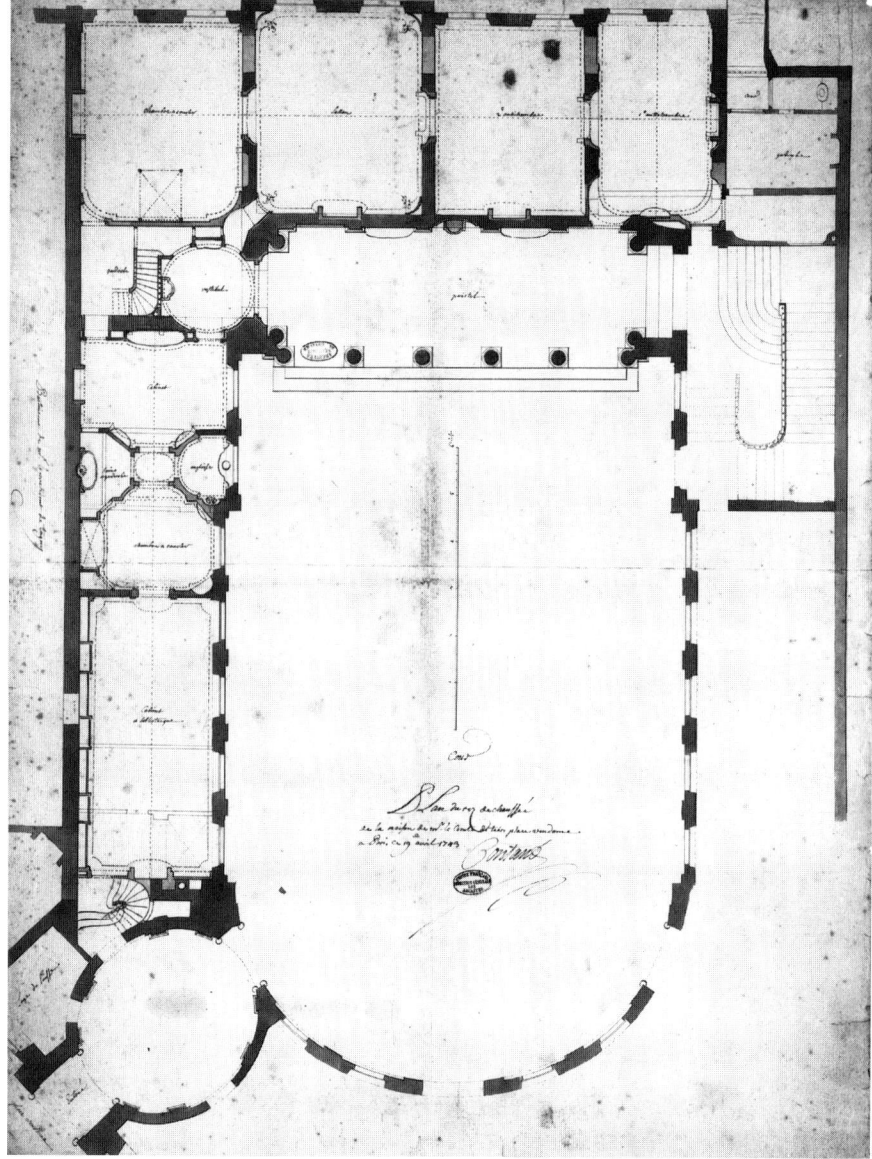

Figure 105
Pierre Contant d'Ivry, project for reconstruction of ground floor, Hôtel de Thiers, no. 19 Place Vendôme (signed and dated April 1743) [photo: Archives nationales, T 188¹, document conserved at Centre historique des Archives nationales, Paris].

installing an armoire in the paneling to accommodate the household altar – one indication of the diminishing importance of the chapel as a social sign, even if, in its reduced state, it still signified that this was a *grand Hôtel*.[42] Beyond a second anteroom, Contant shaped a *sallon d'assemblée*, canting the

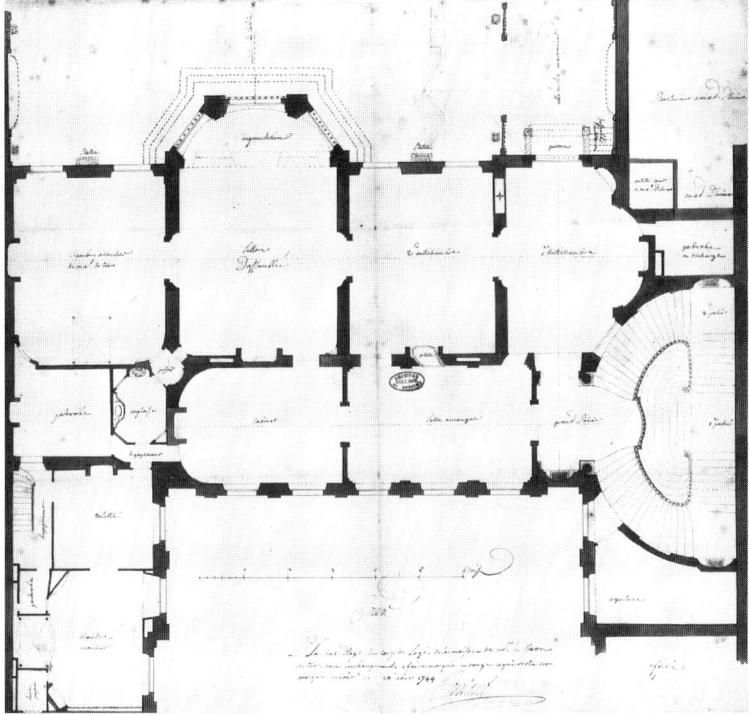

Figure 106
Pierre Contant d'Ivry, project for reconstruction of first floor, Hôtel de
Thiers, no. 19 Place Vendôme (signed and dated August 1744) [photo:
Archives nationales, T 188¹, document conserved at Centre historique des
Archives nationales, Paris].

window wall toward the garden for more extensive vistas, in a projection that
remained unrealized.

Along the court, Contant subdivided the former vestibule-gallery, just as he
had reconceived its counterpart at the Maison Crozat to serve Tugny's intellectual interests; here it accommodated the needs of *compagnie*.[43] The large
dining room was articulated with a fluted Corinthian order and heated by a
stove that also warmed the second anteroom;[44] it opened onto a *cabinet*,
which retained the rounded shape of the former gallery, intended for more
intimate gatherings of *compagnie*.[45] Mme de Thiers's ceremonial bedroom
terminated the garden *enfilade*. In each of the extant projects, Contant shaped
a private suite, opening off Mme de Thiers's *chambre de parade*, that was as
complex and refined as the one for her husband; in 1744, it included an
octagonal *angloise* and, along the court, a *cabinet de toilette* and a private
bedroom with canted corners and an alcove for a bed.[46]

The term *sallon d'assemblée* suggested a room more public than a *salle de
compagnie*, but less ceremonial than a *grand salon*.[47] Contant treated the
room less grandiosely than Tugny's *salon*, applying a more modest pilaster

Figure 107
Pierre Contant d'Ivry, rebuilt grand stair (*in situ*), Hôtel de Thiers, no. 19
Place Vendôme, 1744 [photo: after Jules Vacquier, *La place Vendôme,
dite aussi de Louis le Grand ou des Conquêtes* (Paris: F. Contet, 1913)].

order and playful decorative details (Figs. 109 and 110).Blondel praised the
"nobility and magnificence" of decor in the first-floor suite along the garden.[48]
Differences in character between Thiers's *sallon d'assemblée* and his brother's
grand salon seem subtle, but they may be significant. Tugny, now a retired
magistrate allied with a robe clan, may have felt less comfortable with associations linking the realm of *compagnie* with a "bourgeois" mode of use; Thiers

Figure 108
Pierre Contant d'Ivry, rebuilt grand stair, view to first-floor landing (*in situ*), Hôtel de Thiers, no. 19 Place Vendôme, 1744 [photo: author].

was a successful military officer allied with the Laval-Montmorency court family, and he may well have enjoyed a higher degree of social confidence.

When the marquis du Châtel died in 1750, Pierre Crozat's art collection passed to Thiers;[49] then Tugny died shortly after, and Thiers inherited, as well, the former Maison Crozat and Tugny's collections.[50] Such a concentration of assets in the hands of a male heir had been arranged through familial bequests (a dynastic strategy that would soon be frustrated, since the only legitimate offspring produced by Crozat's sons were female). In late 1750 and 1751, Thiers sold works from both collections, about half of those he had inherited, but he retained over two hundred of his uncle's most valuable paintings.[51] To those, he added works he had himself collected, predominantly Dutch, Flemish, and French. By 1755, Theirs had reshaped a collection of almost four hundred paintings.[52]

Thiers's father had employed the Neopolitan painter Matteis in the decoration of no. 17 Place Vendôme, and he owned some valuable pieces, but he was not an art collector.[53] For the unmarried Pierre, whose motives were no doubt complex, collecting had brought with it, among other rewards, a social prestige that his brother had pursued through other means.

Thiers had architect Pierre Varin rebuild parts of nos. 17 and 19.[54] Varin provided the first-floor ceremonial bedroom of no. 19 with direct access to Tugny's library at no. 17.[55] He shaped a new *appartement de commodité* for

Figure 109

Pierre Contant d'Ivry, *salon d'assemblée (in situ)*, Hôtel de Thiers, no. 19 Place Vendôme, c. 1744 [photo: after Jules Vacquier, *La place Vendôme, dite aussi de Louis le
Grand ou des Conquêtes*, (Paris: F. Contet, 1913)].

Thiers in the *entresol* overlooking the square, extending it into the *entresol* of
the adjoining house. Below it, on the ground floor, Varin planned a new
bathing room and a wardrobe, procuring for this apartment "all the *commo-
dités* desirable, which, joined to its exposition, makes it a preferred place for
the retreat of the master of the house."[56]

Blondel counseled "persons interested in the fine arts to go to visit this
house, one of the most beautiful in Paris . . . perhaps one of those (after the
Palais Royal) that contains the richest collection of paintings of different
schools, without counting the great number of rare objects of great price dis-
tributed and arranged with a taste worthy of the Proprietor who owns these
different marvels."[57] Thiers regularly opened his collection to visitors, and for
their use he had J.-B. La Curne de Saint-Palaye prepare a catalogue, published
in 1755.[58]

The catalogue provided a room-by-room tour. On the ground floor at no.
19 (Fig. 105), Thiers installed the largest part of his uncle's collection in the
four rooms along the garden. In the first anteroom, he displayed less valuable
pieces, mostly Italian, but he set among them Leonardo's *Saint Sebastian.*[59]
Beginning with the second anteroom, walls were completely lined with important works, mostly Italian, plus select Dutch, Flemish, and French paintings.
In a large ground-floor room in the left wing, labeled *cabinet et bibliothèque*
on Contant's plan, Thiers hung some of the most highly valued works of his
collection: two each by Rubens and Pietro da Cortona, a Correggio, a Guido

Figure 110
Pierre Contant d'Ivry, detail of paneling, *salon d'assemblée*, Hôtel
de Thiers, no. 19 Place Vendôme, c. 1744 (*in situ*) [photo: after
Jules Vacquier, *La place Vendôme, dite aussi de Louis le Grand
ou des Conquêtes* (Paris: F. Contet, 1913)].

Reni, an Albani, a Domenichino, a Titian portrait, Veronese's *Marriage of
Saint Catherine*, a *Judith and Holofernes* by Giorgione (then attributed to
Raphael), and a Poussin and a Bourdon.[60] Thiers also filled the first-floor
rooms with more works by Italian masters, Rembrandt, Rubens, and others.[61]

Thiers accorded to his uncle's collection the pride of place in the public
rooms. In his private suite, nestled in the *entresol*, Thiers preferred the sorts
of works that had become most popular among Parisian collectors by mid-
century – Dutch, Flemish, and French paintings, many of them smaller in size.
Among impressive collections of such works already installed at the square
were those of his neighbor Fonspertuis (no. 21) and of Mme Hocquart's
brother Emmanuel-Jacques Gaillard de Gagny, Treasurer General of the *ma-*

réchaussées of France (possibly installed at the Hocquart residence, no. 12).[62] Thiers supplemented those works with a few Italian pieces and family portraits.[63] He devoted the *entresol* and first-floor rooms appropriated from the former Maison Crozat almost entirely to Dutch and Flemish paintings, reserving the *cabinet* off the library at no. 17 for the "French School."[64]

In 1755, Thiers gave the former Maison Crozat to his youngest daughter, upon her marriage to the marquis de Béthune, but it was his middle daughter and her husband, the maréchal de Broglie, who intermittently occupied the house.[65] In 1765, the Béthune signed a lifetime lease to general tax farmer Chalut de Vérin, with Thiers retaining "the *cabinet* and the gallery of the first floor in the right wing, where . . . [he] has his library, and the small apartment in the *entresol* along the Place de Louis le Grand. . . ."[66] At about that time, Claude-Nicolas Ledoux executed "an interior decoration" for Thiers.[67]

In his copy of the 1755 catalogue of Thiers's paintings, Gabriel Saint-Aubin sketched Louis XV visiting the celebrated collection in 1772, shortly before its sale.[68] Perhaps nothing reveals more tellingly the evolution in status enjoyed by at least some families at the Place Vendôme. Louis XIV had, of course, never visited the house of a financier at the royal square that bore his name. Collecting was an important social leveler, but in 1772, Louis XV was not visiting a financial dwelling; he was visiting one owned by the duc and duchesse de Broglie. Thiers had allied his daughters with distinguished court families, and his niece (du Châtel's daughter) was the duchesse de Choiseul.[69] The mobility of Crozat's children echoed among their counterparts, especially the président Hénault. In the twenties, the lawyer Barbier labeled him *homme de rien*, a common appellation for sons of financiers, but by 1749, he was the queen's "great friend," according to d'Argenson, and he was lodged at Versailles in a room adjoining her own.[70]

If a remarkable collection of paintings had effectively served the mobility of the Crozat clan, it no longer seemed essential to the generation that followed. When Thiers died in late 1770, the duchesse de Broglie sold his collection to Catherine the Great, in a transaction brokered by Diderot.[71]

7

The *Caisse,* Collecting, and the *Boudoir*: The Place Vendôme at the End of the Old Regime

> Finance is not at all today what it had been earlier. . . . There are several among them [financiers] who love and cultivate letters, who are sought by the best circles. . . . [1]

At the end of the Old Regime, leading financial families mingled with greater ease among the court and high robe, and noble avocations like collecting art and specimens of natural history became more significant elements of their self-presentation. Sensitivity to subtle gradations of rank never disappeared, however, and a newly calibrated hierarchy emerged among types of financiers.[2] Critics suggested that the rococo style, now widely dispersed, had become inadequate in expressing social distinctions. Theorists argued for a reintroduction of the language of the classical orders with its rules of proportion and decorum. Some, like Blondel, believed that the reestablishment of the orders would, properly, reinforce representational distinctions; in practice, however, the new neoclassical style coincided with the ascent of financial families and others of ambiguous status.

A hybrid elite commissioned dwellings in the new style, but leading patrons included many newly confident financial families and their progeny. Within those dwellings, the female realm expanded, absorbing some formerly gender-neutral spaces, including the *salon* and the dining room, and it became a focus of refinement.[3] Some women who previously would have assumed a low profile (widows, separated wives, and mistresses of prominent men) also built quite conspicuously and opulently in the new style.[4]

By the late seventies, financial families increasingly abandoned the Place Vendôme, with its strongly corporate image, for larger parcels along or beyond the ramparts. In new districts, there was a greater fusion of elites, especially among clients of a younger generation; older members of prominent court families, however, tended to remain in the Faubourg Saint-Germain.[5] Impressive courtiers did not completely abandon the square; but they resided there less frequently as the century wore on, even if the widow of Charles-Anibal de Rohan-Chabot rented no. 21 during the sixties, the duc de Lauzun resided there briefly in the mid-seventies, and, following his wife's death, the duc de Fitz-James rented no. 20 in the eighties.[6] On the eve of the Revolution, as other elites left, bankers filled the void. As private businessmen rather than state office holders (and many among them foreign and Protestant), bankers had rarely shared the social mobility of financiers. Their confidence rose sharply, however, at the end of the Old Regime, ascending with the fortunes of the Genevan Jacques Necker.

Within the dwelling, the *salon* – as a room and as an informal institution – became more closely connected with the mistress of the house. Associated with social advancement, *salons* appeared at and near the Place Vendôme, as wives of financiers and bankers more assiduously displaced their noble predecessors.[7] *Salons* could attract high-ranking guests, and Mme Necker, who resided during the mid-seventies at no. 20 Place Vendôme, apparently began her *salon* at least in part to advance her husband's career.[8] For decades, Mme Geoffrin's *salon* met a few doors west of the square, in a house "bourgeois enough" (as d'Argenson put it), along the rue Saint-Honoré (Fig. 95);[9] she hosted predominantly male guests at dinners followed by readings and conversation.[10] From 1770, those who attended her assemblies convened on Fridays at Mme Necker's *salon*.[11] But as estates mingled in the *salons* of Mme Geoffrin and Mme Necker, their husbands seem to have merged less seamlessly with that company, which still associated them with the ignoble world of commerce.[12]

Financiers, too, increasingly claimed additional space for noble pursuits – especially collecting – that could attract high-ranking visitors to their dwellings; during the last decades of the Old Regime, the Place Vendôme formed one of the most impressive concentrations of private collecting in Paris. Other financiers used the lure of the table – dining or gaming – to attract prominent courtiers, as Samuel Bernard had done so effectively earlier in the century.

In this chapter, I consider the impact of these trends on the dwellings of the Place Vendôme. New corporate distinctions, an expanding female realm, collections of art and natural history, the lure of refined cuisine, the enticement of the gaming table – all of these shaped the use and design of houses at the square during the last decades of the Old Regime. I begin with the new distinctions that arose among types of financiers.

Corporate Distinctions and the Rise of Tax Farmers

May the happy revolution which purges France of the scourge of financiers be one of the glorious epoques of the reign of Louis *le Bien-Aimé* [(Darigrand), *L'Anti-financier*, 1764].[13]

At the conclusion of the Seven Years War, the French Crown found itself in desperate financial circumstances, akin to those at the end of the War of the Spanish Succession.[14] Popular resentment focused on financiers, but the nobility did not call for a Chambre de Justice. Instead, Louis XV officially banned a proliferating critique of the general tax farmers, most closely associated in popular imagination with fiscal corruption. By 1763, they had emerged as the most powerful financial elite.

Corporate distinctions among financiers had become more pronounced during the century, contributing to a hierarchy, although single clans often occupied a range of financial posts.[15] Among general tax farmers, large portions of family assets were sometimes invested for generations, with posts passing from father to son (or nephew); it has been argued that they were on their way to acceptance as a new branch of the second estate.[16] The decade following the Seven Years War marked the apex of their presence at the Place Vendôme, with over twelve percent of their corps residing at the square by 1775, and many more huddled nearby.[17]

Among the Place Vendôme residents rivaling tax farmers in wealth were general treasurers. A proliferation of treasurers had interfered with the Crown's ability to manage its revenues; it had to borrow to cover shortfalls in one sector, when funds lay idle in others. Between 1771 and 1781, reforming ministers reduced the number of treasurers to just a handful, deepening the Crown's dependence on just a few men. The new top-ranking treasurers were among the wealthiest and most powerful, but the autonomy that was so profitable also left them vulnerable to temporary problems of liquidity that could lead to bankruptcy.[18]

The square also remained the abode of some leading receivers general. As a group, they had become less powerful than tax farmers, apparently due to a looser corporate structure; they were not, however, as independent as treasurers, and they maintained a common fund to sustain members of their group. Some leading clans colonized the Place Vendôme – including the Randon and Marquet families, both enjoying ties to tax farming.[19]

Corporate differences appeared in the sphere of *bureaux*, which consumed more space in many houses, but not among general tax farmers, whose rise was accompanied by an increasing extraction of business from private dwellings. That removal affected social geography, and it operated as a social sign.

Tableaux and *Bureaux:* Blondel de Gagny (No. 15)

Among the most renowned collectors of his epoque was Augustin Blondel de Gagny, a contemporary of Crozat's sons and himself the son of a treasurer in the Bâtiments du roi. In 1750, he became Treasurer General of the new Caisse général des amortissements, which redeemed state debt. A widower since 1730, he had moved to the Place Royale with his first *commis* Claude Darras in 1745 (Fig. 52).[20] From 1758, Blondel and Darras rented no. 15 Place Vendôme, where they lived and worked in an almost entirely male household (Figs. 72, 73, and 111). In 1775, the year before Blondel died, Darras bought the house.

Famous for the size and quality of Blondel's art collection, the dwelling was also an unusually active place of business. Visitors entered through a passage leading to an enclosed "peristyle" – a vestibule lined with pilasters – that opened onto a stair hall in the wing. Beyond the stair extended an apartment, presumably a traditional one earlier in the century; in the sixties and seventies,

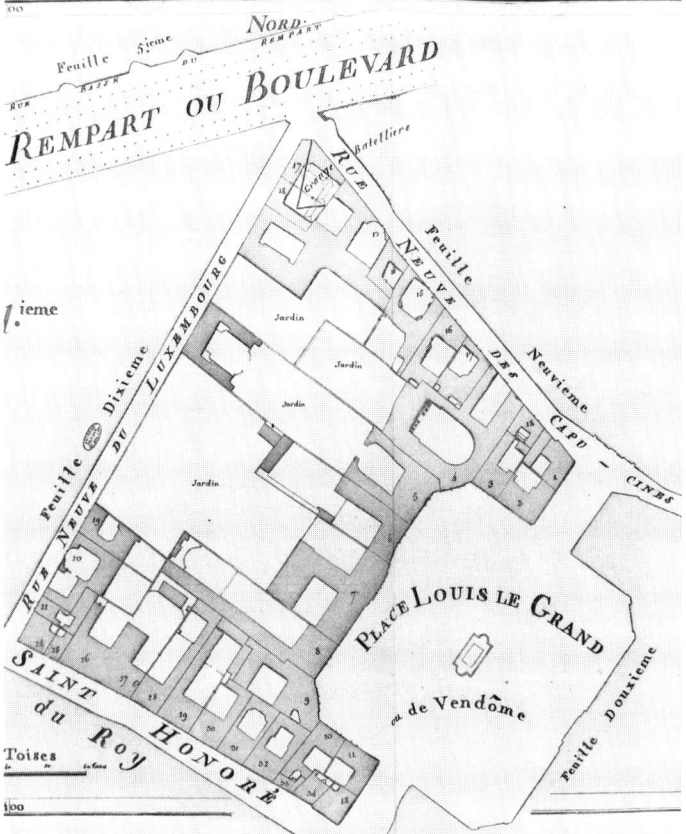

Figure 111

Place Vendôme, west range, *Atlas de la censive de l'archevêché dans Paris*, detail, *feuille* 11 (Paris, 1786); for numbers of houses today, see Fig. 9 [photo: after reprint ed., Paris, 1906].

it served as a "working" apartment consisting of an *antechambre, grande salle*, ample *grand cabinet*, and *cabinet de lieux à l'angloise*.[21]

The "asylum of so many beauties" that "one could not leave without pain" – as the abbé Antonini described Blondel's collections during the late forties – had been moved to the first floor of no. 15 and concentrated in rooms overlooking the square.[22] Use had changed markedly since the widowed maréchale de Boufflers briefly resided in this house in the late thirties. As a duchess, she had the privilege of a canopied dais for official reception; she placed it in a large anteroom "called the *salle du dais*" preceding her ceremonial bedchamber and *cabinet* along the square.[23] The house had been rented during the fifties to the prince d'Ardore, ambassador of the king of Naples, who may have retained that ceremonial apartment. When Blondel and Darras occupied it, however, the former ceremonial suite along the square served the realm of *compagnie*, with a *salle à manger*, a *salle de compagnie*, and a music room.[24]

On the landings of the grand stair, pedestals carried busts of mythological figures by Coustou and Le Lorrain, and reliefs by Le Lorrain crowned first-floor doors leading to the two principal apartments.[25] An anteroom, lit along the court and serving as a *buffet*, opened immediately off the landing; among the works Blondel hung on its walls were views of Rome and Venice by Vanvitelli and Canaletto, a "perspective" and a painting "of architecture" by Le Maire, a Venus by Lancret, and, in 1776, Rigaud's portrait of Blondel's father. The last is telling – Blondel's forbears were not "faceless."[26]

The anteroom preceded a large dining room overlooking the square, filled with impressive paintings rather than decorative works, most prominently a large "Adam and Eve" by Santerre, a *tableau capital* attributed to Rembrandt, works by Wouwerman, Teniers the Younger, Elsheimer, Bril, and Vernet, plus Roman views by Vanvitelli and overdoors with architectural scenes by de Machy and Servandoni. Around the room's perimeter, Blondel placed pedestals, consoles, tables, and *commodes* – including several Boulle père pieces – all carrying small works of sculpture and vases of marble, porphyry, and porcelain.

In the *salle de compagnie* that followed, Blondel hung some of his most prized paintings on walls lined in crimson damask: mostly Dutch and Flemish, several French, and a few Italian and other works.[27] Blondel furnished the room with a large crystal chandelier, and marquetry *commodes*, consoles, and pedestals by Boulle (carrying vases and sculpture).[28] He devoted the adjacent *salon de musique*, lined in green damask, almost exclusively to Dutch and Flemish works.[29]

Behind that suite, along the court, was Blondel's large bedchamber (lined in green damask), which may have also functioned as a *grand cabinet*; the bed was in the form of a sofa, and Blondel kept a large writing table in the room. It is clearly the room sketched by Saint-Aubin in 1771 (Fig. 112), and it, too, was filled with paintings, symmetrically hung and stacked to the cornice. To the left, above the heads of Blondel's visitors in Saint-Aubin's sketch, Blondel crowned a group of Northern paintings (including a Ruisdael landscape) with Noël-Nicolas Coypel's celebrated *Rape of Europa*. On the far wall, two more large works flanked a painting of a female Moor (by Bon Boullongne or his father Louis Boullongne the Elder), set into the paneling above the mirrored *trumeau* of the fireplace; below were many smaller paintings, including works by Terborch, Metzu, Wouwerman, and Teniers the Younger. Around the perimeter of the room (atop a writing desk of antique lacquer, the fireplace mantel, and a variety of tables), Blondel displayed part of his extensive collection of porcelain.[30]

The more public apartment, along the right wing, had a different character. Blondel lined an anteroom with Beauvais tapestries woven after designs by Boucher, a fashionable version of a traditional decor; that left little room for paintings, but Blondel filled the room with prized marquetry pieces by Boulle. In the *salon* that followed, large tapestries of La Fontaine's fables after designs by Oudry were complemented by a sofa, and twelve armchairs uphol-

Figure 112

Gabriel de Saint-Aubin, Blondel de Gagny's bedchamber, Maison Blondel de Gagny, no. 15 Place Vendôme, 1771, Musée du Louvre [photo: Réunion des Musées Nationaux].

stered with tapestry coverings bearing similar themes. The *salon* opened onto a *grand cabinet* used as a library, and there Blondel displayed landscapes, views of Venice by Canaletto and Vanvitelli, and five of his twenty-eight paintings by Teniers the Younger;[31] in the *grand cabinet* and a smaller *cabinet* opening off of it, Blondel displayed porcelain and paintings that included a Teniers the Younger, "ruins" by de Machy, small views of Rome by Vanvitelli, a battle by van der Meulen, and landscapes by Claude and Elsheimer.[32]

Like Crozat's sons, Blondel collected mostly Dutch, Flemish, and seventeenth and eighteenth-century French works. His devotion to opulent marquetry pieces by Boulle père, associated with the reign of Louis XIV, was perhaps somewhat conservative; Blondel far surpassed other collectors, including his neighbor Thiers, who owned about a dozen pieces.[33] Those furnishings and the many architectural views embellishing overdoors and walls would probably have been understood to embody a "male" taste.[34] As the son and nephew of a treasurer and intendant in the Bâtiments du roi, Blondel – who himself served briefly in the Menus Plaisirs – clearly embraced a genre associated with the fortunes of his clan. The paintings of architecture probably served as a kind of familial "attribute."

Mrs. Thrale, who visited France in 1775, called Blondel's house a "Fairy Palace," but remarked, "nothing here was counted curious but in proportion to its being expensive" – barely veiling a charge often leveled at *nouveaux riches*.[35] A decade later, Thiery offered a variation of the stereotype in describing the collection of tax farmer Chalut de Vérin; he implied that Chalut had filled no. 17 with so many paintings, bronzes, and works of porcelain that his interest must have been quantity rather than quality.[36]

Blondel's notary called Darras a first *commis*, but Darras had probably been, for some time, the executor of the post of Treasurer General of the *Caisse*, and he succeeded Blondel. Following Blondel's death, Darras claimed the first-floor wing as an extended working suite, with a *grand cabinet, bureau,* and *arrière cabinet*. He devoted more than half of the house to the *Caisse*, including a partly subterranean zone and the *entresol* along the square, plus the entire second floor and part of the third.[37]

The *Cabinet* and the *Boudoir:* the Maison Dangé (No. 9)

The role of collecting in self-presentation among financiers and the refinement of realms presided over by their wives emerge in the transformation of no. 9 by François-Balthazar Dangé. Residence at the square came at the culmination of his career. Born in 1696, the same year as Tugny and a year after Blondel, Dangé was the son of a receiver of the *taille*. His advancement hinged on the favor of the d'Argenson family, beginning with Marc-René de Voyer de Paulmy, *garde des sceaux* during the Regency (and father of the memoirist), who probably arranged Dangé's 1721 marriage to Anne Jarry, a niece of the Regent's chaplain. Dangé joined the general tax farm in 1736. During the forties, the marquis d'Argenson, then Secretary of State for Foreign Affairs, wed his own son to Dangé's daughter. In 1750, Dangé purchased no. 9. A few years later, he installed a large household, including children of a younger brother, whom he sponsored in military, robe, and financial careers and alliances.[38]

Dining was a focus of the renovation. Like Tugny, Dangé transferred the dining room from the *entresol* (Fig. 78) to the wing of the *noble étage*.[39] With the growing importance of dining as a social sign, conspicuous display of a laden *buffet*, for a time considered "bourgeois," reappeared among Parisian elites;[40] here, beyond the landing of the stair, Dangé installed an elaborate *buffet* in an anteroom.[41] It opened onto a large dining room painted with frescoes, including one of a statue flanked by columns that served as a backdrop to two marble fountains. Just beyond was a *cabinet* lined in green damask, where Dangé hung ten prized paintings, including four by Boucher; off that "green *cabinet*" was a "*cabinet doré*" filled with porcelain.[42]

The prelude to the renovated first-floor public rooms in the main range was an oval anteroom, lit by a window along the court and articulated with fluted Ionic pilasters and niches harboring illusionistic paintings of statues. In a second anteroom (or "first *salon*") facing the square, Dangé hung more paintings, including two Vernet seascapes and portraits of himself and his wife; after Mme Dangé's death in 1772, he installed his famous gaming tables in this room.[43] But the focus of display was the *salon* that followed, and there Dangé installed large Gobelins tapestries and unusually opulent furnishings.[44]

The *salon* had displaced the *chambre de parade* as the main reception room along the public realm, just as it had in most houses at the square. Mme Dangé's expensively outfitted ceremonial bedroom opened off the first ante-room along the court, and she kept in it a single painting, a portrait of the pope, the sort of "devotional" work financial wives often hung in their bed-chambers, if less frequently than earlier in the century.[45]

Dangé's apartment, installed in the *entresol* (Fig. 78), consisted of an ante-room along the court, followed by three rooms facing the square: a library (formerly the dining room of the Maison de Villemaré), a large *cabinet* (also lined with armoires for books), and a small, but opulent bedchamber with a sleeping alcove. After Mme Dangé's death, Dangé installed a second bed in the *cabinet*, and he apparently preferred to sleep there at the end of his life.[46]

Mme Dangé's sphere was associated not with collecting or books, but with personal adornment and conversation – the realms of *toilette* and *compagnie*. Elite women now required extensive private and semiprivate suites, focusing on the *cabinet de toilette* and *boudoir*, the latter defined by some as a small *cabinet* "in which one sulks unobserved, when one is in bad humor."[47] Sulking was not, however, the sort of behavior expected of a bourgeois woman, which is what contemporaries would have considered Mme Dangé. When Louis

Figure 113

Louis Tocqué, portrait of Mme Dangé, 1753, Musée du Louvre [photo: Réunion des Musées Nationaux].

Figure 114
Paneling from *boudoir* of Mme Dangé, no. 9 Place Vendôme, c.
1756, reinstalled at Musée des Arts Décoratifs, Paris [photo: Musée
des Arts Décoratifs].

Tocqué did her portrait shortly before the renovations began, he painted her
in a manner akin to Aved's presentation of Mme Crozat (Figs. 49 and 113).

Mme Dangé's single-bay *boudoir*, made more intimate by a dropped ceiling, was lined in paneling painted with wooded scenes from La Fontaine's
fables (Figs. 114 and 115). The scenes were perhaps intended to embody the
conceit of a "natural" setting, which became popular in *boudoirs*; in J.-F.
Bastide's novella *La Petite Maison*, published at about this time, a *boudoir*
was treated as a fictively "natural" setting conducive to seduction.[48] The term
boudoir carried an association with erotic activity, but Mme Dangé's *boudoir*
was clearly not a site for illicit seduction. Set along the square, it opened off
the *salon* as a semiprivate space for receiving a few friends, bridging the realms
of *compagnie* and *commodité*. Mme Dangé furnished it with a small sofa and

152

Figure 115
Detail of paneling from *boudoir* of Mme Dangé,
no. 9 Place Vendôme, c. 1756, Musée des Arts
Décoratifs, Paris [photo: Musée des Arts Décor-
atifs].

a few chairs covered in white embroidered satin.[49] It was Dangé, not his wife,
who was infamous for extramarital liaisons and for too "proudly" adopting
other noble codes of behavior – especially gambling – in constructing a social
self.[50]

The rest of Mme Dangé's private suite included a *cabinet de toilette* with a
bed alcove, some wardrobes, and a *lieux à l'angloise*. Associated with her
realm, too, was a bathing room on the ground floor along the square; like
many such rooms, the walls were lined in a white textile (here one with blue
flowers, produced in Orange), the same fabric that covered two canopied beds
and seven chairs.[51] Mme Dangé's private realm within the house was, thus,
refined and complex, but far more inventive (and opulent) was the private
apartment François Bélanger would design for Mme Baudard de Sainte-James
at no. 12 Place Vendôme.

"Nature" at the Maison Baudard de Sainte-James (No. 12)

By the eighties, the Place Vendôme was still an important nexus for collecting,
but *cabinets* of natural history predominated. Such collections had long been
a sign of elite cultivation, without inviting charges like those of Mrs. Thrale.

In the eighties, the most admired *cabinets* were to be found in dwellings at the Place Vendôme, including the Maison Baudard de Sainte-James.[52]

Born in Angers in 1738, Baudard was more than forty years younger than Blondel and Dangé. He inherited his post as Treasurer General of the French Colonies in America, borrowing heavily to add to it responsibility for the Navy, and anglified the name of an inherited seigneurie (Sainte-Gemmes-sur-Loire).[53] In 1777, he purchased no. 12 Place Vendôme (Fig. 67), and two years later, he commissioned renovations by the architect of the comte d'Artois, Bélanger, who installed an interior decor celebrated for its opulence.

Some claimed, apocryphally, that 300,000 *livres* had been spent on the *salon* alone (Fig. 116).[54] It is instructive to compare Bélanger's *salon* with those his teacher, Contant d'Ivy, installed for Crozat's sons three decades earlier (Figs. 104, 109, and 110). Contant used the orders to render certain rooms – especially the *salon* – more public in character; Bélanger now set a colossal Corinthian order above a dado, and (like Contant) used extensive mirrors to enhance the effect of a freestanding peristyle. He produced a character so monumental that it seemed to contest its domestic setting. Mme Vigée-Le Brun complained that after dinner at the Maison Baudard, "guests

Figure 116
François Bélanger, architect; Jean-Jacques Lagrenée, painter; *salon*, Maison Baudard de Sainte-James, no. 12 Place Vendôme, (*in situ*), begun 1779 [photo: after Jules Vacquier, *La place Vendôme, dite aussi de Louis le Grand ou des Conquêtes* (Paris: F. Contet, 1913)].

went into a superb drawing-room fitted out entirely with mirrors, which, however, did not . . . [promote] the sort of confidence and intimacy that goes to
make up the charm of conversation."[55]

Beyond the colossal, gilded order, other decorative features displayed a new
level of social confidence. Contant's ornamental details in Thiers's *salon
d'assemblée* – peacocks, putti, musical instruments – were inventive but generic. Here Baudard's powerful post as Treasurer General of the Navy was
celebrated. Jean-Jacques Lagrenée populated an illusionistic sky overhead and
four overdoors with mythological figures that included a Neptune presiding
over the sea. Bélanger framed the overdoors with gilded marine motifs, reiterated in trophies "hung" on the doors (seashells and prows of ships replacing
shields and armor), and installed a floor inlaid with wood to form a large
radiating compass. The ornamental lexicon alluded to Baudard's career, but
the *salon* was by then considered part of the realm presided over by his wife.

So was the dining room. In the tradition of Samuel Bernard, Baudard's
"table" was famous for its expense.[56] Financial families competed successfully
with court nobles in that realm, leaving behind much of the robe. Traditional
robe clans preserved the custom that made dinner, at two or three in the
afternoon, the most important social meal. By the late sixties and seventies,
court nobles, the most elite financial families, and the progeny of financiers
renounced that convention and made supper the meal for which "society"
gathered. "Seigneurs and financiers sup regularly," wrote one observer in
1768, "the robe never. . . ."[57]

To accommodate the importance of the table, Baudard – like Tugny and
Dangé – transformed the first-floor wing. The prelude was a *salle des buffets*,
where a large painting of architectural and sculptural fragments amidst bas-
kets of flowers and fruit presided over three buffets. In the ample *salle à
manger* that followed, Bélanger placed marine scenes into arcades facing the
three windows, and he installed mirrors into the shorter sides of the room to
reflect those seascapes.[58] Marine subjects reiterated allusions to Baudard, but
the idea of dining "in nature" suggests a room associated with the female
realm.

The most refined rooms included those of Mme Baudard's private suite.[59]
From the *salon*, guests could enter her ceremonial bedchamber, and some
might proceed to a *boudoir* – all overlooking the square. Bélanger lined the
boudoir walls and alcove with painted paneling and mirrors adorned with
arabesques, crowning the small room with a ceiling illusionistically open to
the sky.[60] A fictive "nature" also penetrated the bathing room, here set behind
the bedroom and *boudoir*; Bélanger dissolved its walls with painted trellises
that seemed to screen an open landscape.[61] Completing Mme Baudard's private suite were several wardrobes, an octagonal *cabinet de toilette* (with mirrors set into the four canted corners and prints hung on the walls), and a
cabinet à l'angloise (lit from above).[62]

Baudard claimed the *entresol*, as Peyrenc had done as early as the mid-
twenties, Thiers and Dangé in the fifties. A grand flight from the entrance

passage opened onto a large vestibule; a few additional steps provided access to his suite. Facing the square were Baudard's *cabinet d'histoire naturelle, grand cabinet*, bedchamber, and *cabinet*. In the *cabinet d'histoire naturelle*, Baudard hung prints of the ports of France, more "attributes" of his post, but the "nature" on display was quite different from the refined artifice of Mme Baudard's realm. Opposite the mirrored *trumeau* of the fireplace, Baudard installed five mobile armoires filled with minerals, seashells, and "objects of natural history"; curiosities included a preserved serpent, miniature trees, and glass cages with stuffed birds. "Curiosities" spilled into the adjoining *grand cabinet*, where Baudard also hung twelve paintings, including a portrait of Louis XV, and installed richly carved armoires for books; natural "curiosities" appeared even into his bedchamber, where Baudard displayed four family portraits and two paintings of "natural history" surrounded with sea shells under glass. A corridor separated those rooms from smaller rooms along the court, including one only recently adopted by elite males – a *cabinet de toilette* – plus an *angloise* and a bedroom for a domestic.[63] Baudard devoted the wing to *bureaux*: four large and two small offices.[64] Of three sons and a daughter, Baudard's eldest and youngest sons still resided in the house in 1787, on the second floor.[65]

Baudard installed more *bureaux* on the first floor of a small building at the east end of the court. The parcel formerly had been planted with a garden, but before 1764, general tax farmer Hocquart had sacrificed the garden for expanded stables and carriage stalls, to serve his large household (Figs. 9 and 67).[66] Deprived of a garden at the Place Vendôme, Baudard installed one of the most celebrated "English" gardens of the epoque, just west of Paris.

   The garden had always been a prime sign of a noble *hôtel*. When planted in *parterres*, small versions could be incorporated at the Place Vendôme. "English" gardens required large parcels, however, so when Parisian elites embraced them during the seventies and eighties, the constraints of the square may have seemed especially problematic – although, even outside the square, such gardens were rare within the city limits.[67]

   At about the time he purchased his Place Vendôme house, Baudard (displaying his fashionable "anglomania") hired Bélanger to design an "English" garden with a neo-Palladian villa in Neuilly, facing the garden of the comte d'Artois at Bagatelle. Despite a certain fusion of elites, to build so conspicuously on a site so close to that of the king's brother was considered a "revolting" breach of decorum;[68] rules of social geography had grown more flexible, but they had not been dismantled.

   In 1787, Baudard was suddenly forced into bankruptcy. The Crown's pressure for additional funds pushed Baudard into a precarious state, which further degenerated when the state seized his financial records. Contemporaries blamed his bankruptcy on expenditures for his dwelling at the Place Vendôme and his garden and villa at Neuilly – both impounded by the state – but it was probably triggered by the process of inquiry itself.[69]

The Marquet

Almost all those rich financiers have died poor. . . . [70]

Mme Oberkirch's assessment overstated the situation of 1787, but major bankruptcies touched other Place Vendôme families, including the Marquet. Three of four sons of munitions dealer Maurice Marquet resided at the square, and their houses shed light on corporate distinctions, even within a single clan.[71]

The first to arrive was Louis Marquet de Mont Saint-Père, whose alliance with Louise-Michelle Pâris-Duverny in 1744 launched his clan within the Recette générale.[72] In the late forties, they rented the former Maison Peyrenc (no. 23); two decades later the youngest brother, Jean-Daniel Marquet de Montbreton, Receiver General of Finance for Dauphiné, and his wife Marie-Elisabeth Dumas (daughter of the Receiver General for Orléans) purchased that house.[73]

In 1776, the most powerful member of the clan, Jacques Marquet de Bourgade (1718–84), acquired no. 2, which encompassed four bays along the south entry street and six bays on the rue Saint-Honoré (Fig. 67). A major munitions dealer during the War of the Austrian Succession, Bourgade was later the principal adviser to Controller General of Finance Joly de Fleury, and he used his influence to undermine reforms to the Recette générale that had substantially reduced his clan's profits.[74]

Like Pierre Crozat, Marquet de Bourgade never married, and he structured an almost entirely male household in an unusual way.[75] Despite his own prominence, he accorded the *noble étage* to his nephew, Marquet Desgrèves, who had succeeded his father (Mont Saint-Père) as Receiver General for Bordeaux. Bourgade occupied an extensive *entresol* apartment that wrapped around the corner, overlooking both the entry street and the rue Saint-Honoré. His accommodation on that floor spanned the realms of informal reception, private life, and work, with an apartment that included an anteroom, a *salon de compagnie*, a bedchamber, a bathing room, a *cabinet de toilette*, and a wardrobe, plus a *cabinet de travail* opening directly onto one of two *bureaux*. That office was staffed by François Bernard, who occupied a suite off another *bureau* on the second floor.[76] Bernard explained that he "managed the *caisse* . . . with the title of trusted friend (*ami de confiance*) and without any wages or appointment."[77] Bourgade provided him with a well-furnished apartment and placed the second-floor *bureau* in a room embellished with paintings and mirrors.

The modest parcel had no garden, and unable to accommodate even a small one on the site, Marquet pursued a strategy akin to that of Baudard. He purchased a garden north of the boulevard, near the rue de la Chaussée d'Antin, but built no villa or "folie" on it. His tax farmer brother, however, moved north of the boulevard, to a site permitting a new house and an extensive garden. That move reveals a significant distinction that had arisen among men of finance.

Among the first to penetrate the newly fashionable quarter north of the boulevard were those with a high level of social confidence, general tax farmers and their sons; they included Marquet de Peyre and the président Hocquart, son of the tax farmer whose dynastic household had resided at no. 12 from 1739 to 1764. In 1763, the président Hocquart commissioned a new dwelling from Ledoux, and two years later, Marquet de Peyre bought a house and began accumulating parcels along a street that would become a magnet for members of the tax farm, the rue Bergère. Having assembled 1,757 square *toises* extending south to the boulevard, Marquet de Peyre built a spacious dwelling that dwarfed the accommodation of his brothers at the Place Vendôme and incorporated noble signs denied to them: extensive stables and an expansive garden. Set along a terrace that rose above the rampart, his ample garden – with its arbors, *parterres*, and fountains – incorporated the tree-lined boulevard into its prospects.[78]

Two Marquet brothers had chosen to reside at the Place Vendôme even after their tax farmer brother began building his palatial dwelling in a more fashionable quarter. They were certainly not alone. Prices through the decade of the seventies were still considerably lower in the new *faubourgs* than they were at the Place Vendôme.[79] For many financiers, the public character of the square and the concentration of colleagues seemed better suited to households in which *bureaux* were still significant. The institutional character of the square had increased after the Seven Years War. In the late sixties, Radix de Sainte-Foye maintained his residence on the rue des Bons Enfans near the Palais Royal, but as Treasurer General of the Navy, he kept his *bureau* at the Place Vendôme, presided over by *commis* Sandré.[80] In 1769, Receiver General for Bordeaux Charles-François Michel rented no. 25, the smaller of the houses built for Peyrenc, to the Dépôt des Chartes, a financial archive supervised by lawyer Jacob-Nicolas Moreau.[81]

General tax farmers continued to maintain *bureaux* in their houses, but their principal activities increasingly shifted to consolidated offices.[82] By 1764, tax farmer Hocquart and his son (an adjunct in the tax farm) needed just a single *bureau* at no. 12, which seems to have been tucked into an *entresol* built above Hocquart's apartment in the wing of the first floor.[83] Treasurers like Baudard de Sainte-James, who purchased no. 12, were more independent and required increasingly extensive *bureaux* as responsibilities were concentrated in fewer hands.[84]

General tax farmers had become freer to adopt a more noble mode of living, in dwellings where their business activities were far less in evidence. A corporate structure that had permitted removal of many business activities from their houses may have also contributed to their social rise. Members of the general tax farm never disappeared from the Place Vendôme, but their presence declined markedly during the last decade of the Old Regime, and later arrivals tended to be newer members with more modest origins. By the eighties, prices of houses at the square began to fall, and by 1788, just two general tax farmers and one adjunct son resided at the Place Vendôme.[85]

Bankers in Paris

At the end of the Old Regime, bankers formed a significant presence at the Place Vendôme. With the exception of the court banker and members of Catholic clans also engaged in finance, bankers had not generally enjoyed the prestige attached to royal fiscal offices. The social confidence suggested by their claiming of the square coincided with a greater collaboration in funding the Crown's debt. It seems rather ironic that a century after the revocation of the Edict of Nantes – commemorated in inscriptions adorning the pedestal of the colossal equestrian statue – Protestant bankers clustered at the square.[86]

When Protestant bankers returned to Paris during the War of the Spanish Succession, they settled in a small district in the center of the right bank. Their physically restricted quarter was compounded by a "spiritual ghetto," since Protestant bankers found "doors would scarcely open for them, but for commercial transactions."[87] After the Regency, they began to find society more open, and the boundaries of their quarter expanded.

By the thirties, several leading Protestant firms had moved to the Place des Victoires, which became a banking nexus. When the powerful court banker Samuel Bernard had arrived in late 1702, Catholic *agents de change* (agents of exchange and banking) were already there: Louis Rolland (at no. 10 since 1691), Étienne Cornette (at no. 12), and Claude-François Le Gras (at no. 1 *bis*).[88] Major Genevan firms constituted an important presence during the thirties and forties (Thélusson; Tronchin & Cie; Tourton & Baur), and more bankers – many of them foreign – appeared in the fifties (Goofens; Lambert; Woulfe), sixties (Papelier & Ebers), seventies (Nicolas Boggiano), and eighties (Pourrat; Lavabre Doerner & Cie).[89]

The fortunes of Protestant bankers shifted with the rise of Genevan Jacques Necker.[90] When Necker financed the American War of Independence with debt, he relied heavily upon his compatriots. Perhaps emboldened by Necker's prominence, Protestant bankers adopted a higher profile in Paris, and at the end of the Old Regime, they appeared at the Place Vendôme.

Their first appearance was modest, and it apparently began with a formerly Protestant banking family with branches in Holland and England, the Cottin. Since 1708, they had maintained a bank in Paris, installed for decades in the banking district.[91] In 1760, Jean Cottin, a director of the Compagnie des Indes, purchased no. 26 (Figs. 7 and 67).[92] The house he selected was easily accessible from the rue Neuve-des-Petits-Champs and, set at a corner of the square with the entry street, among those most bourgeois in character – with ten bays along the public realm. He installed his firm, Cottin & fils, and figured among the major bankers called upon by Necker to reinstate the Caisse d'Escompte in 1778. During 1765–6, Cottin & fils were the depositary trustees for Genevan banker François Mollet, who rented an apartment in the neighboring house, no. 28.[93]

The second wave appeared later, on the eve of the Revolution, and it was led by Necker. Minister of the Republic of Geneva, Necker leased no. 20 in

1774, just before his precipitous rise within the French fiscal system.[94] In 1777, Simon-Emmanuel-Julien Le Normand, of a banking family from Cadix, rented no. 14, then purchased it the following year.[95] It was not until late in the following decade, however, coincident with Necker's return to power in 1788, that Protestant bankers colonized the square: In 1787, banker Paullin rented no. 9 and Louis Pourrat bought no. 19; members of the prominent Catholic banking firm the Le Couteulx, one of whom married Pourrat's daughter, installed *bureaux*;[96] in 1788, Pache frères & Cie leased no. 20 and Guillaume Sabatier, among the directors of a restructured Compagnie des Indes, purchased no. 5;[97] Magon de la Balue, of another major Catholic banking house, now occupied the dwelling he had acquired in the late sixties (no. 22), when he had served as a general tax farmer.[98]

For most of the century, bankers (with a few exceptions) had tended to observe rules of propriety dictating a more modest presentation than financiers, which may have made the Place Vendôme as unreachable – for the Protestants among them – as the Faubourg Saint-Germain had been for most financiers. But the financial families that abandoned the Place Vendôme during the seventies and eighties, for more noble *hôtels* in newer quarters, would only briefly occupy their new dwellings. Their hard-won prestige largely protected them now from attacks from above, but it did not safeguard them from assaults that came from below.

When the Revolution came many financiers, like countless members of the nobility, fled France. Many of those who remained shared the fate of the group with which they had so long toiled to fuse. "The regime of terror had weighed particularly heavily on my clientele, which was *la haute banque* . . . ," recalled lawyer Pierre-Nicolas Berryer. "[The Place Vendôme] . . . was emptied by the arrests of the Committee of General Safety, almost immediately following the promulgation of the law of December 4, 1793."[99] General tax farmers and a number of other financiers and bankers were condemned to death. "Of all the proscriptions accumulated by the regime of the Terror, the most revolting to my eyes, the most unexpected and the most tragic, was that of the venerable M. Magon de la Balue and his family," recounted Berryer. "The true and unique cause of the revolutionary condemnation . . . was that he had been reputed very rich. The patriot-vandals were persuaded that the basement rooms of M. Magon de la Balue, [at the] Place Vendôme, were filled with gold. Their disappointment converted to rage. . . ."[100]

Conclusion

"INGENIOUS FRENCH, our century beholds with astonishment the brilliant extent of your talents," proclaimed Le Camus de Mézières in 1780, reiterating the widespread belief among eighteenth-century French architects that their greatest contribution had been in the realm of domestic design.[1] Jean Courtonne had boasted in 1725 that the French "have surpassed their neighbors [in the domestic realm] and left them nothing but the glory of imitating us."[2] In 1752, Blondel announced simply, "since about fifty years ago, . . . [French architects] have . . . invented a new art [of domestic planning]."[3]

The formal virtuosity and extraordinary refinement of French planning and interior decor, as well as French dominance in the production of the luxury goods that filled domestic spaces, have long been celebrated. French architects, decorative artists, and other craftsmen – prodded by their elite clientele – devoted their talents to every nuance of domestic design. This book acknowledges that virtuosity and artistry, but it is primarily a consideration of how these ensembles of planning and decoration served the representational needs of the most mobile French elite. Dwellings encoded multiple and complex social meanings that became affixed to spaces and objects through systems of representation – both strategic and ideological.

During the eighteenth century, the Place Vendôme was the most prominent site claimed by the financial elite. Evolving identities seem to have become embedded in fundamental ways in the physical fabric of its dwellings – linked by their shared facade, the singularity of the site, and inherent typological dilemmas. Many aspects of those identities were obvious to the designers of these houses and their clients; others were, no doubt, less consciously encoded in these designs.

Typological choices, division of space into gendered realms, the "social geography" of the household, the absence or presence and placement of a range of signs from ample stables to galleries, as well as decorative elements from armorial emblems to the classical orders or the eroticized vocabulary of the rococo – all these carried distinct social meanings within the particular signifying system of the eighteenth-century Parisian dwelling. The houses of financiers were "hybrid," even outside of the Place Vendôme, since financial families *used* their dwellings differently from nobles of the sword and robe. When similarities among plans and decorative ensembles suggest consistency of meaning across different elites, it is essential to recognize that social signs carried distinct meanings in different contexts. Mrs. Thrale and the guidebook writer Thiery would have had different reactions, no doubt, to the accumulated wealth of objects in the houses of Blondel de Gagny and Chalut de Vérin if those collectors had descended from old noble clans.

Historians have debated the extent to which elites "merged" in the course of the eighteenth century. The notion of a single elite of wealth may be a useful antidote to analyses stressing a rigid class structure. But if members of that elite truly no longer made distinctions based upon lineage, one is hard pressed to explain why, at the end of the Old Regime, Sénac de Meilhan felt the need to argue that financiers were so different from their predecessors and why he painted their forbears as those who rose "out of the mire to inhabit palaces."[4] If distinctions were no longer made in "society," to whom were his arguments addressed? Scholars have questioned the extent of an "aristocratic reaction" at the end of the Old Regime, but the notion has certainly not been disproved.[5] Even when applied to the last decades of the Old Regime, the concept of a merged elite seems too crude to explain a society of privilege that still savored all sorts of distinctions.

The status of the Place Vendôme as a *place royale* factored into the social meanings it embodied. The prestige of the setting both attracted financiers and fueled resentment. Some tension was always present between the public space of the square and the private realm of individual dwellings. Those spheres intersected along its noble facades in a relationship that was not always harmonious.

The program and form of the Place Vendôme had evolved as a compromise, and eighteenth-century critics increasingly found the resolution problematic. The Crown had originally conceived the public space of square as a site of spectacle, a space for grandiose ceremonies representing the sovereignty of the monarchy, enacted by royal officials and witnessed by lesser subjects.[6] As finally realized, however, the Place Vendôme had lost its public purpose. When Mansart and his collaborators reconceived it as a domestic square, its reshaped space remained open to the public, but royal spectacles bringing large numbers of people into the square rarely occurred. A potential for conflict was inherent in its hybrid program.

Anomalous activities periodically claimed its public space. In 1720, when John Law transferred trading in shares of his bank to the square, feverish speculation brought an unruly crowd of mixed social strata into the public space, requiring guards to protect the residents.[7] From 1762 to 1771, during the month-long Foire Saint-Ovide, a fair connected with the Capuchin convent north of the square, makeshift theaters, acrobats, musicians, souvenir sellers, cafés, bakeries, wine and beer shops, and other boutiques filled the square, engulfing the equestrian statue of Louis-le Grand.[8] In 1770, a year before it was transferred to the more open Place Louis XV (de la Concorde), residents obtained an order reducing the duration of the fair, prohibiting loud musical instruments and requiring boutiques to close at ten in the evening.⁹ Public and private uses of the square had obviously collided.

Those conflicts erupted in violence on August 10, 1792. What began as an attack with regicidal intent on the Tuileries palace spilled into the public space of the Place Vendôme. A crowd from the Tuileries stormed the former Feuillant monastery where some royalists were imprisoned, immediately south of the square. The inflamed crowd brought nine prisoners into the Place Vendôme, decapitated them and paraded with their heads on pikes; the square would be renamed the Place des Piques in commemoration.¹⁰ The next day, the Legislative Assembly ordered the destruction of all of the royal statues in Paris, including that of Louis XIV at the Place Vendôme. That the Place Vendôme had ceased to be a royal square became even clearer six months later. The body of the martyred Le Peletier de Saint-Fargeau, assassinated after voting for the king's execution in January 1793, was removed from his brother's house at the Place Vendôme (no. 8) and publicly displayed on the pedestal that had borne the equestrian statue of Louis XIV for ninety-three years.

Notes

List of Abbreviations

AN Archives Nationales
  MC Minutier Central des Notaires Parisiens
AR Almanach royal
BIF Bibliothèque de l'Institut de France
BMJ Bibliothèque de la Ministère de la Justice
BN Bibliothèque Nationale
  Est. Estampes
  Ms. Manuscrits
  P.O. Pièces originales
J.-F. Blondel, *AF* Blondel, Jacques-François. *Architecture Française*, 4 vols. (Paris, 1752–6)
Brice, *Description* Brice, Germain. *Description (Nouvelle) de la Ville de Paris*
BSHAF Bulletin de la Société de l'histoire de l'art français
BSHPIF Bulletin de la Société de l'histoire de Paris et de l'Ile-de-France
[D]AAVP [Délégation à] l'Action Artistique de la Ville de Paris
Favre-Lejeune, *SR* Favre-Lejeune, Christine. *Les Secrétaires du roi de la grande chancellerie de France: Dictionnaire biographique et généalogique (1672–1789)*, 2 vols. (Paris, 1986)
GBA Gazette des Beaux-Arts
NMS Nationalmuseum, Stockholm
  CC Cronstedt Collection
  THC Tessin-Hårleman Collection
Seine Archives du Département de la Seine

Introduction

1. They include Yves Durand, *Les Fermiers généraux au XVIIIe siècle* (Paris, 1971); Guy Chaussinand-Nogaret, *Les financiers de Languedoc au XVIIIe siècle* (Paris, 1970); Herbert Lüthy, *La banque protestante en France de la révocation de l'édit de Nantes à la Révolution*, 2 vols. (Paris, 1959–61); J. F. Bosher, *French Finances 1770–1795: From Business to Bureaucracy* (Cambridge, 1970), and " 'Chambres de Justice' in the French Monarchy," in his *French Government and Society 1500–1850: Essays in Memory of Alfred Cobban* ed. J. F. Bosher (London, 1973); David Bien, in several articles, including "The *Secrétaires du Roi*: Absolutism, Corps, and Privilege under the Ancien Régime," *Vom Ancien Régime zur Französischen Revolution*, ed. Ernst Hinrichs et al. (Gottingen, 1978); and Daniel Dessert, *Argent, pouvoir et société au Grand Siècle* (Paris, 1984).

2. See, for example, Pierre Goubert, *The ancien régime: French society 1600–1750*, trans. S. Cox (New York, 1974), and Chaussinand-Nogaret, *La noblesse au XVIIIe siècle: de la féodalité aux lumières* (Paris, 1976).

3. See Julian Dent, *Crisis in Finance: Crown, Financiers and Society in Seventeenth-Century France* (Newton Abbot, 1973), 242.

Chapter 1

1. In 1698, the king considered plans to sell all of the parcels behind the facades of the Place de Nos Conquêtes to individuals, for the construction of private houses (memoirs and correspondence: AN, O¹ 1576; plans: AN, N III Seine 628; Q¹ 1141, f°18; BN, Va 441 and 234; NMS, THC 6315). Public response was tepid. An investment group led by general tax farmer Alexandre Luillier offered between 600,000 and 800,000 *livres*, but the king resisted [*Mémoires du marquis de Sourches*, ed. Arthur Bertrand (Paris, 1886), VI:50–1; *Les relations artistiques entre la France et la Suède 1693–1718: Nicodème Tessin le jeune et Daniel Cronström Correspondance (extraits)*, ed. R. A. Weigert and C. Hernmarck (Stockholm, 1964), 199–200].

2. On the Place de Nos Conquêtes, see R. Ziskin, "The Place de Nos Conquêtes, and the Unraveling of the Myth of Louis XIV," *Art Bulletin*, LXXVI:1 (March 1994), 147–62.

3. De Cotte played a key role in the shaping of its space and in the execution of the design [see Robert Neuman, *Robert de Cotte and the Perfection of Architecture in Eighteenth-Century France* (Chicago and London, 1994), 113–14]. Less clear is the contribution of architect Pierre Bullet, an investment partner. In early April 1699, a few days after Mansart and Claude Bosc, *prevôt des marchands*, signed the first official plan (AN, Q¹ 1141), Bosc wrote (presumably to Mansart) asking him to "listen favorably to the proposals of Sirs Bullet and Prédot, without which there will be no contract concluded with them . . . ," (AN, O¹ 1576, f°69). A few days later Bosc sent a new plan and elevation prepared by Bullet "following your orders" and stressed the desire of the investors that these be used (AN, O¹ 1576, f°70). For more on Bullet's possible role, see Runar Strandberg, "Les dessins d'architecture de Pierre Bullet pour la Place Vendôme et L'Hôtel Reich de Pennautier-d'Évreux," *GBA* (1965), 72–3. Germain Boffrand, whose name has sometimes been associated with the design, made drawings of the Place de Nos Conquêtes for Mansart, but after April 1699, he disappeared from the payment ledgers of the Bâtiments du Roi and did not reappear until after Mansart's death [Jörg Garms, *Germain Boffrand 1667–1754: L'aventure d'un architecte independant* (Paris, 1986), 23].

4. Quoted by Jacques Saint-Germain, *Les financiers sous Louis XIV: Paul Poisson de Bourvalais* (Paris, 1950), 204. (At the Place Royale, they have put your father / amid people of quality. / One sees on the Pont-Neuf your debonair grandfather, / near the common people who were the object of his generosity. / For you, guardian prince of financiers, / at the Place Vendôme – among them – you have been installed.)

5. AN, O¹ 1576, f°116 (1-VI-1698); Arthur de Boislisle, "Notices historiques sur la place des Victoires et sur la place de Vendôme," *Mémoires de la Société de l'histoire de Paris et l'Ile-de-France*, 15 (1888), 143–7.

6. In 1701, Fontanieu would become Treasurer General of the Navy.

7. His daughter wed Gabriel in 1698 (see Dessert, *Argent, pouvoir et société*, 538–9).

8. The purchase price of 620,000 *livres* was reduced following the king's gift of a

large parcel to Mansart. Initially, each partner invested proportionally to form a fund of 500,000 *livres* (AN, V⁷ 332 and Seine, DQ¹⁰ 700, n°3779, f°10). On the day before the inauguration, Sauvion bought a large six-bay-wide parcel along the west range (nos. 9 to 11) (Fig. 9). Soon after, Besnier and Herlaut together purchased 1,392 square *toises* extending along much of the east range (nos. 10 to 20); Besnier ceded one-eighth of his total holdings to Urbain Aubert, Receiver General of Finance for Caen, and Herlaut ceded 15 percent of his interest in the partnership to Jacques de Farcy. Details of early sales appear in BN, Collection Moreau, Ms. 1067; AN, Q¹ 1141 and *série* S, and in papers of the notary Savalette. See Maurice Dumolin, "La Place Vendôme," *Procès verbaux de la Commission du Vieux Paris*, mars 1927 (Paris, 1931), 20–21; and F. de Saint Simon, *La Place Vendôme* (Paris, 1983), passim.

9. Boislisle, "Notices," 179.

10. The site appears in BIF Ms. 1308 I:2, f°ˢ156–7, and NMS, CC 1301v°.

11. Sourches, *Mémoires*, VI:50–1; Madame de Maintenon, *Lettres*, ed. Marcel Langlois (Paris, 1939), V:358.

12. AN, O¹ 1576, f°101; Boislisle, "Notices," 105–6.

13. AN, MC XCIV, 71 (8-XI-1682); Q¹ 1159; T 599²⁻³.

14. Mansart subdivided the parcel and sold smaller lots to Jacques V Gabriel, de Cotte, Pierre Le Maître, Jean Aubert, and Jacques Mazière [cited in AN, Z¹ʲ 1088 (8 and 18-VI-1782); MC XXXVI, 354 (17-IV-1715); Q¹ 1141; Q¹ 1099, 130v°; 131]. In 1697, the king had given Mansart 128 square *toises* on the north side of the street (AN, Q¹ 1141), and in 1701, Mansart acquired 95 square toises along the south side, immediately east of his larger parcel [AN, MC XCV, 36 (1-II-1701)].

15. In December 1700, de Cotte bought a parcel just east of the convent and built a house on it for the Tubeuf family. A few years later, he acquired two adjacent lots west of the convent; for that site, he designed the Maison Legendre d'Arminy, built in 1713 (Dumolin, "Place Vendôme," 23, 26; AN, Q¹ 1141). Previously, de Cotte had invested at the Place des Victoires (see ch. 7), and he later invested more heavily along streets surrounding the Place Vendôme (the rue Neuve-des-Capucines, the rue Neuve-des-Petits-Champs, and the rue Saint-Honoré) [AN, MC CXV, 376 (4-X-1718); Q¹ 1140; Q¹ 1141; Q¹ 1158; Q¹ 1159; Z¹ʲ 899 (2-II-1766); Z¹ʲ 1088 (18-VI-1782); BN, Coll. Moreau, Ms. 1067]. De Cotte's investments at the Place Vendôme appear in ch. 3; for a detailed account of his speculative activity, see François Fossier, *Les dessins du fonds Robert de Cotte de la Bibliothèque nationale de France* (Paris, 1997), 49–52.

16. AN, V⁷ 332.

17. Boislisle, "Notices," 168.

18. Dumolin's estimate, "Place Vendôme," 24.

19. Copy of contract confirming sale of no. 14 to Paparel in June 1704 (AN Q¹ 1141).

20. AN, Q¹ 1141. The shares may have been equalized as additional funds were needed; Bullet may have rendered services in exchange for a larger share.

21. Dumolin described the partition ("Place Vendôme," 24–5) and reconstructed the plan.

22. Dessert's term (*Argent, pouvoir et société*, 98–107).

23. On types of financiers, see the works cited in the introduction; on *traitants* and *partisans*, see William Doyle, *Venality: The Sale of Offices in Eighteenth-Century France* (Oxford, 1996), 6–8; and William Beik, *Absolutism and Society in Seventeenth-Century France: State Power and Provincial Aristocracy in Languedoc* (Cambridge, 1985), 254–7.

24. On bankers, see Lüthy, *La banque protestante*; Dessert, *Argent, pouvoir et so-ciété*, 191–203; and Jean Bouchary, *Les Manieurs d'Argent à Paris à la fin du XVIIIe siècle* (Paris, 1939–43), 3 vols.

25. Mme de Grignan, explaining the marriage of her son to a daughter of a receiver of the *taille*, said it was occasionally necessary "to fertilize with manure [even] the best lands," Saint-Simon, *Mémoires*, XII:289.

26. See Dent, *Crisis in Finance*, 175; François Bluche, *Les magistrats du Parlement de Paris au XVIIIe siècle*, 2nd ed. (Paris, 1986), 56.

27. See ch. 6, n. 70.

28. "Taste is like philosophy. It belongs to a very small number of privileged souls. . . . It is unknown in bourgeois families, where one is constantly occupied with the care of one's fortune" [Voltaire, "Goût," *Dictionnaire philosophique*, quoted and translated by Robert Darnton, "The High Enlightenment and the Low-Life of Literature in Pre-Revolutionary France," reprinted in *French Society and the Revolution*, ed. Douglas Johnson (Cambridge, 1976), 62]. See Michael Moriarity, *Taste and Ideology in Seventeenth-Century France* (Cambridge, 1988); and Pierre Bourdieu, *Distinction. A Social Critique of the Judgement of Taste*, trans. R. Nice (Cambridge, Mass., 1984).

29. J. Marion argued that Jourdain was a parody of Colbert, Controller General of Finance ["Molière a-t-il songé à Colbert encompasant le personnage de M. Jour-dain?" *Revue d'Histoire Littéraire de la France*, 45 (1938), 145–80]; see, too, P. J. Yarrow, "M. Jourdain and Colbert," *Seventeenth-Century French Studies*, 9 (1987), 122–30.

30. Sénac de Meilhan, *Considerations sur les riches et le luxe* (1787), quoted in Bosher, "Chambres de Justice," 38–9.

31. "Hôtel," *Encyclopédie* (1765 ed.; reprint, Stuttgart-Bad Cannstatt, 1967), VIII: 319.

32. See Elias, *Court Society*, 45.

33. See Jean-Pierre Babelon, "Le passage du corps d'hôtel simple au corps d'hôtel double," *XVIIe Siècle*, 162 (January–March 1989), 9.

34. See Martin Lister on "great Gates" announcing "Houses of Persons of Distinc-tion," *A Journey to Paris in the Year 1698* (Urbana, Ill., 1967), 9. In 1704, Lieutenant General of Police d'Argenson, apparently responding to complaints, wrote to minister Jérôme de Pontchartrain that there had "never been any ordi-nance that determined the condition of those who can put the inscription '*hostel*' on the frontispiece of their houses; birth and dignity have alone established this distinction, without the authority of laws . . . ," *Correspondance administrative sous le règne de Louis XIV*, ed. Georges B. Depping (Paris, 1850–5), II:836.

35. J.-F. Blondel explained that he included the *maison bourgeoise* of M. Guillot (Fig. 20) because he found its "distribution treated with decorum (*convenance*)" (*AF* III:1).

36. Functional arguments, however, could be made [Jean-Baptiste-Alexandre Le Blond, 1710 supplement to Daviler's *Cours d'architecture* (1720 ed.), I:185–2].

37. For a summary of the history of the apartment in France, see Robin Middleton, "Introduction," in Nicolas Le Camus de Mézières, *The Genius of Architecture; or, The Analogy of That Art with Our Sensations*, trans. D. Britt (Santa Monica, 1992), 32.

38. See Peter Thornton, *Authentic Decor: The Domestic Interior 1690–1920* (Avenel, 1993), 26.

39. These facilities had various names. Daviler defined the *aisance* as a "*lieu commun* or *de commodité*," usually on the ground floor, or connected with a wardrobe, or above the stair; a *cabinet d'aisance* was a "*lieu de commodité* with a seat (*siège*) that is also called *garderobe* and *privé*" [*Cours d'Architecture* (1693 ed.),

II:4, 34]; J.-F. Blondel often used the term *lieux de soupape* to designate additional plumbing (see, e.g., [*Maisons de Plaisance*, I:136–37]).

40. See ch. 4.

41. *Chaises de commodité* appear in inventories of noble households throughout the century.

42. According to Louis Savot, the house of a *grand seigneur* required at least two *salles*: one where persons of "quality" waited to be received, a second for servants, and – among important noblemen – a third for *fêtes*, balls, ballets, and large assemblies [*L'Architecture françoise* (Paris, 1624; reprint of 1685 ed. Geneva, 1973), 35–6].

43. Le Blond, supplement to Daviler, *Cours d'architecture* (1720 ed.), I:185–8.

44. Separate dining rooms had been introduced several decades earlier; see Claude Mignot, "De la cuisine à la salle à manger, ou de quelques détours de l'art de la distribution," *XVIIe Siècle*, 162 (January–March 1989), 17–36.

45. As Middleton notes, most theorists recommended placement of the stair to the right, some arguing that it was the direction to which a visitor naturally turned (Le Camus de Mézières, *Genius of Architecture*, 187, n. 23).

46. See Gérard Sabatier, "Politique, histoire et mythologie: La galerie en France et en Italie pendant la première moitié du XVIIe siècle," *La France et l'Italie au temps de Mazarin*, ed. Jean Servoy (Grenoble, 1986), 283–301.

47. See Savot's description of typical decorative programs and François Blondel's comments in *L'Architecture françoise* (reprint of 1685 ed.), 102. Despite the example of the Luxembourg palace, built for Marie de Medici as Regent, galleries attached to women's apartments were rare; two exceptions were those of the comtesse de Verrue (separated from her husband) and her sister, the widowed marquise de Saissac.

48. "The chapel is necessary principally in the country," explained Savot; "in cities, to have them is a privilege belonging only to Princes, or to the grandest seigneurs." He warned, however, that "women must not lodge either above or below it" (ibid., 35, 65); Katie Scott argues that such locations were considered "impure" [*The Rococo Interior: Decoration and Social Spaces in Early Eighteenth-Century Paris* (New Haven and London, 1995), 97]. On the "devout sex," see Wendy Gibson, *Women in Seventeenth-Century France* (New York, 1989), 209.

49. Béat-Louis de Muralt, *Lettres sur les Anglais et les Français* (reprint, Lausanne, 1972), 93. Editor Perrette Chappuis suggests 1694 as the probable date of these letters (220–2). On Muralt, see Katie Scott, "Decoration and Cultural Distinction in Paris, c. 1680–c. 1750," Ph.D. dissertation, University of London, 1988, 378, n. 80.

50. Even after the professionalization of the army, when the payment of a commutation in exchange for service became more common, nobles of the sword continued to pursue military careers in great numbers; see Franklin Ford, *Robe and Sword: The Regrouping of the French Aristocracy after Louis XIV*, 2nd ed. (New York, 1965), 17.

51. *Court Society*, 52. The interpretation that follows owes an important debt to Elias's analysis.

52. Hugh Murray Baillie, "Etiquette and the Planning of the State Apartments in Baroque Palaces," *Archaeologia*, 101 (1967), 186–7.

53. 6th ed., rev. (Paris, 1682), 21–2; Baillie, "Etiquette," 186–7.

54. The prestige of the bed presumably emerged from its role in the continuation of the dynasty. When the king appeared at a session of Parlement to order registration of a royal edict, he reclined on cushions, and the appearance was called a "lit de justice"; Baillie, "Etiquette," 186–7.

55. The *chambre de parade* was "inhabited by preference by the mistress of the house

when she is indisposed; she receives ceremonial visits and uses it for her *toilette* for special distinction . . ." (J.-F. Blondcl, *AF*, I:33).

56. In 1723, it was sold, still unfinished, to M. de Matignon [see Françoise Magny and Bruno Pons in DAAVP, *La rue de Varenne* (Paris, 1981), 27–33].

57. J.-F. Blondel, *AF*, I:31.

58. Baillie, "Etiquette," 186. In his published lectures, J.-F. Blondel noted that noblemen rarely still received audiences under the canopy of a *salle du dais*, so that "often this mark of dignity is but ceremonial in the majority of the dwellings of the *grands*," *Cours d'architecture, ou traité de la décoration, distribution, & construction des Bâtiments contenant les leçons données en 1750, & les années suivantes . . .* (Paris, 1771–7), IV:248.

59. Le Blond explained that Daviler presented a manner of planning that was "almost not at all in use at the current time," *Cours d' architecture* (1720 ed.), preface.

60. For an overview, see the plates assembled by Jean Mariette, *L'Architecture française* (Paris, 1727–38/39; reprint, Paris and Brussels, 1927–9), 3 vols.; J.-F. Blondel republished those plates, with some new ones, in *AF* (Paris, 1752–6; reprint, 1904), I – III.

61. On these dwellings, see Françoise de Catheu, "Le Développement du faubourg Saint-Germain du XVIe au XVIIIe siècle," *BSHPIF*, LXXXVII – LXXXVIII (1955–6), 31–9; Neuman, *Robert de Cotte*, 128–32; H. Rault and M. Constans in DAAVP, *La rue de Grenelle* 2nd ed. (Paris, 1985), 22–3, 32–3.

62. P. de Crousaz-Crétet, *Paris sous Louis XIV* (Paris, 1923), I:81; courtiers may have also called ordinary porters "Swiss guards," as Elias suggests (*Court Society*, 47).

63. Le Blond, supplement to Daviler's *Cours d'architecture* (1720 ed.), I:185–5.

64. *Traité de la perspective pratique avec les remarques sur l'architecture* (Paris, 1725), 97.

65. See Le Blond's *hôtel* with a frontage of 40 *toises*, supplement to *Cours d'architecture* (1720 ed.), I:185.

66. Le Blond argued that meat and water spoiled more easily underground (ibid., I: 185–3).

67. According to the early seventeenth-century jurist Charles Loyseau, only nobles had the right to display such emblems, but the custom was widespread among wealthy commoners [Roland Mousnier, *The Institutions of France under the Absolute Monarchy 1598–1789*, trans. Brian Pearce (Chicago and London, 1974), I: 113–14].

68. Ranking well below them were ennobled municipal officers, such as the *capitouls* in Toulouse, classified as *noblesse de la cloche*.

69. See François Bluche, "The Social Origins of the Secretaries of State under Louis XIV, 1661–1715," *XVIIe Siècle* 42–43 (1959), reprinted in *Louis XIV and Absolutism*, ed. Ragnhild Hatton (London, 1976), 85–97.

70. Ford, *Robe and Sword*, 128.

71. They also tended to form dynasties, with offices passed from father to son, but as the century progressed marriages with the sword and sons entering the military became more frequent, as did intermarriage with finance to replenish family fortunes (Bluche, *Magistrats du Parlement*, 81–90; Ford, *Robe and Sword*, 143–5).

72. See Doyle, *Venality*; Ford, *Robe and Sword*, 115. *Gages* on offices were interest payments on investments, not wages paid for work.

73. Its decoration was, properly, "regular and serious (*grave*), and the place spacious, according to the importance of the employment of the master who holds his audiences there" (J.-F. Blondel, *AF*, I:31). Daviler had employed the term *salle*

for the room "in the houses of Ministers of State and Magistrates . . . where they give audiences," reserving *salle d'audience* for a "room in the *grand appartement* of a Prince, for receiving and giving audiences to ambassadors and other ministers of foreign princes," *Cours d'Architecture* (1693; 1720 ed.), II:846.

74. J.-F., Blondel, *AF* I:117.

75. According to Daviler, a *bureau* was primarily a "room where accounts are kept or where payments are made," but, he noted, the term was still employed for "the place where the directors of hospitals and communities assemble" [*Cours d'Architecture* (1693), II:34]. *Bureaux* in robe dwellings were more akin to the latter. For example, conseiller d'État Henri-François de Paule d'Aguesseau situated a room he called *les bureaux* on the first floor of his *hôtel*, between his library and *cabinet*; in 1765, it was embellished with expensive mirrors, armoires for books, twenty-two armchairs, and a table draped with the cloth (bearing the family arms), on which his father had once affixed the Seal of State. *Bureaux* could also be more modest rooms for assistants (if never as spartan as those of financiers), such as the one on the second floor of the house of conseiller d'État Michel-Jean Amelot de Gournay, equipped in 1724 with little more than six armchairs [AN, MC LI, 1033 (16-I-1765); MC LXVII, 389 (26-VI-1724)].

76. Ford, *Robe and Sword*, 217–21; Bluche, *Magistrats du Parlement*, 185–7; J. H. Shennan, *The Parlement of Paris* (London, 1968), 133. Lassurance provided a vast first-floor library in the dwelling he built for Colbert's uncle, conseiller d'État Henri Pussort; a more considerable suite of rooms appeared in the house of the cardinal de Rohan, designed by Alexis Delamair in c. 1705 (J.-F. Blondel, *AF*, III: pl. XXVI; II: pl. XVIII).

77. "Discours sur la vie et la morte de M. d'Aguesseau, conseiller d'État; par M. d'Aguesseau, Chancelier de France, son fils" [*Oeuvres complètes du Chancelier d'Aguesseau* (Paris: 1819), XV:302–3]; see Isabelle Storez, *Le Chancelier Henri François d'Aguesseau (1668–1751): monarchiste et libéral* (Paris, 1996), 66.

78. "Discours sur la vie . . . de M. d'Aguesseau," 373.

79. Ibid., 283.

80. Saint-Simon thought it presumptuous when the widow of the président de Nesmond had the title "Hôtel de Nesmond" inscribed at the entrance to her house (Bluche, *Magistrats du Parlement*, 135). Guidebook writers typically adhered to that distinction in terminology.

81. An early example in Paris is that of the sixteenth-century financier Pierre Legendre, where the principal living quarters were removed to ranges along the garden and a narrow third wing was set along the street; see André Chastel, "Les Vestiges de l'hôtel Le Gendre et le véritable hôtel de la Trémoïlle," *Bulletin Monumental*, CXXIV (1966), 129–65. There were more modest dwellings, too (including that of the sixteenth-century royal architect Philibert de l'Orme), that emulated the noble type.

82. Michel de Frémin, *Mémoires critiques d'architecture* (Paris, 1702; reprint, Farnborough, 1967), 55.

83. For a comparison with English counterparts, see Colin Campbell, "Understanding Traditional and Modern Patterns of Consumption in Eighteenth-Century England: A Character-Action Approach" [*Consumption and the World of Goods*, ed. John Brewer and Roy Porter (London and New York, 1993), 41]. Among the wealthiest commoners, dynastic goals focusing on a merger with the nobility appear to have been more pervasive in eighteenth-century France than in England.

84. *Cours d'architecture*, II:236–7.

85. On the vulnerability of financiers, see ch. 4.

86. Many original proprietors of the Place Royale (including some major financiers) were connected with the minister Sully, but most rented the dwellings to less elite

families [see Hilary Ballon, *The Paris of Henri IV: Architecture and Urbanism* (Cambridge, Mass., 1991), 103–10, and AAVP, *De la place royale à la place des Vosges* (Paris, 1996), 162–398].

87. See Babelon, "Le passage du corps d'hôtel simple au corps d'hôtel double," 8. Le Blond noted cases when one might place the *corps-de-logis* along the street, supplement to Daviler's *Cours d'Architecture* (1720 ed.), I:185–2.

88. Elias, *Court Society*, 90–104.

89. "After supper, since the weather was so beautiful, M. d'Épinay suggested that we make a tour of the *place* [Vendôme]" [*Mémoires et correspondance de Madame d'Épinay*, ed. J.-P.-A. Parison (Paris, 1818), I:144–5]. On the Place Royale as a space for promenade, see Ballon, *Paris of Henri IV*, 68–9.

90. Military reviews lapsed by the middle of the century [Annibale Antonini, *Mémorial de Paris et ses environs* (Paris, 1749), I:154]; on the Foire Sainte-Ovide, see the conclusion.

91. Financiers long had a tendency to cluster; see Françoise Bayard, "Manière d'habiter des financiers de la première moitié du XVIIe siècle," *XVIIe Siècle*, 162 (January–March 1989), 61.

92. For an analysis of the concentration of magistrates in different quarters throughout the city, see Bluche, *Magistrats du Parlement*, 130–1.

93. Jean-Marie Apostolidès, *Le roi-machine: Spectacle et politique au temps de Louis XIV* (Paris, 1981), 16; see James S. Ackerman, *The Architecture of Michelangelo*, 2nd ed. (Chicago, 1986), 152; Richard Cleary, "The Places Royales of Louis XIV and Louis XV," Ph.D. dissertation, Columbia University, New York, 1986, 11; Ziskin, "The Place de Nos Conquêtes."

Chapter 2

1. Brice, *Description* (1706 ed.), I:184.

2. F. de Saint Simon, *Place Vendôme*, 249.

3. "In one of the richest quarters of the city, between twenty superb houses, one distinguishes the house. . . . The facade is among the most magnificent . . ." [*Médailles sur la Régence; avec les tableaux symboliques du sieur Paul Poisson de Bourvalais, 1er maltôtier de Royaume, & le songe funeste de sa femme* (Paris, 1716), 8]. La Vieuxville was to demolish construction on the site and build a new public facade, both the responsibility of the partnership in all other cases; the partners undertook the sculptural decoration of the frontispiece, however, including the reclining figures, royal arms, and column capitals [AN, Q^1 1141 (22-IX-1699); MC XXXI, 25 (8-VIII-1702); MC XXXI, 29 (22-V-1704)]. A site plan accompanying the September 1699 contract already indicated the massing of the house.

4. A construction contract was signed in April 1700. In 1701, Pierre Le Maître estimated that 86,130 *livres* were needed to complete the building ("Recherche des titres de proprieté . . . occupé par la Chancellerie, Place Vendôme no. 13," 14-IV-1826, BMJ).

5. AN, MC XXXI, 25 (25-VII-1702).

6. He wed Marie-Guillaume (b. 1681) to Pollart de Villequoy, *conseiller au parlement*, and Henriette-Guillaume (b. 1685) to Pierre Poulletier de Nainville. Luillier got the house through a "donation," but paid 117,520 *livres* ["Recherche des titres," BMJ; Michel Antoine, *Le Gouvernement et Administration sous Louis XV: Dictionnaire biographique* (Paris, 1978), 105; Favre-Lejeune, *SR*, 1107; Dessert, *Argent, pouvoir et société*, 576, 672–3; 576].

7. Bourvalais paid 230,000 *livres*, plus a 6,000 *livre pot au vin*, a considerable sum for a house ("Recherche des titres," BMJ).

8. Ibid.; Marie and her son Pierre-Guillaume later returned to the square. She lived in an *entresol* apartment at no. 26, the house of Fontanieu's son Gaspard-Moïse, who wed her granddaughter [AN, Y13503 (30-V-1742)]; Pierre, who became the archbishop of Bayonne, subleased an *entresol* suite at no. 5 from his relation François Neyret, *conseiller au Parlement* [AN, Y11153 (30-VI-1734)].

9. The uses of the principal rooms, described in construction specifications of 1702–3, did not change.

10. *Description* (1706 ed.), I:188.

11. He bought approximately 317 square *toises* from the heirs of the duc de Luxembourg (Seine, DQ¹⁰ 0370, n°14020).

12. *Description* (1717 ed.), I:259–60; Brice also described Bourvalais's seigneuries, "numerous and rich possessions [that] are not very old."

13. On Italian bankers in France, see ch. 1.

14. *Médailles sur la Régence*, 10–11.

15. For example, a "Hagar and Ishmael" became an analogue for Bourvalais's treatment of his mother, whom he insolently expelled from his house; in the woods, she met the Devil, who promised to take care of her progeny ("which he has executed until now in good faith"), etc. (ibid., 13).

16. Attributions in Bauyn's inventory include works by Rembrandt, Rubens, Albani, Giorgione, Annibale Carracci, Veronese, Poussin, and Wouwerman, plus Raphael drawings [AN, MC CXVI, 134 (22-II-1701)]. Brice mentioned a Rubens, a Veronese, and a Poussin in Bourvalais's collection, noting the house in which they were installed had been "formerly inhabited by illustrious Magistrates, very distinguished by their wisdom and disinterestedness, which procured for them the esteem and love of the Public . . . that which has very much changed," *Description* (1706 ed.), I:225–6.

17. As well as Pierre Crozat and Samuel Bernard [Jean-Pierre Samoyault, *André-Charles Boulle et sa famille* (Geneva, 1979)].

18. On Bourvalais's base origins: *Pluton Maltôtier, nouvelle galante* (Cologne, 1708); Bois Jourdain, *Mélanges historiques, satiriques et anecdôtes de M. de B . . . Jourdain, écuyer de la grand écurie du roi (Louis XV) . . .* (Paris, 1807), III:456–7. Challes reported that Bourvalais had been Thévenin's lackey and that "those who claim to have information about his birth" said he was "the bastard of the *curé*" of his native village (Mémoires, 205–6).

19. Quoted by Saint-Germain, *Poisson de Bourvalais*, 4.

20. See *Médailles sur la Régence*, 176.

21. BN, f°Fm 3506; BN, 4°Fm 19 868.

22. Saint-Simon, *Mémoires*, VI:230; XXIV:227–33.

23. The dowry appears in BN, Ms. Fr. N.A.F. 9702, f°201, and in BN, f°Fm 3506 and 4°Fm 19 868. According to two "notices" published by Bois Jourdain, Mlle Guihou brought to the marriage just 400 *livres*, saved from her modest wages, and her husband supplied the rest (*Mélanges historiques*, III:457, 464). Perhaps Mlle Guihou was pregnant, but the union was ultimately childless.

24. Bois Jourdain, *Mélanges historiques*, III:464; *Pluton Maltôtier*, 169–70. Significantly, cuisine (increasingly a battleground for social distinction) appeared as the realm where Mme Bourvalais revealed her modest origins.

25. Bruslon and Villamur pursued robe careers, but were probably also involved in finance; Chendret was married to Mme Bourvalais's niece Louise-Thérèse Guihou (BN, Ms. Fr. 7586, 17v° – 18; AR, 1709, 1712–16; Dessert, *Argent, pouvoir et société*, 558, 599–600; Favre-Lejeune, *SR*, 1095–6).

26. Dumolin, "Place Vendôme," 37.

27. According to Brice, Boullongne was "lodged" at the square, in a house neighboring Bourvalais's [*Description* (1717 ed.), I:260]; his residence appears in royal

almanacs and in Adolphe Jal, *Dictionnaire critique de biographie et d'histoire*, 2nd ed. (Paris, 1872), 266. Boullongne's financier nephew Jean later bought no. 23 Place Vendôme.

28. Among them "Miser [*sic*], *syndic*," who also served as Bourvalais's *maître d'hôtel* (*AR*, 1713; BN, 4°Fm 19 868).

29. *Description* (1717 ed.), I:261. By late 1716, Duquesnoy resided at the Place des Victoires (BN, Ms. Clair., 768, tax roll 4).

30. Challes claimed Crozat was "the son of a mender of old clothes (*ravaudeuse*), who had her small boutique at the corner of the rue de Cléry" (*Mémoires*, 236); on the nobility attached to the office of *capitoul*, see Marcel Marion, *Dictionnaire des institutions de la France aux XVIIe et XVIIIe siècles* (Paris, 1923; reprint, New York, 1968), 71.

31. Claude Michaud, *L'Église et l'argent sous l'ancien régime* (Paris, 1991), 390–1.

32. Challes, *Mémoires*, 229; Lüthy, *La banque protestante*, I:251. Lüthy concluded that the Crozat were probably also converted Protestants.

33. See Chaussinand-Nogaret, *Financiers de Languedoc*, 92–101. There were some unusually prominent witnesses to the marriage: the chevalier de Lorraine and François de Harlay (archbishop of Paris), as well as Philippe d'Orléans and his "favorite," Philippe d'Harcourt; Mme Crozat's dowry was 100,000 *livres* plus 50,000 *livres* added by the chevalier de Lorraine (Michaud, *L'Église et l'argent*, 390–1).

34. The *entresol* extended along the square and above the carriage stalls and stables.

35. The first-floor plan engraved by Blondel presupposed a connection with no. 19, introduced after 1706; earlier, the only source of light was a small court (Figs. 27 and 28).

36. See Annik Pardailhé-Galabrun, *Birth of Intimacy: Privacy and Domestic Life in Early Modern Paris*, trans. Jocelyn Phelps (Philadelphia, 1991), 137. Among his plans for country houses (1737), J.-F. Blondel placed one bathing suite in an Orangerie wing (warm in winter, shaded in summer) (*Maisons de Plaisance*, I:71–5); Le Camus de Mézières recommended an eastern exposure (*Genius of Architecture*, 123).

37. AN, Y11157 (7-VII-1738).

38. "He painted a gallery at M. Crozat's house in 1702 that all the great connoisseurs of painting come to see and admire, even the princes S. A. Mgr le prince de Conty [and] M. le duc d'Orléans, who want him to work for them . . . [making] all the able painters of this city jealous" ["Lettres de filiation accordées par les religieux augustins de Paris à Paolo de Mattei, peintre napolitain (13-IX-1703)," *Nouvelles archives de l'art français* (1880–81), 377]; see Arnauld Brejon de Lavergnée, "Plaidoyer pour un peintre 'de pratique': le séjour de Paolo de Matteis en France," *Revue de l'art*, LXXXVIII (1990), 72.

39. "The gallery was painted in 1703 by a Neapolitan named Paul Mattei, who worked with more speed and activity than correctness and good taste. . . . The choice of this master has made it easy to realize that poor taste and presumption still reign in certain places in Paris, despite the justice that one should render to our able painters, who would have, without doubt, done much better than this foreigner, widely acclaimed for his merit," *Description* (1706 ed.), I:188. Just two years before Matteis's arrival, the Crown had invited Luca Giordano and fellow Neapolitan Francesco Solimena to work at several royal palaces; see Sabatier, "La galerie en France," 283–301. Antoine Schnapper argues that Brice's critique embodied genuine French opposition to the rapid technique of Matteis and other Italian painters, but acknowledges the possibility of some "aigreur chauvine" ["Antoine Coypel: La galerie d'Énée au Palais-Royal," *Revue de l'art*, V (1969), 33].

40. "The king is informed that luxury has returned to its vigor in Paris particularly with respect to houses, and he named to me, among others, sirs Crozat and Thévenin, who have taken the liberty of gilding their galleries," wrote Jérôme de Pontchartrain to the Lieutenant General of Police in late September 1703. "His Majesty is very astonished that you pay so little attention to the edict which has been given on this subject and ordered me very precisely to advise you that he is not content to see you relax on this point . . . ," in *Correspondance administrative*, II:810. For these luxury laws, renewed in 1700, see Nicolas Delamare's *Traité de la police*, 2nd ed. (Paris, 1722), I:451–7.

41. Philippe Ariès, *Centuries of Childhood*, trans. R. Baldick (New York, 1962), 269–71. At the Place des Victoires house of tax farmer Bauyn de Cormery (whose paintings Bourvalais would purchase), young sons shared a second-floor bedroom with a preceptor; an adjoining *cabinet* was filled with armoires of books for their studies [*Inventaire*, AN, MC CXVI, 134 (22-II-1701)].

42. Alix de Janzé, *Les financiers d'autrefois* (Paris, 1886), 60. A portrait by Matteis, engraved for the title page, appears in Brejon de Lavergnée, "Plaidoyer pour un peintre," Fig. 3; and F. de Saint Simon, *Place Vendôme*, 291.

43. Ariès, *Centuries of Childhood*, 331–33. Bourgeois families educated daughters at home, but Parisian magistrates and financiers often sent them to the Couvent de Sainte-Marie on the rue Saint-Jacques [Edmond and Jules de Goncourt, *The Woman of the Eighteenth Century*, trans. J. Le Clercq and R. Roeder (London, 1928; reprint, Westport, Conn., 1981), 14]; d'Aguesseau's daughter Claire-Marie lived at that convent for eleven years, from age four to fifteen (Storez, *Chancelier . . . d'Aguesseau*, 145).

44. On servant lodgings at Crozat's house, see ch. 5.

45. Crozat's notary described them as *lits jumeaux* [*Inventaire*, AN, MC VIII, 1024 (7-VI-1738)].

46. No evidence has emerged to indicate who, in fact, occupied those rooms; on the Maison Villemaré, see ch. 3.

47. Saint-Simon, *Mémoires*, XII:231. Later he wrote that Mme de Pontchartrain "had been too long steeped in the bourgeoisie for there to have not remained with her some small odor" (XXVI:228). Pontchartrain was, of course, noble, of a robe family from Brittany with a distinguished record; Villemaré, too, was of a robe family (occupying more modest offices), but he actively participated in finance.

48. "It seems that they are each condemned to keep aloof from one another," wrote Charles Sorel in 1663, commenting on the independence of noble marriage partners. "To conduct themselves differently is to live like commoners (*les bonnes gens*) of times past, at least among those who adopt the airs of fashionable society. It is enough to turn the stomachs (*soulever le coeur*) of gallant persons simply to see husband and wife in the same carriage," quoted by Gibson, *Women in Seventeenth-Century France*, 66.

49. *Description* (1706 ed.), I:187.

50. *Mémoires du marquis de Sourches*, X:251.

51. Michaud, *L'Église et l'argent*, 500. Among those objecting was the Cardinal Bouillon, who responded: "one cannot rejoice at a marriage . . . so disproportionate with respect to birth" [BN, N.A.F., Ms. 6677, f°32 (6-II-1707)].

52. It was unusual, but not unheard of, for girls to be married so young (see Bluche, *Magistrats du Parlement*, 264). The most infamous case at the Place Vendôme occurred during the Regency, when financier Jean André (no. 14) signed a contract for a daughter not yet two years old; André promised to pay the marquis d'Oise (then age thirty-three) 20,000 *livres* annually, and his father another 6,000 *livres* annually, even if André's daughter refused when legally of age. André met

these obligations, which began immediately, until 1725; when he could no longer do so, the marquis d'Oise sued him and won [*Journal et Mémoires de Mathieu Marais, avocat au Parlement, sur la Régence et le règne de Louis XV (1715–1737)*, ed. M. de Lescure (Paris, 1863–8), I:267].

53. All the charges were eventually dropped (*Michaud, L'Église et l'argent*, 513–28).

54. See Babelon, "Le passage du corps d'hôtel simple," 7–16. The rooms comprising the ground-floor apartment (*Salle, Anticabinet, Grand cabinet*, and *cabinet*) strongly suggest a male user; on the first floor, a ceremonial bedchamber replaced the *grand cabinet*.

55. Minimal construction had occurred [AN, MC LXXVII, 96 (5-VIII-1706)].

56. Dumolin, "Place Vendôme," 26.

57. See Brice, *Description* (1725 ed.), I:310.

58. Bullet labeled it "galerie" (Fig. 45); J.-F. Blondel called it a "vestibule en galerie" (Fig. 41).

59. See Blondel on appropriate placement of the room (*AF*, I:32). Bullet and his son had situated the dining room of the Maison de Pennautier to the left of the entry on the ground floor (Fig. 34).

60. Challes revealed this in his account of d'Évreux's passing "from indifference to his wife to callousness, walling up the door that led from her apartment to that of Mme Crozat, her mother, ... to whom she frequently went to lament the unhappiness of her marriage and the wretched conduct, from her point of view, of the Count, her husband" (*Mémoires*, 237). Mme Crozat's apartment was in the range along the square.

61. "Croizat [*sic*] married his daughter to M. le comte d'Évreux, of the house of Bouillon, who, in truth, took one million, five or six hundred thousand *livres* of dowry and never slept or lived with his wife..." (Barbier, *Journal* I:338–9). Occasionally, agreements were made that a marriage would not be consummated until a young wife reached a more suitable age [see, e.g., the duc de Luynes, *Mémoires ... sur la cour de Louis XV (1735–1758)*, ed. L. Dussieux and E. Soulié (Paris, 1860–5), IX:29]. Contemporaries, however, seemed surprised at the extreme degree of d'Évreux's detachment from his wife.

62. See Michael Dennis, *Court and Garden: From the French Hôtel to the City of Modern Architecture* (Cambridge, Mass., 1986), 91.

63. The passage (later blocked up) appears open in a ground-floor plan for no. 19 (NMS, THC 6874).

64. *Recueil de Maurepas: chansons, épigrammes et autres vers satiriques sur divers personnages des siècles de Louis XIV et Louis XV* (Paris, 1865), III:35.

65. Marais, *Journal* (1722), II:345.

66. "Only Mlle Crozat's mother did not lose her good sense; she received the visits [of nobles asked to call on her by d'Évreux's mother] with a very respectful air, but tranquilly, responding that this was an honor so above her that ... she believed it better to mark her respect by not returning at all to thank [her callers] ... and [by] not going to visit anyone" (*Mémoires*, XIV:363).

67. In two classic satires, Molière's *Bourgeois gentilhomme* (1670) and Le Sage's *Tucaret* (1711), married financiers, in their quests to be recognized as noble, pursued court noblewomen. Crozat, like many financiers, had a mistress (see ch. 5), but society remained fairly intolerant of the extramarital affairs of wives of financiers and bankers. That it was still the case later in the century is most clearly revealed by the public reaction to the Kornmann affair of the 1780s [see Sarah Maza, *Private Lives and Public Affairs* (Berkeley, 1993), 295–311].

68. See Dennis, *Court and Garden*, 91.

69. On their house, see ch. 6.

Chapter 3

1. See ch. 1. On the extended architectural clan of Hardouin-Mansart, see, especially, Allan Braham and Peter Smith, *François Mansart* (London, 1973), I:179–83.

2. *Inventaire . . . J.-H. Mansart*, AN, MC CV, 1087 (6-VI-1708).

3. Ibid.

4. AN, MC XCV, 51 (9-II-1703; 3-III-1703).

5. For example, the Hôtel de Coulanges (see Dominique Fernandes, AAVP, *De la place royale*, 170–8). About thirty years before Mansart had renovated the Hôtel de Chaulnes, built along three sides of its site at the Place Royale [see J.-P. Babelon, "L'oeuvre de Jules Hardouin Mansart à l'Hôtel de Chaulnes, 9 place des Vosges, à Paris," *BSHAF* (1970), 37–46; and idem., AAVP, *De la place royale*, 200–9].

6. Mansart's parcel included a small extrusion to the northwest, approximately fifteen by four *toises* [AN, MC XCV, 51 (3-II-1703)]. He apparently sold part of it to Bullet, who had acquired neighboring lots on the rue Saint-Honoré when the partnership dissolved; de Cotte later acquired Bullet's lots and built houses on them (today nos. 366–70 rue Saint-Honoré) [AN, MC CV, 376 (4-X-1718); Z[1j] 899 (3-II-1766); see Jean de La Monneraye, *Terrier de la Censive de l'Archevêché dans Paris 1772*, II:142–43].

7. It was later called "a kind of anteroom" [AN, Z[1j] 1112 (30-III-1784)]. Fragments of paneling, apparently once installed in an *entresol* room of this house, are today preserved in the Musée des Arts Décoratifs in Paris. These are illustrated by Bruno Pons in *Waddesdon Manor: Architecture and Panelling* (London, 1996), Figs. 414–15.

8. Pons recently argued that some paneling in the Louvre, long believed to have been installed at no. 9, had been removed instead from no. 7 (*Waddesdon Manor*, 428–47); Pons convincingly associated an unusual section of paneling with a description of the fireplace wall of a first-floor *cabinet* along the court [AN, Z[1j] 1112 (30-III-1784)]. The *cabinet* appears along the south party wall in a study of nos. 7 to 11 (Fig. 53) and in a revised plan (NMS, THC 6411). Pons misidentified Bullet's unexecuted plan for the first floor of no. 22 (Fig. 66) as a possible study for no. 7.

9. In another study (NMS, THC 6410), Mansart divided the rooms along the square into two smaller suites.

10. *Description* (1706 ed.), I:108.

11. Dumolin, "Place Vendôme," 39. "His friendship for her was not without scandal," Saint-Simon recounted. "Besides the continuous and considerable gifts, he defrayed the expenses of her house all year long, and gave her one entirely furnished; also, he lived with her when he was in Paris, rousing great jealousy in all his other heirs" (*Mémoires*, XIX:45–6; see, too, XXXIII:100).

12. Register of notary Lefevre CXIII (31-I-1719). "Of the most worldly of all women, the most occupied with her appearance, with personal adornment, with all sorts of comforts and with magnificence, and the most passionate gambler," according to Saint-Simon, "she became the most retiring, most modest, most prodigal towards the poor and the most miserly for herself" (*Mémoires*, XXXIII:100).

13. Le Tellier left his considerable collection of books and manuscripts to the Couvent de Sainte-Geneviève [*Testament*, AN, MC CXIII, 229 (22-II-1710)].

14. The honoring of Louis XIV would certainly have underscored the eminence of the Le Tellier ministerial clan, but it could have been intended, as easily, to convey the royal favor enjoyed by Mansart and Montargis.

15. When Mme Le Bas de Montargis died in 1748, eight gilded plaster busts of Roman emperors crowned the armoires [AN, MC LXXIX, 59 (4-III-1748)]. At the end of the century, a notary described the color of the armoires as *vert d'eau* [*Inventaire . . . Madame veuve Pollersky*, AN, MC XXIII, 847 (3-VIII-1791)]. Technical analysis has convinced Brian Considine, Conservator of Decorative Arts and Sculpture at the J. Paul Getty Museum, that the blue-green paint is the original layer. If it is, colored paneling, which was quite popular by the thirties, may have been introduced earlier than is commonly believed. Pons remained uncertain about the date of the paint (*French Period Rooms*, 182; *Waddesdon Manor*, 430, 563). Le Camus de Mézières later explained that green was an agreeable color for libraries because it was "restful to the eyes" (*Genius of Architecture*, 135).

16. Some exceptions may be found in Ernest Quentin Bauchart, *Les Femmes bibliophiles de France (XVIe, XVIIe & XVIIIe siècles)* (Paris, 1886), 2 vols.

17. *French Period Rooms* (Dijon, 1995), 184; see his reconstruction, 180–1. *AR*, 1720, 1721.

18. *Waddesdon Manor*, 446.

19. It is indicated as a bedchamber in Fig. 53, but according to a revised plan (NMS, THC 6411), Mansart had it built with a regular perimeter. In 1728, it was embellished by a single mirrored *trumeau*, and Hénault equipped it with a desk, some seating, and armoires holding six hundred books [*Inventaire . . . Catherine-Henriette Le Bas de Montargis*, AN, MC CXVII, 362 (6-VII-1728)].

20. *Testament . . . C.-H. Le Bas de Montargis*, AN, MC LIII, 245 (16-VI-1728).

21. Mme Hénault's notary had been mute about the range at the rear of the court, no doubt because it formed part of the *entresol* suite rented to d'Alary. On the club de l'Entresol, see L. Lanier, "Le Club de l'Entresol (1723–1731)," *Mémoires de l'Académie des Sciences, des Lettres et des Arts d'Amiens*, 3e série, VI (1880), 1–56; Paul Janet, "Une Académie politique sous le cardinal de Fleury de 1724 à 1731," *Séances et Travaux de l'Académie des sciences morales et politiques*, 5e série, IV (1865), 107–26; Robert Shackleton, *Montesquieu: A Critical Biography* (Oxford, 1961), 63–6; Isaac Krammick, *Bolingbroke and His Circle* (Cambridge, Mass., 1968), 16; and Reinhart Koselleck, *Critique and Crisis. Enlightenment and the Pathogenesis of Modern Society* (Oxford, 1988), 67–68.

22. "The abbé Alary was lodged at the place Vendôme, in the *hôtel* of the président Hénault, where he leased a pretty apartment *en entresol*," recounted d'Argenson (*Mémoires*, I:87–8). D'Argenson remembered windows in d'Alary's apartment overlooking a "pretty garden," which must refer to a room in the rear range that would have had a view of the garden of a house on the rue Saint-Honoré.

23. D'Argenson, *Mémoires*, I:96.

24. Ibid., I:92.

25. Regular members included the marquis de Balleroy; Lévesque de Champeaux, later minister at Geneva and then at Hamburg; the comte de Plélo, named ambassador to Copenhagen in 1729; the comte de Caraman, son-in-law of the *premier président* of the Parlement of Paris; François-Dominique Barberie de Saint-Contest, later ambassador to Holland and then Secretary of State for Foreign Affairs; the abbé de Bragelone, named an associate of the Academy of Sciences in 1728; and Andrew Michael Ramsay, a Jacobite and friend of Fénelon. "Honorary" members included François de Franquetot (later the duc de Coigny, who resided at no. 15 Place Vendôme in the thirties); the marquis de Matignon; the marquis de Lassay; the duc de Noirmoutiers; Dominique-Claude Barberie de Saint-Contest, plenipotentiary minister for France at the treaty of Baden in 1714 and the congress of Cambrai in 1721; Pierre-Blouet de Camilly, a knight of the Order of Malta named ambassador to Copenhagen in the twenties; and the abbé

Pomponne, son of the former Secretary of State (ibid., I:88–91). Hénault, whose interests were more literary, was not a regular member.

26. Despite Mme d'Arapajon's high-ranking husband, the duchess liked to call her "my *bourgeoise*" (Saint-Simon, *Mémoires*, XXXII:235); she was residing again at no. 7 Place Vendôme when her husband died in 1736 at the Palais du Luxembourg [*Scellé . . . d'Arapajon*, AN, Y13645 (24-VIII-1736)].

27. *AR*, 1741.

28. *Inventaire*, AN, MC LXXIX, 59 (4-III-1748). Mme d'Arapajon leased the house to Louis Phélypeaux, comte de Saint-Florentin, Secretary of State [AN, MC LXXIX, 59 (11-III-1748)]; when she sold the dwelling to general tax farmer Nicolas Dedelay Delagarde eleven years later, she was living with her daughter and son-in-law at the Hôtel de Noailles in the Faubourg Saint-Germain [AN, MC XXIII, 626 (27-IX-1759)].

29. According to Dessert (*Argent, pouvoir et société*, 586–7) and Favre-Lejeune (*SR*, 567–8), Mme Fontanieu was the sister of Charles-Gaspard Dodun, who became Controller General of Finance in 1722; according to Pons, she was his cousin (*Waddesdon Manor*, 213).

30. *Mémoires du Président Hénault* (Paris, 1911), 182; Favre-Lejeune, *SR*, 567.

31. See the caption of Fig. 60.

32. "Plan d'une maison à Mr. Delpeche à la place de Vandosme par le Maître arch" appears on a copy of the ground-floor plan (Fig. 62); see Michel Le Moël, "Archives architecturales parisiennes en Suède," *L'Urbanisme de Paris et l'Europe 1600-1680*, ed. P. Francastel (Paris, 1969), 119. On Le Maître the Younger, see H. Lemonnier, *Procès-verbaux de l'Académie royale d'architecture, 1671–1793* (Paris, 1911–20) III:xv. Both fathers were *secrétaires du roi*, and de Monchy long resided at no. 4 Place des Victoires, which Mme Delpech later inherited (BN, P.O. 989, 22143, f°16; Favre-Lejeune, *SR*, 456, 977).

33. Indicated here, and in what follows, are room uses indicated in Paul Delpech's 1752 *scellé* [AN, Y13378 (22-XII-1752)].

34. BIF., Ms. 1038, f°2.

35. In a third, nearly identical, plan (limited to the range along the square), a chapel appears off the elongated anteroom (NMS, THC 6420); in 1757, when Mme Delpech died, agents of Châtelet mentioned a chapel in that location [AN, Y13383 (7-VII-1757)].

36. Delpech's daughters leased the dwelling to the prince and princesse de Chimay, then to Montargis's nephew, general tax farmer Le Bas de Courmont. In 1766, Receiver General for Poitiers Elie Randon de Massane bought the house; he left it to his daughter, wife of Michel-Étienne Le Peletier de Saint-Fargeau [*Succession*, AN, MC XXIII, 721 (30-VI-1772)]. It was here that her famous stepson, the martyred Le Peletier de Saint-Fargeau, died in 1793 (see the Conclusion).

37. The *salle, antechambre, grand cabinet, chambre*, and *garderobe* comprising the ground-floor suite were presumably for a male user; on the first floor, the ceremonial apartment consisted of a *grande salle, antechambre, "chambre parée," cabinet*, and *garderobe*, probably for a female occupant.

38. On houses at the Place Royale, see Ballon, *The Paris of Henri IV*, 104–7, and the catalogue of houses in AAVP, *De la Place Royale*; on "*hôtels sur rue*," see Hautecoeur, *Histoire de l'architecture classique*, III: 212–13.

39. The only galleries built at the square were those at the Maisons Crozat.

40. Villemaré and his wife Anne Crocq (+1729) lived at no. 9 with five children: Germain (1688–1715), a *conseiller* in the Parlement of Paris; Anne and her husband, the marquis de Plumartin; Louise-Françoise, who stayed until the early thirties with her husband Pierre Poncet de la Rivière, a *président* in the Parlement of Paris; Paul-Marie Le Lay du Plessis, who apparently remained until his mar-

riage in 1734 to Marie-Madeleine Delpech (daughter of the Delpech at no. 8); and Jean-Bonaventure Le Lay de Guébriant, a *conseiller* in the Parlement of Paris, who still resided there in the late thirties [BN, P.O. 1683 (39,167); AN, G⁷ 1837 and MC LXXVII, 998 (22-IV-1750); *AR*, 1733, 1738].

41. *Traité de la perspective pratique avec les remarques sur l'architecture* (Paris, 1725), 62. Alternative schemes for the vestibule appear in NMS, THC 6685. Some panels of *boiserie* today preserved at the Louvre were long thought to have been installed at no. 9 by Villemaré, but Pons argued that some of these (perhaps all of the early panels) may have been removed instead from no. 7 (*Waddesdon Manor*, 428–47; see n. 8, earlier). Some panels at the Louvre are connected with F.-B. Dangé's later renovations (see ch. 7).

42. AN, MC CXVII, 254 (17-I-1714). On the duchesse de Gramont, a former servant who became the mistress and then the wife of the duke, see Saint-Simon, *Mémoires*, XII:85–90; Luynes, *Mémoires*, I:206; F. de Saint Simon, *Place Vendôme*, 259–62.

43. Son of a leading Receiver General of Finance and *secrétaire du roi*, Rioult pursued a military career (Favre-Lejeune, *SR*, 1155).

44. Brice, *Description* (1717 ed.), I:261.

45. Rioult still resided in the dwelling in 1738, although he and his wife had officially separated with respect to finances; he then occupied a suite on the second floor, extending along ranges facing the rue Neuve-des-Petits-Champs and the square. Mme Rioult, two daughters, and a son-in-law, the marquis de Mauconseil, also lived in the house [*Inventaire . . . Rioult*, AN, MC CXVII, 422 (2-IX-1738)].

46. NMS, THC 6245 and THC 6994.

47. NMS, CC 1946–54 are studies for a house of three bays, probably for a site at the Place Vendôme. The houses of two and three bays do not correspond precisely with parcels assigned to Bullet, suggesting he may have prepared them for the investment partnership.

48. As a group, these small houses were more modestly constructed than others at the square. For example, the main stair, necessarily constrained, was often built of stone only to the *entresol*, with wood steps above; in larger dwellings, the grand stair was invariably built of stone.

49. Dumolin, "Place Vendôme," 26. Beaudet was the director of the royal tree nurseries [AN, MC CXVII, 251 (3-VIII-1713)].

50. Plans are perserved in BN, Est., Ha 18, t. III; a complete set of final plans and a section accompany the construction contract [AN, MC XXVI, 268 (26-XII-1712)].

51. The house was leased for most of the century, sometimes to impressive occupants like the comte de La Marck, *grand d'Espagne*, who resided there during the fifties; on the eve of the Revolution, the tenant was general tax farmer Jacques-Alexis Paulze, Lavoisier's father-in-law.

52. Exceptional were the large *salon* Bullet and his son planned for the Maison de Pennautier and a small oval *salon* in Bullet's unexecuted plan for the first floor of no. 22.

53. Similarly, when court nobles occupied houses at the square during the Regency, they considered *chambres de parade* to be essential and *salons* expendable.

Chapter 4

1. Jean Buvat, *Journal de la Régence (1715–1723)*, ed. Émile Campardon, (Paris, 1865), I:124.

2. *Les correspondants de la Marquise de Balleroy*, ed. Edouard de Barthelemy, (Paris, 1883), I:100.

3. " 'Chambres de Justice,' " 24; see Pierre Ravel, *La Chambre de justice de 1716* (Paris, 1928), and Dom H. Leclercq, *Histoire de la Régence pendant la minorité de Louis XV* (Paris, 1922), I:295–313.

4. Buvat, *Journal de la Régence*, I:124–9; AN, G⁷ 1837.

5. Paparel was not involved in extraordinary finance, according to a memoir pleading for leniency, but could not repay 1,200,000 *livres* he owed the Crown (AN G⁷ 1837).

6. He had been Pontchartrain's "homme des affaires," (Antoine, *Gouvernement et Administration sous Louis XV*, 12). In 1715, Aubert and his wife still lived at no. 12 with their son Louis-Urbain (the future intendant of Bordeaux), daughter Marie-Catherine, and widowed daughter Catherine-Suzanne, who had been given the house as part of her dowry in 1703, when she wed Léon-Etienne Le Camus, *maître des requêtes*. [AN, MC XCVI, 238 (26-VI-1715)].

7. See Dangeau, *Journal*, VI:377–8; Leclercq, *Histoire de la Régence*, I:302, n. 56.

8. "The Regent wanted to exempt from the investigation by the Chambre, sirs Menon, Le Bas de Montargis, Fargès, the two Crozat, Samuel Bernard, the four Pâris [brothers], Prondré, and one other, but the M. le duc de Bourbon forcefully insisted [they be included] . . ." (Buvat, *Journal de la Régence*, I:195–6). Only Pierre Crozat was spared.

9. BN, P.O. 2312 (52, 272), fᵒˢ2–5. The Chambre awarded all of Paparel's property to his son-in-law, the marquis de La Fare, who promised to pay funds owed the Crown and other creditors (Ravel, *Chambre de Justice*, 77–90); instead, La Fare immediately sold no. 14 (part of his wife's dowry three years earlier), used 140,000 *livres* from the sale to purchase the charge of *mestre de camp général des dragons*, and abandoned his wife. D'Argenson charged that La Fare had denounced Paparel to win confiscation of his property (*Mémoires*, IV:102–3). By 1719, a backlash prompted Paparel's release and the annulment of the sale. Salomon Le Clerc, attached to the household of the duchesse d'Orléans, acquired no. 14 for his daughter, wife of Jean André (soon notorious for a fortune amassed speculating in shares of Law's bank) [AN, MC XLII, 316 (12-XII-1719)].

10. Samuel Bernard asked not to be fined, since it might weaken his credit outside France, and instead offered to renounce six million *livres* owed to him by the Crown (Dangeau, *Journal*, XVI:500). Crozat's fine was even larger, but he paid just 1,474,995 *livres* in cash, the rest waived when he renounced his monopoly on trade with Louisiana (which he had found unprofitable and had wanted to abandon) [Edgar Faure, *La banqueroute de Law* (Paris, 1977), 126–7]. On Montargis's anxiety during the tribunal, see Saint-Simon, *Mémoires*, XIV:387; his fine, after some moderation, was 1,650,000 *livres* plus the suppression of his post (AN, G⁷ 1837; Boislisle, *Mémoires du Saint-Simon*, XI:206, n. 5).

11. AN, MC XCVI, 246 (26-I-1717). Pons was convinced that Jacques V Gabriel built no. 10 before 1705 (*De Paris à Versailles*, 113–14), but the parcel was empty when Aubert acquired it in 1711 [AN, MC CV, 1012 (20-III-1711)]; evidence of Gabriel's involvement with some decoration at Aubert's house in 1707 presumably referred to no. 12, where Aubert had resided since 1702. From August 1715 until 1723, no. 10 was the residence of the large La Live-Fayard clan, which included Receiver General for Poitiers Jean-François-Christophe La Live de Pailly (1674–1753); his wife Marie-Catherine Fayard; her banker father Gaspard Fayard; Laurent Fayard de Champagneaux, Receiver General for Grenoble; Pailly's younger brother, general tax farmer Louis-Denis La Live de Bellegarde (1679–1751); and, briefly, their sister Antoinette-Françoise and her husband Joseph Terisse, also a General tax farmer [*AR*, 1716-24; AN, MC LIII, 203 (15-IV-1720)]. During the twenties, the clan formed an enclave nearby, along the rue Saint-Honoré and the rue Neuve-du-Luxembourg.

12. Buvat, *Journal de la Régence*, I:136; *Scellé*, AN, Y14054 (6-II-1719). Among those taxed was "Jean Bullet de Chamblain, Architecte et Interesé" (BN, Ms. Clair. 768, tax roll 6): He was modestly involved in extraordinary finance (presumably through Bourvalais).

13. *Journal de la Chambre de justice*, AN, G^7 1837.

14. BN, Lb^{38} 76. Some satirical songs and prints are collected in the *Recueil de la Chambre de Justice* (BN, Ms. Clair. 767). See, too, *Médailles sur la Régence*.

15. Prior to the 1661 tribunal, financial families had adopted a high profile in the capital, among them the Lambert (for whom Le Vau built the dwelling on the Ile Saint-Louis in the forties) and the Aubert de Fontenay (whose house, built in the fifties, was called the "Hôtel Salé").

16. AN, G^7 1837. The tribunal ruled that dowries financiers gave their daughters, several of whom had married into court families, would be neither scrutinized nor taxed; property given to sons, who tended to marry into financial or robe clans, would be considered as still belonging to their fathers and, thereby, subject to taxation.

17. BN, Ms. Fr. 7586; Ms. Clair. 768; AN, G^7 1837.

18. Officers of the tribunal found the room empty (AN, G^7 1837).

19. *Journal de Dangeau*, XIV:459.

20. AN, V^7 41; *AR*, 1717. "Bourvalais, one of the richest *traitants* and among the most mistreated by the *chambre de justice*," Saint-Simon recounted, "was stripped of a superb house that he had built at the Place Vendôme and of a country house at Champs, which he had rendered charming and . . . [had] made the country seat of a large and beautiful estate . . ." (*Mémoires*, XXXII:111–12). The duc de Noailles, close to the d'Aguesseau family, lobbied for d'Aguesseau's appointment and secured for him Bourvalais's former house. At the Crown's request, the comte de Simiane (husband of Mme Bourvalais's niece) ceded no. 11, in exchange for extensive lands in Dauphiné plus an annual income of 2,400 *livres* (Dumolin, "Place Vendôme," 38).

21. *Mémoires*, XXXI:28.

22. Claire-Thérèse (b. 1699) lived until age fifteen in a convent, but resided briefly at the Place Vendôme before her 1722 marriage to the comte de Chastellux. Marie-Anne (b. 1709) spent her childhood and young adulthood in a convent and probably never resided at the Chancellerie. Six other children died in early childhood, four before 1717, another in 1718, and a son who died during his father's second banishment to Fresnes (1722–7) [Storez, *Chancelier . . . d'Aguesseau*, 140–8, 175; Mme la marquise de la Tournelle, "Essai sur la Vie de Mme la Comtesse de Chastellux," (1772), in ed. D. B. Rives, *Lettres inédites du Chancelier d'Aguesseau* (Paris, 1823), I:1–64].

23. Dangeau, quoted by Boislisle, *Mémoires de Saint-Simon*, XXXII:113, n. 1.

24. Pons illuminated the working relations of de Cotte and his assistants in "L'hôtel de la Chancellerie" [*Monuments historiques*, CLXXII (1990), 105]. Numerous studies for this conversion are preserved in BN, Est. Va 234 (among them a plan and elevation of the "Chambre du Chancellier"), BN, Va 419j, and AN, N III Seine 1208; a study for the cornice of the *grand cabinet* also survives (NMS, THC 7494).

25. AN MC LI, 897 (9-XII-1735); Storez, *Chancelier . . . d'Aguesseau*, 53–4. Leather upholstery still appeared in eighteenth-century anterooms, but it had been far more common during the previous century.

26. Herlaut protested (not very convincingly) that "the least part" of his assets came from "profits made in extraordinary finance . . . and . . . the greatest part . . . came at first from commerce, aided by the counsel of my father, [and] money I have added to it by my thrift and work over a period of about forty years" (BN,

Ms. Fr. 7584, fº40). His testament is lost, but other documents cite its terms (BN, P.O. 659, nº15,446, fº56); in 1709, financier Jean Thévenin left his house to former Controller General Pontchartrain, who refused to accept it (Saint-Simon, *Mémoires*, XVI:398).

27. Herlaut's declaration suggested that Pierre Le Maître the Younger had overseen the decoration of the house in 1705 (BN, Ms. Fr. 7584, fº41); architect Charles Bernard, among Herlaut's creditors, may have been involved in some capacity [*Scellé . . . Herlaut*, AN, Y11138 (11-V-1716)].

28. *Description* (1717 ed.), I:260–1. Herlaut's household formerly had been larger. Claude Marescot, a daughter of his deceased wife, resided there with Magdeleine and her older sister Marie-Anne Baunier (apparently more distant relations). In 1704, Herlaut arranged to wed his stepdaughter to Antoine-Nicolas Barjavel de Saint-Louis, involved in extraordinary finance.

29. Beaudet provided the plans, which are attached to the construction contracts, and six months later, he began overseeing the construction [AN, MC CXVII, 251 (3-VIII-1713) and 254 (4-I-1714)]. The dwelling had entries along the square and on the rue Saint-Honoré. On the first floor, the stair (at the corner, lit along the street) separated two ceremonial suites, one overlooking the square, the other along the rue Saint-Honoré; in the *entresol*, a private apartment faced the square and the dining room overlooked the street. Des Fourneaux apparently never occupied the dwelling; Beaudet's daughter and her husband, treasurer Nicolas Sézille, lived at the square during the Regency, probably in part of this house [AN, MC CXVII, 371 (12-I-1730); *AR*, 1716–18].

30. "Nocé, long a great favorite of the Regent, is the man he loves most" (Barbier, *Journal*, I:214); see Saint-Simon, *Mémoires*, XXVII:117, XXIV:229. On bribes to Nocé and Parabère, including a large one from J.-R. Hénault, father of the *président*, see M. de Lescure, *Les Maîtresses du Régent: études d'histoire et de moeurs* (Paris, 1861), 190.

31. The Regent appointed the comte d'Évreux to the council on war. The marquis d'Asfeld, a member of the councils on war and the navy, arrived at the square in 1716 and remained through the Regency (*AR*, 1717, 1724).

32. On d'Estrées's collecting, see Saint-Simon, *Mémoires*, XI:18–19; Luynes, *Mémoires*, II:211–12; and Brice, *Description* (1717 ed.), I:262. D'Aguesseau also had a resident librarian, the abbé André, plus a second librarian at his *château* at Fresnes (Storez, *Chancelier . . . d'Aguesseau*, 176).

33. "People are laughing a lot at the game played by the maréchale d'Estrées, who pretends to love the Chancellor" [Marais, *Journal* (1722), II:238]; on her affair with Hénault, see the *Chansonnier historique* (1722), IV:114.

34. The duc de Richelieu, a notorious libertine, commissioned portraits of his mistresses dressed as nuns, including the maréchale d'Estrées in Capuchin robes, perhaps alluding to the convent immediately north of the square.

35. *Mémoires*, XI:22.

36. *Bail* (no. 15), AN, MC CXVII, 254 (17-I-1714).

37. Faure, *La banqueroute de Law*, chs. 10–13; Paul Harsin, *Crédit public et Banque d'Etat en France du XVIe au XVIIIe siècle* (Paris, 1933), 28, 55–62; Jean Meyer, *Le Régent* (Paris, 1985), 222–9; J. H. Shennan, *Philippe, Duke of Orleans: Regent of France 1715–1723* (London, 1979), 110–13; George T. Matthews, *The Royal General Farms in Eighteenth-Century France* (New York, 1958), 67. Law left the Place Vendôme, buying dwellings near the Palais Royal for himself and the royal bank, the latter installed in the former Palais Mazarin (Buvat, *Journal de la Régence*, I:424).

38. The Regent's intervention would explain the rebuilding of the portal of the Capuchin church directly north of the square, deemed too modest to terminate the

axis; see François Souchal, "Le Portail de l'Église des Capucines à Paris," *GBA*, 73 (1969), 193–205. On Gabriel's designs, see Pons, *De Paris à Versailles*, 112–27.

39. Pons, *De Paris à Versailles*, 114. Law sold some houses before completion or when still nearly devoid of interior decoration; he retained a few, promising extensive decoration that he did not always complete [*Réception . . . entre Mr. de Fonspertuis et le créanciers du Sr. Law*, AN, Z^{1j} 570 (21-XI-1724)].

40. BN, P.O. 659, 15446. Mme de Parabère paid 90,000 *livres* plus 36,000 *livres* for the small dwelling on the cul-de-sac and as a settlement to Mlle Baunier [cited in AN, MC XCV, 243 (26-VIII-1755)].

41. She would have a passage built to connect her bathing apartment on parcel no. 20 with her new dwelling [cited in AN, MC LXXXVIII, 529 (10-VI-1732)].

42. *Bail à vie*, AN, MC CXV, 387 (7-III-1720). Parabère retained use of the garden extension of no. 20 and the pavilion at the cul-de-sac, where she may have installed her bathing apartment [cited in AN, MC LXXXVIII, 529 (10-VI-1732)]. Widowed in early 1716, she became pregnant a few months later, and court gossip named Nocé as the father [*Les correspondants de la Marquise de Balleroy*, I:95; Georges Normandy and Fernand Mitton, *Quatre Maîtresses du Régent* (Paris, 1911), 110]. Nocé had already bought parcel no. 26 in 1717, but in 1720, he sold a house built on it to speculator L'Heraud de Saint-Germain; two years later, Fontanieu, apparently already leasing no. 26, purchased it for his son, Gaspard-Moïse [AN, MC CV, 1116 (2-VIII-1717) and LVI, rep. 4 (22-XII-1722); *AR*, 1721].

43. At some point during the century, a range was built along the north side of no. 20 (Fig. 67). When Parabère sold no. 22 in 1732, two doors in the party wall were walled up – one connecting the court of no. 22 with the garden of no. 20 and a second opening onto the passage to the bathing suite [AN, MC LXXXVIII, 529 (10-VI-1732)].

44. "I saw (the Regent) at night at Mme de Parabère's house at the Place Vendôme, in a room completely illuminated and completely open" [Marais, *Journal* (1721), II:119]. According to a younger relation, Parabère's behavior during the Regency was so profligate that members of her own family refused to acknowledge her [*Souvenirs de la marquise de Créquy de 1710 à 1803* (Paris, 1855), II:28].

45. From a large anteroom along the court, visitors entered a second anteroom (lit by one window facing the square), followed by Mme de Parabère's *chambre de parade* (two windows), then the *cabinet* in the fourth bay [AN, MC LXXXVIII, 529 (10-VI-1732)]. On Gabriel's role, see Pons, *De Paris à Versailles*, 116–18.

46. See Katie Scott, *The Rococo Interior*, chs. 7–8, and Thomas Crow, *Painters and Public Life in Eighteenth-Century Paris* (New Haven and London), 55–67.

47. Her *toilette* appeared in a song about Controller General of Finance Le Pelletier de La Houssaye, of whom one expected "the most austere probity," visiting to seek support with the Regent; it reveals the kinds of entreaties she may have received at her *toilette* (*Chansonnier historique*, IV:47–8).

48. AN, MC LXXXVIII, 529 (10-VI-1732); the lease to Nocé was canceled at that time.

49. Law sold no. 3 to Charles-Elisabeth de Coëtlogon, son-in-law of a controller in his bank, and no. 5 to Jacques-Daniel de Guetteville d'Orsigny, of an old financial family; he sold a lifetime lease on no. 28 to the unmarried military officer Joseph Brunet de Rancy, son of one of the financiers most heavily taxed during the Chambre de Justice (BN, Ms. Fr. 7584, f°98; P.O. 541, n°12197, f°88, 102).

50. Luynes, *Mémoires*, VIII:261; Bluche, *L'Origine des magistrats du Parlement de Paris au XVIIIe siècle* (Paris, 1956), 62; Saint-Simon, *Mémoires*, XIV:302; *Les correspondants de la marquise de Balleroy*, I:241.

51. A desk was among the contents of this room in 1747 [*Scellé . . . Angran de Fons-*

pertuis, AN, Y14794 (11-VI-1747)]. Much of what follows relies upon an account of interior decoration promised by John Law [AN, Z^{1j} 570 (21-XI-1724)].

52. The suite along the square consisted of a single-bay anteroom (hung with thirteen paintings in 1747), the two-bay bedchamber (hung with twenty-one paintings), and the *cabinet*.

53. AN, Z^{1j} 570 (21-XI-1724); Y14794 (11-VI-1747). Gersaint discussed the porcelain at length, as well as Fonspertuis's Dutch and Flemish paintings and most precious furnishings, in *Catalogue raisonné des bijoux, porcelaines, bronzes, lacqs, lustres de cristal de roche et de porcelaine, pendules du goût . . . tableaux, desseins, estampes, coquilles, & autres effets . . . provenans de la succession de M. Angran, vicomte de Fonspertuis* (Paris, 1747).

54. AN, E 2019, f^{os}185-6v^{o} (23-VII-1720); see Barbier, *Journal*, I:28–38; Marais, *Journal*, I:269; *Mémoires du comte de Maurepas*, 3rd ed. (Paris, 1792), IV:3; Saint-Simon, *Mémoires*, XXXVII:371.

55. AN, V^{7} 254.

56. Architect Armand-Claude Mollet, who had worked for Law at the Banque Royale, and Pierre Perrin, *secrétaire du roi*, acquired no. 1. Perrin lived at no. 1 until 1729; in 1736, his heirs sold it to munitioner and Receiver General for Alsace Jean Fauste Batailhe de Francès [AN, MC XLI, 455 (7-XI-1736); Y11578b (2-VII-1761); Favre-Lejeune, *SR*, 172–3, 1065–6]. Pierre Grandhomme and Guillaume Cressart, *entrepreneurs* who had worked with Mollet for Law, acquired nos. 16 to 18; see Pons, "Les boiseries de l'Hôtel Cressart – 18 place Vendôme au J. Paul Getty Museum," *The J. Paul Getty Museum Journal* (1983), II: 67–88.

57. See Lüthy, *La Banque protestante*, II:788–9; Chaussinand-Nogaret, *Financiers de Languedoc*, 78; 128–35; marquis de Lordat, *Les Peyrenc de Moras (1685–1798): Une famille cévenole au service de la France* (Toulouse, 1959).

58. A complete set of building contracts survive [AN, MC XCV, 74 (28-II-1724)]; see reconstructed plans by Anne Thiry in "L'Hôtel Peirenc de Moras, puis de Boullongne, 23, place Vendôme," *BSHPIF* CVI (1979), 62–6, and by Pons, *De Paris à Versailles*, 123.

59. In the niche of the dining room buffet, Gabriel installed a painting "after Oudry" of game and fruit [AN, Z^{1j} 878 (9-II-1763); Z^{1j} 926 (29-I-1769)].

60. Similar rooms, discussed in ch. 6, would later be called *cabinets d'assemblée*.

61. For photographs before the paneling was dismounted and dispersed, see *Notice sur un très beau salon décoré par N. Lancret dont la vente aura lieu à Paris . . . 1896* (Paris, 1896). Peyrenc sold no. 23 to Jean de Boullongne, *premier commis des finances*; Boullongne lived in the house for two decades with his wife Catherine de Beaufort, daughter of a general tax farmer, but left before he was named Controller General of Finances in the late fifties. Peyrenc died suddenly in 1732, a year after his new dwelling was completed; in 1736, his widow sold its lifetime use to the duchesse du Maine.

62. Charles Pinot Duclos, "Mémoires secrets sur le règne de Louis XIV, la Régence et la règne de Louis XV," *Oeuvres* (Paris, 1821), III:119.

63. Bien, "The *Secrétaires du Roi*," 164–5; and idem., "Officers, Corps, and a System of State Credit: The Uses of Privilege under the Ancien Régime," in *The French Revolution and the Creation of Modern Political Culture*, ed. Keith Baker (Oxford, 1987), 89–114.

64. Matthews, *The Royal General Farms*, 69–76.

Chapter 5

1. *Mémoires du Président Hénault* (Paris, 1911), 26.

2. Hénault continued: "he was insolent in good faith; all that was greatest about him contributed to his folly; . . . he was generous, whatever was the motive . . .

he rendered great services ... in the military above all; he aided great fortunes and he prevented great falls."

3. The "five Controllers General" in a song of 1720 were Le Pelletier de La Houssaye, who succeeded Law, and the Pâris frères (*Chansonnier historique*, III: 238).

4. In 1708, Crozat purchased 703 square *toises* from the Luxembourg executor; in late 1719, he added almost 764 square *toises*, and in 1723, about 240 square *toises* [AN, MC XXX, 320 (12-I-1751); Seine DQ^{10} 0370, n°14020 (1750–1)].

5. During the forties, the Crown acquired land from Crozat's son Tugny and from financier François Castanier, eventually extending the garden of the Chancellerie to the rue Neuve-du-Luxembourg (AN, O^1 1576, f^{os}264–70; AN, N III Seine 940, f^{os}1–2; N III Seine 1208/6; BN, Est. Va 234).

6. "These subsidiary courts should have entrances from the outside, so that the service ... can be done commodiously and without being perceived from the apartments of the masters and from the principal court" [J.-F. Blondel, "Basse-cour," *Encyclopédie* (1765 ed.), II:121].

7. *AF*, III:101; on Dailly, see Michel Gallet, *Les architectes parisiens du XVIIIe siècle* (Paris, 1995), 167–8.

8. AN, Z^{1j} 601 (16-XII-1728).

9. The comtesse d'Évreux died in July 1729, just as the masons completed their work [AN, MC CXVII (5-VII-1731)].

10. On Fonspertuis's house, see ch. 4.

11. AN, Z^{1j} 601 (16-XII-1728); Seine, DQ^{10} 0370, n°14020; *Inventaire ... de Tugny*, AN, MC XXX, 320 (12-I-1751).

12. See the *grand cabinet chinois* that Nicolas Dullin installed at the Hôtel de Richelieu at the Place Royale [J. Wilhelm, "Le grand cabinet chinois de l'hôtel de Richelieu, place Royale," *Bulletin du Musée Carnavelet* (June 1967), 2–14; and Joëlle Barreau in AAVP, *De la place Royale*, 264–7].

13. A construction appraisal seems to locate the apartments of all three sons and their wives at no. 17 [AN, Z^{1j} 601 (16-XII-1728)]; in a plan of no. 19 dated 1724 but executed a few years later, J.-F. Blondel indicated that no. 19 was occupied by a former extraordinary ambassador of Portugal (AF, III:108). When Crozat died in 1738, at least one apartment was in "the pavilion," possibly a reference to the *corps-de-logis* of no. 19 [AN, MC VIII, 1024 (13-VI-1738)]. As late as 1736, Crozat rented the small *entresol* apartment of no. 19 (plus a kitchen on the ground floor) to Sr. and Dame Feuillet [*Scellé ... Lefebvre Feuillet*, AN, Y 13745 (3-VIII-1736)], and he continued to lease the stables to the duchesse d'Orléans.

14. See Robert Forster on the reluctance among the Parisian high nobility "to have several generations living under the same roof. ..." [*The House of Saulx-Tavanes: Versailles and Burgundy 1700–1830* (Baltimore and London, 1971), 204]. Court nobles certainly lodged members of their extended clans, but the practice was more common among financial and traditional robe families.

15. For example, Crozat and his wife pledged "to nourish and lodge with them Sr. and Dame de Tugny, also to feed and lodge their *valets* and *femmes de chambre* and their horses," and promised Thiers and his wife "utensils of a household," [AN, MC XXX, 289 (3-III and 24-IX-1743)].

16. Fossier illustrates two projects for the house and catalogues other plans (*Fonds ... de Cotte*, 325–7). José-Luc d'Iberville-Moreau reproduces excerpts from construction contracts in "Robert de Cotte: His Career as an Architect and the Organisation of the Service des Bâtiments," Ph.D. dissertation, University of London, 1972, 115–17.

17. See J.-F. Blondel, *AF*, III:106. Brunet de Rancy, who resided for two decades at no. 28 Place Vendôme, was also related to the Legendre through the marriage of his aunt (Chaussinand-Nogaret, *Financiers de Languedoc*, 95; Favre-Lejeune, *SR*,

298–9). By the late twenties, the Place Vendôme and its vicinity had become a nexus for directors of the royal trading companies, including Peyrenc at no. 23 Place Vendôme; J.-B.-D. Laugeois de Saint-Quentin, who rented no. 18 Place Vendôme; and Castanier, Desvieux's neighbor on the rue Neuve-des-Capucines.

18. *Scellé . . . veuve Legendre*, AN, Y14523 (11-XII-1726); *Inventaire*, AN, MC II, 426 (13-XII-1726).

19. This discussion draws upon *Inventaire . . . S. Bernard*, AN, MC LXXXVIII, 564 *bis* (27-I-1739); *Inventaire . . . A. Crozat*, AN, MC VIII, 1024 (13-VI-1738); *Scellé . . . Crozat*, AN, Y11157 (7-VI-1738); *Inventaire . . . J.-R. Hénault*, AN, MC CXVII, 417 (10-XII-1737); *Scellé . . . Mme Hénault*, AN, Y11157 (22-VII-1738); *Inventaire . . . L.-A. Duché*, AN, MC CXVII, 419 (10-III-1738); and *Scellé . . . Duché*, AN, Y11157 (4-III-1738).

20. AN, MC CXVI, 91 (24-IV-1690); MC XCV, 49 (22-III-1698).

21. Hénault's father bought the house at no. 7 and bequeathed it to Jean-Rémy before 1700 [F. de Saint Simon, *La Place des Victoires* (Paris, 1984), 210]. Hénault added the small no. 9 in 1709, but he and his wife did not list the Place des Victoires as their address in royal almanacs between 1699 and 1715; in 1716, they lived on the rue Neuve-des-Petits-Champs [BN, Ms. Clair. 768 (tax roll 5)].

22. *AR*, 1721; J. Hillairet, *La rue de Richelieu* (Paris, 1966), 52; 138–41.

23. In 1714, Bernard bought three contiguous houses on the rue Notre-Dame-des-Victoires (for 254,500 *livres*); during 1715–16, he added three more small houses. Projects for joining the larger dwellings and for decoration of a *cabinet* may be found in Fossier, *Fonds . . . de Cotte*, 283–5. Shortly before his death, Bernard bought no. 7 Place des Victoires, but continued to reside next door at no. 5.

24. AN, MC CXVII, 391 (28-IV-1733); *AR*, 1724, 1729; Pons, *French Period Rooms*, 211.

25. Hénault, son of a provincial *secrétaire du roi*, was born in 1648 in the Ile-de-France. Duché, of an ennobled family long serving as *avocat général* of the Cour des Aides in Montpellier, entered into the general tax farm in 1721, with the support of the Regent (*Mémoires . . . du publicanisme*, BN, Ms. Fr. 10477, f°1–92). Bernard was ennobled in 1699 and made chevalier de Saint-Michel in 1702, but he, like Crozat and Hénault, purchased the post of *secrétaire du roi* to bolster his claim to nobility.

26. On Bernard, see Lüthy, *La banque protestante*, I:120–5, 185–225; Jacques Saint-Germain, *Samuel Bernard, le banquier des rois* (Paris, 1960); E. de Clermont-Tonnerre, *Histoire de Samuel Bernard et ses enfants* (Paris, 1914); and Victor de Swarte, *Un Banquier du trésor royal au XVIIIe siècle* (Paris, 1895).

27. Hénault, like Crozat, wed a daughter of a general tax farmer; Bernard married a daughter of a "bourgeois of Paris" allied to finance (Dessert, *Argent, pouvoir et société*, 532, 603). Bernard's wife died in 1716, and four years later, he married Pauline Félicité de Saint-Chamans, of an old noble family from Limousin.

28. Crozat purchased Tugny's post as *président* in 1704, when his son was under ten years of age (Chaussinand-Nogaret, *Financiers de Languedoc*, 100, n. 1).

29. They soon separated, and Bernard's daughter returned to her father's house, occupying an *entresol* apartment overlooking the Place des Victoires; she died there of smallpox in 1716 [*Inventaire*, AN, MC LXXXVII, 379 (18-XII-1716)]. See Hénault, *Mémoires*, 147.

30. A model for Servandoni's setting was retained, contemporaries joked, to serve one day for the marriage of the Dauphin (Marais, *Journal*, II:426–7); they also mocked Bernard's dynastic ambitions: "O temps! ô moeurs, ô siècle déréglé! On voit se dégrader les plus nobles familles: Lamoignan, Mirepoix, Molé; de Bernard épousant les filles, et sont les receleurs du bien qu'il a volé (Oh times! Oh morals! Oh unruly century! When one sees the derogation of the most noble families:

Lamoignon, Mirepoix, Molé, marry the daughters of Bernard, and are the recipients of his stolen goods)" (*Chansonnier historique*, IV:64–5).

31. Crozat and Hénault were featured among those freqenting Mme de Romainville in *Les Parisans Demasquez. Nouvelle Galante* (Cologne, 1707), III:167.

32. They still occupied it in 1739 when Dupin's colleague, tax farmer J.-H. Hocquart, purchased the house (AN, S 1237, fº430).

33. "Her house was as brilliant at that time as any in Paris, and frequented by company which, if it had been a little less numerous, would have been the cream of all society. She liked to receive everyone of any brilliance – noblemen, men of letters, and beautiful women. Only dukes, ambassadors, and men with decorations were to be seen at her house. The Princess de Rohan, the Countess de Forcalquier, Mme de Mirepoix, Mme de Brignolé, and Lady Hervey passed as her friends. M. de Fontenelle, the Abbé de Saint-Pierre, the Abbé Sallier, M. de Fourmont, M. de Bernis, M. de Buffon, M. de Voltaire were members of her circle and came to her dinners" [Jean-Jacques Rousseau, *The Confessions*, trans. J. M. Cohen (Harmondsworth, 1984), 274]. See Gaston de Villeneuve-Guibert, ed., *Le Portefeuille de Madame Dupin* (Paris, 1884), 582–90.

34. "His character . . . appeared made for success among women; for he had wit, grace, delicacy and finesse. He cultivated, with success, music, poetry and light literature. . . . He took . . . [from the Académie française] a taste for study, and acquired there some erudition, but without pedantry. He never had the haughtiness of the magistracy nor the *mauvais ton* of men of the robe . . . There were great ladies who pardoned him for the flaw of his birth, his lack of good looks and even of vigor" (d'Argenson, *Mémoires*, V:91–2). According to Luynes, Hénault, "who always lived with the very best *compagnie*, and who has always seemed to devote himself to the pleasures of society, was nonetheless infinitely well read. . . . This is a man of the world who knows the most in almost all genres, at least in the genres most agreeable and useful to society" (*Mémoires*, V: 444). Hénault was connected with the salons of Mme de Tencin, Mme de Lambert, and his close friend (and, for a period, mistress) Mme du Deffand, but was apparently less interested in the serious political conferences taking place at the club d'Entresol (see ch. 3).

35. "M. du Châtel was extremely intelligent . . . [and Mme du Châtel] had as much intelligence. . . . Her husband had a great reputation at war, for his courage and for his military views . . . [and also] benevolence and a probity equal to all sorts of virtues. He was my intimate friend and I spent my life with him" (Hénault, *Mémoires*, 238); du Châtel and his wife were close to Mme du Deffand (see his "self-portrait" in Deffand, *Correspondance complète*, ed. Lescure, II:748–9). On Mme Doublet's *salon* (1731–71), assembled when Fleury closed the club de l'Entresol, see Robert S. Tate, *Petit de Bachaumont: his circle and the Mémoires secrets* (Geneva, 1968), 122; and Dena Goodman, *The Republic of Letters: A Cultural History of the French Enlightenment* (Ithaca and London, 1994), 154–6.

36. The *compagnie* included the Prince de Rohan, Mme d'Aumont, the maréchal de Villeroy, Mme de Maisons, "in a word, all Paris" (Hénault, *Mémoires*, 23–6).

37. "His table, for dinner alone, cost him fifty thousand *livres* per year" (Barbier, *Chronique de la Régence*, II:418).

38. Saint-Simon was disdainfully expressing surprise that the duc de Vendôme visited Crozat at his country house at Clichy, near Paris [*Mémoires* (1708), XVI:32].

39. Bernard's correspondence contains references to meetings from 6 A.M. until late in the evening (Saint-Germain, *Samuel Bernard*, 80). Crozat clearly worked long hours overseeing his maritime investments.

40. In the forties, Bonnier de La Mosson, Treasurer General for Languedoc, lived

quite nobly in the Faubourg Saint-Germain and kept his *bureau* on the rue Saint-Anne in the financial quarter (*AR*, 1742); two decades later, Radix de Sainte-Foye, Treasurer General of the Navy, resided on the rue des Bons-Enfans near the Palais Royal but installed his *bureau* at the Place Vendôme (*AR*, 1769, 1770).

41. He died in a bedroom at the Place des Victoires.

42. His son's *valets*, however, had rooms alongside those of Bernard's servants, on the third floor of the house at the Place des Victoires.

43. The furnishings of Crozat's gallery were valued at 6,680 *livres* and those of Bernard's gallery at 5,240 *livres*.

44. See Brice, *Description* (1752 ed.; reprint, 1971), 134–5; on Rigaud's clientele, see *Le Livre de raison du peintre Hyacinthe Rigaud*, ed. J. Roman (Paris, 1919).

45. Scott argues that "The Birth of Romulus and Remus" and "The Rape of the Sabine Women" referred to Bernard's dynastic ambitions; the others were "Coriolanus" and "The Continence of Scipio" (*The Rococo Interior*, 235–6).

46. On the Toulouse gallery, see Jean-Daniel Ludmann and Bruno Pons, "Nouveaux documents sur la galerie de l'hôtel de Toulouse," *BSHAF* (1979), 115–28.

47. Crozat's notary counted eleven other paintings in the ceremonial rooms of his house, including Flemish pieces and "histoire de la fable," appraised at 1,200 *livres*; four years later, thirty-three paintings appeared "either in the *cabinet*, in Mme Crozat's chamber or in the library," including five by Wouverman, a Poussin, a Titian portrait, and a Guido Reni [*Inventaire . . . M.-M. Legendre*, AN, MC XXX, 287 (12-IX-1742)]. On Matteis's portrait, see Brejon de Lavergnée, "Plaidoyer pour un peintre," 72.

48. Thirion, *La vie privée des financiers*, 340.

49. Hénault's notary valued the furniture in his *salle* and *cabinet* at a total of almost 4,200 *livres*, that of his bedchamber at 762 *livres*, and his wife's bedchamber at 478 *livres*.

50. Together these were valued at 4,000 *livres*.

51. Duché's notary valued the furnishings of Mme Duché's bedchamber at just 320 *livres*. After her husband's death, she claimed his apartment, and when she died in 1741, her notary appraised its contents (including new bed hangings, new fabric in the zone of the bed, and a new suite of matching curtains, chairs, and sofa) at 10,276 *livres* [*Inventaire . . . Elizabeth Du Breuil*, AN, MC CXVII, 440 (11-X-1741)]. On the realm of *compagnie*, see ch. 6.

52. Gallet, *Stately Mansions*, 93.

53. Bernard's statue, probably a reduction of one of those installed at a *place royale*, was valued (with some small objects and two small armoires) at 7,500 *livres*, about as much as all of the furniture in his *salon*. Crozat's son Thiers owned a reduction of the Place Vendôme statue, possibly among the bronzes left to him by his mother [AN, MC XXX, 287 (6-IX-1742); François Souchal, *French Sculptors of the 17th and 18th centuries* (Oxford, 1977), II:56; P. Remy, *Catalogue des . . . Objets curieux du Cabinet de feu M. Crozat, Baron de Thiers* (Paris, 1772), n°904]; on the reduction owned by Pontchartrain, see Michel Martin, *Les monuments équestres de Louis XIV* (Paris, 1986), 102–4.

54. Fleury had reappointed Duché to the reorganized general tax farm in 1726. After Duché's death, his wife converted a large ground-floor room into a *salle à manger*, embellished with a portrait of Louis XIV.

55. Bonfait found that robe noblemen tended to place royal portraits in their *cabinets*, but financial families often displayed them more prominently, in ceremonial bedrooms, *salons*, and (as the widowed Mme Duché did) in dining rooms ["Les Collections picturales des financiers," 134; "Les Collections des parlementaires parisiens du XVIIIe siècle," *Revue de l'art*, 73 (1986), 32].

56. On domestics, see Audiger, *La Maison réglée* (Paris, 1692), reprinted by Alfred

Franklin in *La Vie privée d'autrefois. La vie de Paris sous Louis XIV: Tenue de maison et domesticité* (Paris, 1898), 1–203; Cissie Fairchilds, *Domestic Enemies: Servants and their Masters in Old Regime France* (Baltimore and London, 1984); Sara Maza, *Servants and Masters in Eighteenth-Century France* (Princeton, 1983); J.-P. Gutton, *Domestiques et Serviteurs dans la France de l'Ancien Régime* (Paris, 1981); and Reed Benhamou, "Parallel Walls, Parallel Worlds: The Places of Masters and Servants in the *Maisons de plaisance* of Jacques-François Blondel," *Journal of Design History*, VII:1 (1994), 1–11.

57. Quoted by Jean Meyer, *La vie quotidienne en France au temps de la Régence* (Paris, 1979), 161.

58. Brice, *Description* (1706 ed.), I:187 (also mentioned in subsequent editions).

59. Crozat's notary valued the furnishings of the intendant's apartment at 669 *livres*, including a fairly expensive bed (100 *livres*), a sofa, three tapestries (200 *livres*), several chairs, two tabourets, and a desk.

60. See ch. 4. Capperonnier resided there until Mme Crozat's death [AN, MC XXX, 287 (12-IX-1742)], then lived with du Châtel, but by 1750, he had a post at the Royal Library (*AR*, 1743, 1751); Tugny kept Capperonnier's portrait on display [AN, MC XXX, 320 (12-I-1751)].

61. Crozat's *maître d'hôtel* had a room in the *entresol*. The *valet* was expected to know how to write, shave, comb hair, clean clothes, and make a bed; the *femme de chambre* was to know how to arrange hair, dress her mistress fashionably and according to her status, oversee the *toilette*, tie ribbons, put on and take off the shoes of a lady, give an enema, make a foot bath, sew, whiten linens, and make beds ("La Maison réglée," 30–1, 73–4).

62. The contents of the two rooms accorded to the first *femme de chambre* were valued at 423 *livres*.

63. Crozat's notary valued the furnishings collectively at 1,200 *livres*, for 24 beds, 40 chairs, and 30 tables.

64. Audiger, "La Maison reglée," 63–4; when satirists claimed that Mme Bourvalais obsessively supervised her kitchen staff, they meant to reveal her bourgeois value system (see ch. 2).

65. *Inventaire*, AN, MC LXXXVIII, 558 (13-I-1738).

66. Storez, *Chancelier . . . d'Aguesseau*, 176–7.

67. She lodged most of them in the mansard roof, but placed one chambermaid next to her bedroom and another on the second floor, where the chef also had a room; the chef's assistant slept in a *petit entresol* above the kitchen and the postilion in a kind of hammock (*suspente*) in the stables [*Scellé . . . Catherine-Charlotte de Gramont, veuve de Louis-François de Boufflers*, AN, Y11158 (25-I-1739)]; on Mme Legendre's domestic staff: AN, Y14523 (11-XII-1726); MC II, 426 (13-XII-1726).

Chapter 6

1. *AR*, 1733, 1735, 1738, 1742–4, 1747–51, 1755; the duchesse d'Antin appears in AN, O¹ 1576, f°270 and Coigny in AN, MC CXVII, 381 (4-VII-1731). Georges-Erasme de Concordes, governor of Beaufort, also resided at the square [AN, MC CXVII, 425 (17-IV-1739)].

2. Nassigny and his wife Claude-Françoise-Antoinette d'Amoressan (sister of Séchelle's wife) apparently lodged with them their son Moreau de Beaumont, *conseiller au Parlement*, and (after 1743) his wife, Marie-Françoise Grimod de la Reynière; their daughter and her husband, Jean-Charles de Bonnevie, *conseiller au Parlement*; and, briefly, Nassigny's brother Moreau de Beauplan, *conseiller au*

Parlement (+1733) [AN, MC LXXXVIII, 593 (14-X-1744); *AR*, 1733, 1735, 1738, 1742–4; Bluche, "L'Origine des Magistrats," 320–1; Favre-Lejeune, *SR*, 983–4].

3. *Chronique de la Régence*, VI:45. Also notable were Villemaré's son, Le Lay de Guébriant, named plenipotentiary minister at Cologne in 1747, and Fontanieu's son Gaspard-Moise, who long served as a royal intendant; see Luynes, *Mémoires*, VIII:304–5; XIV:405, 417–26.

4. J.-F. Blondel, *Maisons de plaisance*, I:33.

5. "Please God that the late King were still alive, because I had more pleasure and happiness then, in one day, than I have had during the six years of the regency of my son! There was really a court then and not this bourgeois life to which I cannot get accustomed . . ." (*Correspondance complète de Madame duchesse d'Orléans*, II:352).

6. Thus, J.-F. Blondel counseled that, for *maisons d'oeconomie* (bourgeois houses), "after having planned the apartments of *compagnie*, it suffices to give each bedroom a well-lit wardrobe" (*Maisons de plaisance*, I:157).

7. Blondel first extensively used the term *compagnie* in his *Maisons de plaisance* of 1737–8; in some plans engraved for Mariette's *L'Architecture française* of 1727– c. 1739 and used in Blondel's reedition of the fifties (*AF*), rooms were renamed to reflect current terminology.

8. *AF*, III:101. Work on no. 17 began in 1744, and by 1746, Tugny spent 120,000 *livres* [Gabrielle Joudiou, "Pierre Contant d'Ivry," *Chevotet-Contant-Chaussard* (Lyon, 1987), 102]; during those years, Receiver General of Finance for Limoges Le Texier de Mennetou paid 100,000 *livres* for no. 5 Place Vendôme – 20,000 *livres* less than Tugny's "renovations" [*Inventaire*, AN, MC XXIII, 719 (30-III-1772)]. Bernard's sons also renovated their Paris dwellings in the forties.

9. Five projects are preserved in AN, T 1881.[1]

10. AN, Z[1j] 746 (24-VII-1745)n°1; Brice had earlier criticized the entrance passage, which rose only to the *entresol* [*Description* (1706 ed.), I:187].

11. *AF*, III:101.

12. Seine DQ[10] 0370, n°14020 (1750–1). Architect Gillet de La Fontaine noted that "pilasters at the beginning of each ramp are crowned with copper vases" and the voussoir below the first-floor landing was embellished with a cartouche "enriched with flutes and rays *à la rocaille*."

13. See, for example, J.-F. Blondel, *AF*, I:212–14.

14. In houses where dining occurred in an anteroom, "one omits mirrors and other ornaments"; otherwise, "since one has regarded the table as the bond of *société*, one renders the decoration . . . susceptible to some richness" (ibid., I:32).

15. By the late thirties, Blondel noted that a laden buffet was no longer considered appropriate to a house "of the first consideration," in "a place destined for the meals of persons of superior distinction," where "one must not affect a frivolous display, which would only give a feeble idea of . . . [the household's] importance" (*Maisons de plaisance*, II:122).

16. Seine DQ[10] 0370, n°14020 (1750–1). Contant reused "a part of the *lambris* formerly in the gallery," now resculpted and integrated with new paneling [AN, Z[1j] 746 (24-VII-1745), n°23].

17. AN, Z[1j] 746 (24-VII-1745), n°25; by 1750, it had been converted into a chapel, with an altar inserted into one of the corners [AN, Y10765 (6-I-1751); AN, MC XXX, 320 (12-I-1751); Seine DQ[10] 0370, n°14020 (1750–1)]; J.-F. Blondel, *AF*, III:102]. The conception seems akin to the *cabinet* lined with *papier des Indes* adjoining the dining room at the Hôtel de Fonspertuis, no. 21 (see ch. 4).

18. Tugny equipped the room with a fountain for hand washing and a variety of

chairs and benches upholstered in leather [AN, Z^{1j} 746 (24-VII-1745), n°s 32–7; Seine DQ^{10} 0370, n°14020 (1750–1); *Inventaire . . . Tugny*, AN, MC XXX, 320 (12-I-1751)].

19. Ibid. Tugny kept several gaming tables and his father's large harpsichord in the room, plus two sofas and several chairs upholstered in yellow and green leather.

20. AN, Z^{1j} 746 (24-VII-1745), n°s 39–44; Seine DQ^{10} 0370, n°14020 (1750–1).

21. Seine DQ^{10} 0370, n° 14020 (1750–1). Tugny's notary described the tall paintings as "une figure d'une homme tenant une hure de sanglier" and "une femme & un petit amour" – possibly Hercules with the head of the Erymanthian boar and Venus and Cupid [AN, MC XXX, 320 (12-I-1751)].

22. *AF*, III:102. This room was more opulently furnished than any had been in the house of Tugny's father; its furnishings (including an octagonal rug, two sofas, and eighteen chairs upholstered in white and pale gray velours and damask, plus some expensive wall lights) were valued at 10,020 *livres* [AN, MC XXX, 320 (12-I-1751)].

23. *Scellé*, AN, Y10765 (6-I-1751); *Inventaire*, AN, MC XXX, 320 (12-I-1751); Seine DQ^{10} 0370, n°14020 (1750–1); J.-F. Blondel, *AF*, III:102. In two early projects, Contant planned rooms embellished with rococo cornices and labeled them *sallons de compagnie* (and, in a third, *cabinet d'assemblée*) (AN, T 188^1); in the projects in which he articulated the room with a classical order, Contant used the term *salon*. A typical *salle de compagnie* at this moment was that of the Hôtel de Soyecourt in the Faubourg Saint-Germain; in c. 1750, architect Pierre-Michel Mouret converted a *salon* into a *salle de compagnie*, clad in exuberant rococo paneling by Verberckt [see J.-F. Blondel, *AF*, I:257–60; Pons, DAAVP, *La rue de l'Université* (Paris, 1987), 85–91].

24. In fact, there was a dressing table set up in a small room in the *entresol* that probably regularly served as the *cabinet de toilette*, located next to the bedroom of one Mme de Tugny's chambermaids [AN, MC XXX, 320 (12-I-1751)]. Whereas the term *boudoir* had been used since the turn of the century [Hélène Himelfarb, "Regards versaillais sur l'hôtel parisien," *XVIIe Siècle*, 162 (January – March 1987), 95], it would be more commonly employed only later in the century.

25. Paintings in the *cabinet des tableaux* included works by Wouwerman, van Ostade, Elsheimer, Rembrandt, Terborch, Titian, Albani, Le Sueur, Claude, Watteau, Pater, and Natoire; some were left to him by his mother, although she bequeathed the majority to his brother Thiers [AN, MC XXX, 287 (6-IX-1742)]. On Tugny's collection, see P.-J. Mariette, *Catalogue des tableaux et sculptures tant en bronze qu'en marbre, du Cabinet de feu Monsieur le Président de Tugny . . .* (Paris, 1751); Charles Blanc published excerpts in *Le Trésor de la curiosité* (Paris, 1867), I:61–2.

26. See Durand, *Fermiers généraux*, 563–4. Bonfait found an average of 2,070 volumes per library among robe noblemen at the turn of the century and 453 volumes among financiers ("Les Collections picturales des financiers," 136).

27. *Partage*, AN, MC XXX, 289 (3-III and 24-IX-1743). Crozat's notary indicated that there were 4,887 volumes in his library, including works of piety, dictionaries, histories of law, and *belles lettres Romaines*, together valued at 10,213 *livres* [AN, MC VIII, 1024 (13-VI-1738)]. When Mme Crozat died four years later, a room along the court was called *la bibliothèque* (probably already used by Tugny), and her notary listed some of the volumes she had added since her husband's death [AN, MC XXX, 287 (12-IX-1742)]. Du Châtel inherited Pierre Crozat's library [AN, MC XXX, 278 (30-V-1740)]; the abbé Crozat's library appears in his inventory [AN, MC LXXVII, 199 (11-VII-1729)].

28. Buvat, *Journal de la Régence*, I:213, n. 1; Antoine, *Gouvernement et Administration*, 105; *Inventaire . . . de Ségur*, AN, MC LXXXVIII, 636 (27-V-1755).

29. Storez, *Chancelier . . . d'Aguesseau*, 183. For comparisons with other libraries at mid-century, see Michel Marion, *Recherches sur les bibliothèques privées à Paris au milieu du XVIIIe siècle (1750–1759)* (Paris, 1978). At the Place Vendôme, general tax farmers Ollivier de Montluçon (no. 3) and Alexis-Rolland Fillion de Villemur (no. 10) also assembled libraries [Ollivier: AN, MC LXXXVIII, 618 (19-IV-1751); Fillion: AN, Y11469b (4-IX-1753)]. In the late forties, the duc de La Vallière briefly leased accommodation at the square and presumably installed part of his considerable library (see Blanc, *Trésor de la curiosité*, II:40).

30. AN, Z^{1j} 746 (24-VII-1745), n°62 and Seine DQ^{10} 0370, n°14020 (1750–1). Contant also reinstalled the original gilded cornice, adding new sections at both ends. During the sixties and seventies, Dezallier d'Argenville continued to remark upon the paintings by Matteis crowning the stair and gallery [*Voyage pittoresque de Paris*, 6th ed. (Paris, 1778), 136]. Tugny's library was sold following his death, and the *Catalogue des Livres de Monsieur le président Crozat de Tugny* (Paris, 1751) listed over 5,000 items, including works of theology; jurisprudence; philosophy; politics; history; geography; travel accounts; genealogical works; numismatics; physics; natural history; botany; medicine; chemistry; art; architecture (including Perrault's translation of Vitruvius and Daviler's *Cours d'Architecture*); archaeology; rhetoric; poetry; comedies; English novels in translation (among them Richardson's *Pamela* and Fielding's *John Andrews*); *histoires galantes*; print folios; printed music; and modern gazettes. Tugny also claimed for his books a suite of four rooms on the second floor, overlooking the square.

31. Thiers equipped his *cabinet* with devices that included a pneumatic machine, a telescope, a microscope, and a movable sphere established on the system of Tycho Brahe [AN, MC LXXIII, 925 (22-XII-1770); P. Remy, *Catalogue des estampes . . . pieces de méchaniques, & autres objets curieux du cabinet de feu . . . Baron de Thiers . . .* (Paris, 1772), 178–80].

32. *AF*, III:102.

33. See Scott, *The Rococo Interior*, 97; Pardailhé-Galabrun, *Birth of Intimacy*, 171–2. Antoine Crozat and his wife favored crimson textiles, but they hung tapestries in the anteroom, ceremonial bedroom, and *grand cabinet* [AN, MC VIII, 1024 (13-VI-1738); MC XXX, 287 (12-IX-1742)].

34. J.-F. Blondel wrote in the late thirties that it was the "taste" to paint rooms blue, green, yellow, etc., but he found it inappropriate in a room of *parade* or *assemblée* (*Maisons de plaisance*, II:111). Even for dining rooms, Blondel advocated walls "lined with carved wood paneling painted white and ornamented with gilded sculpture, this manner of decorating having much more magnificence (*éclat*) . . ." (I:33). A decade later, Contant introduced colored paneling even into Tugny's public apartments, enriched with gilding for *éclat*. See, too, J.-F. Blondel and Jean-François Bastide, *L'Homme du monde éclairé par les arts* (Amsterdam, 1774; reprint, Geneva, 1973), II:77–80.

35. On Contant's contemporary use of the orders in ecclesiastical works, see Robin Middleton, "The Abbé de Cordemoy and the Graeco-Gothic Ideal: A Prelude to Romantic Classicism," *Journal of the Warburg and Courthauld Institutes*, XXVI (1963), 93–5; see, too, Joudiou, "Pierre Contant d'Ivry," 86–182, and idem., "Un architecte Parisien de 'bon goût': Contant d'Ivry," *BSHPIF* 115 (1989), 81–106; F. J. Kretzschmar, *Pierre Contant d'Ivry: Ein Beitrag zur französischen Architektur des 18. Jahrhunderts*, Ph.D. dissertation, University of Cologne, 1981.

36. They left briefly in 1749, when Dumont directed a school for *élèves protégés* of the Academy of Painting and Sculpture [Jal, *Dictionnaire critique*, I:518; Louis Dimier, *Les peintres français du XVIIIe siècle* (Paris and Brussels, 1928), II:232].

37. Saladin, who had acted as intermediary when Moreau de Séchelles rented no. 5, was related to François Geoffrin; he lived on the rue Saint-Honoré during the late forties, probably in Geoffrin's house (*AR*, 1747–9). Luynes called him "a man of intellect and of merit" (*Mémoires*, VII:322). On his friendship with Tugny, see Rohan Butler, *Choiseul I: Father and Son* (Oxford, 1980), 874. Saladin left Paris following Tugny's death (Lüthy, *La banque protestante*, II:80; 295, 738–9; *Correspondance complète de la marquise du Deffand*, ed. Lescure, I:138–42).

38. Fontenay may have been Léopold le Preud'homme, comte de Fontenoy in Lorraine, ensign of the guards of the duc de Lorraine [François Aubert De la Chenaye-Debois, *Dictionnaire de la noblesse* (Paris, 1874; reprint, Nancy, 1980), VIII:373]. Luynes mentioned a M. de Fontenay who served during the forties and fifties as envoy, then minister, of the king of Poland (i.e., Stanislaus I, also duc de Lorraine and father of the French queen) (*Mémoires*, IX:106–7, XVI:43). On the connection of the Legendre with high-ranking Lorraine dignitaries, see ch. 2, n. 33.

39. Durand found that during the forties and fifties, the number of servants in houses of general tax farmers ranged from just six serving Laurent Mazade in 1741 to seventeen (almost a third smaller than Tugny's staff) maintained by Pierre Dedelay de La Garde in 1752 (*Fermiers généraux*, 496–7). Even larger than Tugny's *maison* was the household of general tax farmer Jean-Hyacinthe II Hocquart, born within a few years of Tugny to a financial clan linked to Colbert. He purchased no. 12 Place Vendôme in 1739, and with his wife Marie-Anne-Françoise, daughter of fellow tax farmer Jean Gaillard de La Bouexière, he shaped a *maison* akin to that of Antoine Crozat. Two of three of Mme Hocquart's brothers (all financiers) also lived at the square during the forties and early fifties (*AR*, 1743–5, 1750–1). When Hocquart died in 1764, six adult children still resided with him, some with their noble spouses and children, and to serve them, Hocquart maintained thirty-four domestics lodged in twenty-four rooms [AN, Y15369 (3-V-1764); MC II, 603 (14-V-1764)].

40. Plans dated 1743–4, for three alternative projects, may be found in AN, T188[1].

41. *AF*, III:103.

42. Blondel criticized the placing of small chapels in or near anterooms (*AF*, III:38), but P.-J. Mariette acknowledged that "it is ordinarily near second anterooms that one places chapels in *grands Hôtels*. . . ." [revisions to Daviler, *Cours d'architecture* (Paris, 1738), I:215].

43. An account of the *compagnie* assembling at Thiers's house appears in correspondence between Danish minister Bernstorff and his nephew, both frequent visitors. In 1757, the minister wrote to his nephew: "M. de Thiers has much intelligence, taste and leisure . . . [and] pleasantly passes his life. His wife, who is of higher birth than him, since she is [a] Laval-Montmorency, is full of reason, piety and virtue. . . . In this same house you will find a man of merit, but of little fortune . . . M. de Segui, formerly governor of the duc de Wirtemberg. . . ." Bernstorff's nephew found Segui, "a man of society . . . full of good sense" and very closely "attached . . . to the household of Thiers" [*Bernstorffsche Papiere. Ausgewählte Briefe und Aufzeichnungen die Familie Bernstorff Betreffend aus der zeit 1732 bis 1835*, ed. Aage Friis (Copenhagen, 1904–7), I:174, 186–7].

44. See Theo H. Lunsingh Scheurleer's reproduction of Contant's 1744 section through the first-floor vestibule and dining room (in a private collection), in "Deux projets pour l'Hôtel de Thiers attribués à Contant d'Ivry," *BSHAF* (1934), 293.

45. "In houses that are rather considerable," architect Charles-Étienne Briseux explained, "it is good to have, besides the *cabinet d'assemblée*, a small room where

the master and his family can retire on days when there are no guests: it is pleasing to inhabit smaller spaces when there are few in the group" [*L'Art de bâtir des maisons de campagne* (Paris, 1743; reprint of 1765 ed., Farnsborough, 1966), I:22].

46. In one project, Contant labeled the bedroom along the court "summer bedroom."

47. In two earlier projects, Contant labeled the room *cabinet d'assemblée*, a term often used interchangeably with *salle de compagnie*. Some theorists, however, preferred a more calibrated distinction. According to J.-F. Blondel, *salle d'assemblée* commonly referred to two sorts of rooms, one ceremonial, "serving to receive persons of distinction, who wait there until the hour of the *lever* or the moment when they are introduced to the master," the other better named *salle de compagnie* [*AF*, (1752) I: 31]. In the *Encyclopédie*, however, the chevalier de Jaucourt defined *salle d'assemblée* more inclusively as a room "for receiving *compagnie*" [(1765 ed.), XIV:574]. Later, *menuisier* Roubo fils also advocated a distinction between *salles de compagnie* and *salles d'assemblée*, since "the last are destined to receive visits and treat serious affairs, whereas the first are reserved for recreation and different pleasures, like games, music and dance" [*L'Art de Menuisier* (Paris, 1769; reprint, Paris, 1976), II:192].

48. *AF*, III:104.

49. *Partage*, AN, MC XXX, 281 (30-I-1741). Tugny may have been skipped because he was childless.

50. The widowed Mme de Tugny retired to an apartment attached to a convent in the Faubourg Saint-Germain [AN, Y13560 (5-VI-1777)].

51. Among the paintings from Tugny's collection retained by Thiers were Rembrandt's *Danaë*, Poussin's *The Triumph of Amphitrite*, and some Dutch works [Hélène Meyer, "La collection de Louis-Antoine Crozat, baron de Thiers," *L'Age d'or flamand et hollandais: Collections de Catherine II, Musée de l'Ermitage* (Dijon, 1993), 50–2]. Mariette prepared the sales catalogues: *Description sommaire des statues, figures, bustes, vases, et autres Morceaux de Sculpture . . . & des Modéles en terre cuite, Porcelaines & Fayences d'Urbin, provenans du Cabinet de feu M. CROZAT* (Paris, 1750) and *Catalogue des tableaux et sculptures, Tant en Bronze qu'en Marbre, du Cabinet de feu M. le Président DE TUGNY, & de celui de M. CROZAT* (Paris, 1751); both were reprinted in *Description de la Collection Crozat* (Geneva, 1973).

52. See Margret Stuffmann, "Les tableaux de la collection de Pierre Crozat," *GBA*, 72 (1968), 11–139; and Meyer, "La collection de Louis-Antoine Crozat," 49–56.

53. "Il n'est pas curieux," the painter Vleughels wrote to the duc d'Antin, contrasting Antoine Crozat with his brother Pierre (quoted by Brejon de Lavergnée, "Plaidoyer pour un peintre," 72).

54. For a list of known works by Varin, see Gallet, *Les architectes parisiens*, 467–8.

55. *AF*, III:104.

56. Ibid., III:103.

57. Ibid.

58. *Catalogue des Tableaux du cabinet de M. Crozat, Baron de Thiers* (Paris, 1755; reprinted, Geneva, 1972).

59. By 1770, Thiers displayed many more paintings in this first anteroom [*Inventaire*, AN, MC LXXIII, 925 (22-XII-1770)]. Unless otherwise noted, attributions are those found in La Curne de Saint-Palaye's catalogue or in Thiers's inventory. Hebert described the installation in the sixties [*Dictionnaire pittoresque et historique* (Paris, 1766; reprint, Geneva, 1972), I:33–9].

60. See Meyer, "La collection de Louis-Antoine Crozat," 51. Thiers's notary called this room the *grande gallerie*.

61. The works filling the rooms along the garden included paintings by Giorgione, Giulio Romano, Barocci, Annibale Carracci, Lanfranco, Guercino, Van Dyck, Bril, Jordaens, Poussin, Claude, and Bourdon. Like most collectors, Thiers tended to hang works on the basis of size, with walls arranged to look balanced and fairly symmetrical, as Colin Bailey points out in "Conventions of the Eighteenth-Century *Cabinet de tableaux*: Blondel d'Azincourt's *La première idée de la curiosité*," *Art Bulletin* LXIX:3 (September 1987), 437.

62. See E. F. Gersaint *Catalogue . . . de M. Angran, vicomte de Fonspertuis* (Paris, 1747), and Pierre Remy, *Catalogue Raisonné des Tableaux, Porcelaines, Bijoux et autres effets du Cabinet de feu M. Gaillard de Gagny . . .* (Paris, 1762); excerpts appear in Blanc, *Trésor de la curiosité*, I:45–51, 110–11. Krzysztof Pomian discusses the interest in Dutch, Flemish, and French works in *Collectors and Curiosities: Paris and Venice, 1500–1800*, trans. E. Wiles-Portier (Cambridge, 1990), ch. 5; for case studies, see Bailey, "Aspects of Patronage and Collecting of French Painting in France at the End of the *Ancien Régime*," Ph.D. dissertation, Oxford University, 1985.

63. Heir to many Rosalba pastels from his parents and his uncle (including a portrait of his sister, the comtesse d'Évreux), Thiers displayed them in a *petite galerie* and a *petit salon*; hanging with them were Louis Toqué's portraits of his two eldest daughters.

64. Dutch and Flemish works included many by Teniers and Wouverman, plus paintings by Ruisdael, Jan Steen, Terborch, van Ostade, Metzu, Rubens, Rembrandt, Dürer, and Elsheimer. In the *cabinet* filled with the French School, Theirs hung paintings by La Fosse, Stella, Claude Lorrain, Bourdon, Mignard, Parrocel, Largillière, Poussin, Bon Boullongne, de Troy the Elder and Younger, van der Meulen, the Le Nain brothers, Antoine and Charles Coypel, Watteau, Natoire, Chardin, Pater, Raoux, Boucher, and, by 1770, Lancret and Vien. See the account of his own interest in the French School written by La Live de Jully – whose financier father had resided at the Place Vendôme during the Regency – published by Bailey in *Ange-Laurent de La Live de Jully. A Facsimile Reprint of the Catalogue Historique (1764) and the Catalogue Raisonné des Tableaux (March 5, 1770)* (New York, 1988).

65. The maréchale de Broglie, named *dame de compagnie* of the princesses of France in 1754, resided at Versailles when her husband served in the Seven Years War; in 1762, the king banished Broglie to his country estate [Dominique de Broglie, *Les Broglie: leur histoire* (Paris, 1972), 108–115].

66. *Bail à vie*, AN, MC VIII, 1162 (18-V-1765). Thiers retained, in a new service structure that Tugny had built along the rue Neuve-du-Luxembourg (Fig. 111), "two small apartments" for an intendant and cashier, who were guaranteed entry through the Place Vendôme from 6 A.M. to midnight; clearly, the investments inherited from Antoine Crozat still required special financial assistants.

67. It appears on a list Ledoux prepared in November 1767 for his candidacy to the royal Academy of Architecture [Gallet, *Claude-Nicolas Ledoux* (Paris, 1980), 261].

68. Stuffmann, "Les tableaux de la collection de Pierre Crozat," *GBA* 72 (1968), 35.

69. Two daughters married into the Béthune clan. The eldest, born in 1731, had wed the comte de Béthune; later, as a widow, she returned to her father's house (no. 19) and occupied the first-floor suite along the square [AN, Y13546 (16-XII-1770)]. During the sixties, Thiers formed a regular member of an intimate circle surrounding the duchesse de Choiseul [see *Horace Walpole's Correspondence*, ed. W. S. Lewis (New Haven, 1939), IV:passim].

70. *Chronique de la Régence*, I:339; d'Argenson, *Mémoires*, III:271.

71. See Pomian, *Collectors and Curiosities*, 153–55.

Chapter 7

1. Charles Pinot Duclos, "Les confessions du comte de ***" (1742), in *Oeuvres de Duclos* (Paris, 1821), I:266–7.

2. I agree with William Sewell's argument that, for the newly ennobled, France remained an "elaborate hierarchy" in which "social status was never secure" [*A Rhetoric of Bourgeois Revolution: The Abbé Sièyes and What is the Third Estate?* (Durham and London, 1994), 64].

3. Le Camus de Mézières, *Genius of Architecture*, 105.

4. Critics labeled some of their dwellings "temples."

5. *AR*, 1789. Sébastien Mercier, voicing a popular perception, wrote that the dwellings in new quarters belonged to "userers, embezzlers, speculators – indefatigable agents of oppression" [*Tableau de Paris* (Amsterdam, 1782–8), VII:89].

6. *Scellé . . . Henriette-Charlotte de Jarnac*, AN, Y14554 (28-VIII-1769); *AR*, 1775; *Inventaire . . . duc de Fitz-James*, AN, MC LVI, 336 (24-V-1787).

7. See Carolyn Lougee, *Le Paradis des Femmes: Women, Salons and Social Stratification in Seventeenth-Century France* (Princeton, 1976).

8. "It was not at all for us, not at all for herself, that she took such care [at her *salon*], it was for her husband. We became acquainted with him, accorded him our wit, praised him in society, and launched his renown; that was the principal object of the foundation of her literary society" [*Mémoires de Marmontel*, ed. Maurice Tourneux (Paris, 1891), III:15; see, too, Grimm et al., *Correspondance littéraire, philosophique, et critique*, ed. Maurice Tourneux (Paris, 1877–82), VIII:438]. On the Necker residence at the Place Vendôme: BN, Ms. Fr. 11671, f^os189–234; *AR*, 1775.

9. D'Argenson, *Mémoires*, V:97.

10. See Marmontel's account, *Mémoires*, II:82–110; Goodman, *Republic of Letters*, 74–9; Daniel Gordon, *Citizens Without Sovereignty: Equality and Sociability in French Thought, 1670–1789* (Princeton, 1994), 190–4; and Roger Picard, *Les Salons littéraires et la société française, 1610–1789* (New York, 1943), ch. 6. A painting of a reading in Mme Geoffrin's *salon* is illustrated by Lorenza Minoli in "Oltre le pareti delle'esclusione: Il caso dei salotti politico-letterari," in *Esistere come donna* (Milan, 1983), 67.

11. Goodman, *Republic of Letters*, 79–82.

12. M. Geoffrin was the man who "who never said a word" (d'Argenson, *Mémoires*, V:98). Marmontel described Necker as "there only as a silent and cold spectator," a man "accustomed, since his youth, to the mysterious operations of a bank and buried in the calculations of commercial speculation, knowing little of *le monde* . . . very little even of books . . . [who] had to, by discretion, by prudence, by self-respect, be reserved . . ." (*Mémoires*, III:16–17).

13. Translated, the full title is *The Anti-financier; or, Summary of some of the malversations [through] which the Farmers General daily render themselves guilty and the molestations that they commit in the Provinces.*

14. James C. Riley, *The Seven Years War and the Old Regime in France* (Princeton, 1986), 213–14.

15. Bosher, *French Finances*, chs. 4–5.

16. Matthews, *The Royal General Farms*, 239.

17. *AR*, 1774, 1775; Durand, *Fermiers généraux*, 457–8.

18. Bosher, *French Finances*, ch. 5.

19. Ibid., 76–81, 105–6, chs. 8 and 9.

20. Blondel's son Barthélemy-Augustin (1719–94) pursued a military career and became an art collector; he lived with them until his 1752 alliance with a niece of the wealthy tax farmer La Haye. Blondel had a daughter who lived in a convent

and a second son, who died in 1754 [Joudiou, "Un architecte Parisien," 85, n.10; Bailey, "Conventions of the Eighteenth-Century *Cabinet*," 434; Josette Proust-Perrault in AAVP, *De la place Royale*, 328].

21. AN, Z¹ʲ 993 (8-VI-1775); *Le Provincial à Paris ou État actuel de Paris* (1787) listed the Place Vendôme houses of three treasurers and a banker as *bureaux*, rather than *maisons*: no. 15 ("Bureau des la caisse des amortissemens"), no. 12 ("Bureau du trésorier général de la marine, M. Baudard de Sainte-James"), no. 3 ("Bureau du trésorier général des États de Languedoc, M. Joubert"), and no. 9 ("Bureau de M. Poullin, banquier") (IV:117).

22. *Mémorial de Paris et de ses Environs* (Paris, 1749), I:210.

23. AN, Y11158 (25-I-1739). Five decades later, the duc de Fitz-James also installed a dais – of red velvet with gold ornament, bearing his arms – at no. 20, also in a room overlooking the square [AN, MC LVI, 336 (24-V-1787)].

24. AN, Z¹ʲ 993 (8-VI-1775); MC LVII, 529 (27-VII-1776)]. Marmontel described Blondel's avid interest in French music (*Mémoires*, II:117).

25. Hebert described the installation in *Dictionnaire pittoresque* (Paris, 1766; reprint, Geneva, 1972), 20–31.

26. The portrait appears in AN, Y13969b (9-VII-1776)]; on "faceless" ancestors, see ch. 5.

27. Paintings included works by Teniers the Younger, Gerard Dou, Van Ostade, Santerre, Claude, Watteau, and Lancret; Teniers's *Prodigal Son* sold for 29,000 *livres*, Metzu's *Herb Garden in Amsterdam* for 25,800 *livres* [*Catalogue des tableaux . . . Blondel de Gagny* (Paris, 1776), n°81, n°107].

28. Hebert, *Dictionnaire pittoresque*, 23–4.

29. The sixty paintings included two by Terborch, two attributed to Rembrandt (one purchased from Fonspertuis's collection), eight Wouwermans, a van Ostade, several landscapes by Jan I Brueghel and Bril, a Holbein portrait, and a Poussin; furnishings included more Boulle pieces, vases, and small sculpture.

30. See Hebert, *Dictionnaire pittoresque*, 26–7. In 1775, an architect from the Chambre des Bâtiments described a painting of "a Moor," set into a "circular border" crowning the fireplace bay [AN, Z¹ʲ 993 (8-VI-1775)]. Agents of Châtelet mentioned the presence of a large writing table and of a painting of "une negresse avec une corné d'abondance" by Bon de Boullongne [AN, Y13969b (9-VII-1776)]; that, however, may be a work that appears in the sale catalogue as "une negresse" by Louis de Boullongne the Elder (*Catalogue . . . Blondel de Gagny*, n°214). Blondel's notary described a "lit en canapé" with a "baldaquin" [AN, MC LVII, 529 (27-VII-1776)].

31. *Catalogue . . . Blondel de Gagny*, n°ˢ 81–101.

32. Blondel displayed thirty-eight paintings and a drawing by Rubens in the *petit cabinet*. The chandelier and sconces flanking the fireplace in the *grand cabinet*, which was filled with porcelain, were themselves fashioned from pieces of antique porcelain (Hebert, *Description pittoresque*, 30–1).

33. Some of Thiers's pieces were the legacy of his parents and uncle [Remy, *Catalogue des estampes, vases de poterie etrusques, figures, bas-reliefs & bustes de bronze, marbre & de terre cuite, ouvrages en marqueterie du célèbre Boulle père . . . & autres objets curieux du cabinet de feu M. Crozat, Baron de Thiers . . .* (Paris, 1772), 180–3; Pierre Verlet *Les Bronzes dorés français du XVIII siècle* (Paris, 1987), 291–2; Ris, *Amateurs d'autrefois*, 357].

34. Architectural paintings also formed a striking feature of a house Contant d'Ivry had built for Blondel in the Faubourg Saint-Honoré and of Blondel's country house at Garches, which Contant renovated in the fifties [Dezallier d'Argenville, *Voyage pittoresque de Paris* (1778 ed.), 142; Joudiou, "Pierre Contant d'Ivry," *Chevotet-Contant-Chaussard*, 93–4, and "Un architecte Parisien," 87–9].

35. *The French Journals of Mrs. Thrale and Dr. Johnson*, ed. Moses Tyson and Henry Guppy, (Manchester, 1932), 113.

36. *Guide des amateurs et des etrangers voyageurs à Paris* (Paris, 1786–7), quoted in Bailey, "Conventions of the Eighteenth-Century *Cabinet*," 445. Chalut and his wife were known for their charity, especially their support of the foundling hospital, from which they adopted a daughter in 1776; she wed Nicolas Deville, who succeeded Chalut as a general tax farmer and purchased no. 17 in 1787; see Pierre-Nicolas Berryer, *Souvenirs de M. Berryer, doyen des avocats de Paris, de 1774 à 1838* (Paris, 1839), I:153; Bachaumont et. al., *Mémoires secrets*, XXXI: 76–7; and, on Mme Chalut, Marmontel, *Mémoires*, II:17–22; 204–5.

37. *Scellé . . . Darras*, AN, Y13980 (19-V-1788); *Inventaire*, AN, MC LXXXVI, 859 (21-VIII-1788). In 1767, Darras became a *secrétaire du roi*; his grandniece (and heir) wed Louis Marquet de Montbreton, whose family resided at no. 23 (Favre-Lejeune, *SR*, 423–4).

38. "People claim he had been the lackey and then *commis* of M. d'Argenson" (*Mémoires pour servir à l'histoire du publicanisme moderne*, BN, Ms. Fr. 10448, f°38); the Regent supplied the 3,000 *livres* Anne Jarry brought to the marriage [AN, MC LXXXVII, 1138 (27-III-1772)]. In the fifties, Dangé lodged Henry-Felix Duché, son of a captain of the Swiss Guards of the duc d'Orléans, in a second-floor suite in the wing [AN, Y15954 (10-XII-1757); MC LXXXVII, 1043 (10-XII-1757 and 23-XII-1757)]. By the seventies, two of four nephews – maréchal des camps Dangé d'Orsay (b. 1733) and adjunct tax farmer Dangé de Bagneux (b. 1739) – plus their wives and d'Orsay's two young sons, still lived with Dangé; also resident were a niece and her husband, the marquis de Floressac, and their two sons [AN, Y10902 (22-III-1772); MC LXXXVII, 1165 (10-IV-1773, dep. 7-III-1777); Y10911 (6-III-1777); MC LXXXVII, 1165 (17-III-1777); BN, Nouv. Acq. Fr., Ms. 20533, f°ˢ487–9. For paneling associated with Dangé's renovations, see illustrations in Jules Vacquier, *La place Vendôme, dite aussi de Louis le Grand ou des Conquêtes* (Paris, 1913)].

39. *Scellé . . . Villemaré*, AN, Y11161 (29-X-1743).

40. See J.-F. Blondel's argument in ch. 6. Adoption of behavior formerly considered "bourgeois" is an aspect of what Norbert Elias called the "bourgeoisification" of the noble elites [*The Civilizing Process*, trans. Edmund Jephcott (New York, 1978) I: 103].

41. A painting of Louis XIV, probably installed by Villemaré, crowned the zone above the buffet table.

42. AN, Y10902 (22-III-1772); MC LXXXVII, 1138 (27-III-1772). The financiers and their sons who figured among Boucher's most important patrons included Pierre-Louis Randon de Boisset, Receiver General for Lyon, who may have occupied no. 18 in the early fifties, and Pierre-Jacques-Onésyme Bergeret, son of a general tax farmer who long resided at the Place des Victoires (Durand, *Fermiers généraux*, 515–17).

43. Châtelet agents called the room a "second anteroom," but Mme Dangé's notary suggested it was more important, using the term *premier sallon* [AN, Y10902 (22-III-1772); MC LXXXVII, 1138 (27-III-1772)]. After 1772, Dangé installed another *buffet* into the contiguous first anteroom, and he sometimes used this "second anteroom" for dining, in a setting quite different in character from the *salle à manger* in the wing [AN, MC LXXXVII, 1165 (17-III-1777); Z¹⁾ 1031 (26-III-1778)].

44. A large sofa and ten chairs upholstered in white velours, almost twenty armchairs of various sorts, marble tables, porcelain vases, a clock, a d'Aubusson rug, and a crystal chandelier were together valued at over 13,600 *livres* [AN, MC LXXXVII, 1138 (27-III-1772)].

45. Bonfait, "Les Collections picturales des financiers," 133.
46. AN, Y10911 (6-III-1777); Z^{1j} 1031 (26-III-1778).
47. *Dictionnaire domestique portatif* (Paris 1764), III: 236; see, too, the definition in the *Dictionnaire de Trévoux* (1752) quoted in E. Lilley, "The Name of the Boudoir," *JSAH*, LIII:2 (June 1994), 194; and see Pardailhé-Galabrun, *Birth of Intimacy*, 64. In 1775, Mrs. Thrale referred to Mme d'Argenson's *boudoir* as a "pouting Room" (*French Journals*, 116). Roubo fils defined *boudoirs* as "types of *arrière-cabinets*, in which one retires to remove oneself from a lot of people ..." [*L'Art de Menuisier* (1769–71), II:202]. But the *boudoir* was usually associated with women, and according to Roland Le Virloys, it was "where a woman retires to think, or to read, or to work, in a word, to be alone" [*Dictionnaire d'architecture, civile, militaire et navale* (Paris, 1770), quoted by Middleton in Le Camus de Mézières, *Genius of Architecture*, 190–1, n. 30]. In *L'Homme du monde éclairé par les arts* (1774), J.-F. Blondel and Jean-François Bastide apparently considered the *arrière cabinet* and *serre papier* to be the male counterparts to the *cabinet de toilette* and *boudoir* (II:39).
48. Mercier de Compiègne's *Manuel des boudoirs, ou Essais érotiques sur les Demoiselles d'Athènes* (1727) already associated the room with erotic activity. On Bastide, see Middleton, "Introduction," in Le Camus de Mézières, *Genius of Architecture*, 54–5; Cleary, "Romancing the Tome; or an Academician's Pursuit of Popular Audience in 18th-Century France," *JSAH* 48 (June 1989), 142–4; and Anthony Vidler, "Preface," and Rodolphe el-Khoury "Introduction," to Bastide, *The Little House: An Architectural Seduction* (Princeton, 1996).
49. Its furnishings, including a "garnishing" of porcelain, were valued at a relatively modest 509 *livres*, quite different from the 13,600 *livres* of furniture in the adjacent *salon* [AN, MC LXXXVII, 1138 (27-III-1772)].
50. Dangé's extramarital affairs appeared in police records (Durand, *Fermiers généraux*, 323); a song about visits to "la Dame Paris" appears in *Noms et origines des Messieurs les Fermiers Généraux ...*, BN, Ms. Fr. 14078, f°39, with related notes in *Mémoires pour servir à l'histoire du publicanisme*, BN, Ms. Fr. 10477, f°95. See Bachaumont et al., *Mémoires secrets*, where Dangé was labeled "this Tucaret" (X:62–3). Dangé's devotion to the noble pastime of gambling was the source of a joke circulating after his death – that one could now pass through the Place Vendôme "sans danger" (without danger) (ibid., X:75).
51. A room devoted to bathing was typically associated with the female realm; Blondel and Bastide still considered it so in 1774 (*L'Homme du monde*, II:39). However, unmarried tax farmer Ollivier de Montluçon had installed a small bathing suite in the *entresol* of no. 3 [AN, MC 618 (19-IV-1751)], and in the forties and fifties, Contant d'Ivry and Varin provided bathing rooms specifically for Thiers (see ch. 6). White textiles often appeared in bathing rooms and adjoining chambers; for example, in a *chambre des bains* at the Maison Crozat, white embroidered cotton, ornamented with lace, was used to line the walls and for bed hangings and door curtains [AN, MC VIII, 1024 (13-VI-1738)].
52. Among over seventy *cabinets d'histoire naturelle* that Thiery listed in 1785, he described at length only those of Philippe-Laurent Joubert, Treasurer General of the Estates of Languedoc, who purchased no. 9 from Dangé's heirs, and Receiver General for Châlons Jean-Baptiste-François Gigot d'Orcy, son of a *secrétaire du roi* involved in tax farming, installed at no. 26. "Few *cabinets* present themselves like this one, either by the beauty of locale or by the choice, arrangement and number of objects," Thiery said of Gigot's collections. "Three large rooms offer respectively the three kingdoms of Nature; a fourth is reserved for petrified material" [*Almanach du voyageur à Paris* (1785 ed.), 132–4].

53. Denise Ozanam, *Claude Baudard de Sainte-James: Trésorier général de la Marine, 1738–1787* (Geneva, 1969), 4–14.

54. Jean Stern, *A l'ombre de Sophie Arnould, François-Josèph Bélanger* (Paris, 1930), I:145; the "*Salon* decorated by M. Bellanger," appeared in the *État Actuel de Paris*, IV:117. The Crown sold the whole house for 347,000 *livres* in 1788 [AN, Z^{1a} 854 (18-III-1788)].

55. *Memoirs of Madame Elisabeth Louis Vigée-Le Brun, 1755–1789*, trans. Gerard Shelley (New York, n.d.), 186. See Charles Giraud's painting of this *salon* in 1886 (private collection), reproduced by Pons, *French Period Rooms*, 62–3.

56. Janzé, *Les Financiers d'autrefois*, 233.

57. *Dictionnaire critique, pittoresque et sentencieux*, quoted by Durand, *Fermiers généraux*, 528. Among those sons of financiers was Hénault, who moved to "a pretty house . . . on the rue Saint-Honoré," where, according to Luynes, "he freqently gives suppers, brings good cheer to a great number of friends, and lives with all who are the most eminent and the most likable of men and women" (*Mémoires*, V: 444–5). His renowned chef and table attracted court nobles, foreign dignitaries and men of letters (*Horace Walpole's Correspondence*, vols. 3 to 8, passim). See, too, Barbara Ketcham Wheaton, *Savoring the Past: The French Kitchen and Table from 1300 to 1789* (Philadelphia, 1983), 153.

58. AN, Z^{1j} 1171 (11-X-1787).

59. Julie-Augustine Thibault-Dubois was a daughter of the first *commis* of the Secretary of State for War; she wed Baudard in 1764 (Ozanam, *Baudard de Sainte-James*, 6).

60. AN, Z^{1j} 1171 (11-X-1787). In a *boudoir*, Le Camus de Mézières recommended lining the recess for a daybed or ottoman with mirrors and "carved tree trunks artfully arranged and leafed and painted to resemble nature" (*Genius of Architecture*, 116), close in conception to Bastide's fictional *boudoir*. Mme Baudard installed rose-colored textiles (red was too harsh, according to Le Camus de Mézières) in the curtains, a sofa, six armchairs, and a screen; she also installed a writing desk and fireplace sconces that were covered in arabesques, two white marble *girandoles*, small marble sculpture, and a small, expensive clock (*Procès verbal de scellé et inventaire . . . de M. Baudard de Ste-James*, Bibliothèque Marmottan, Rés. 03020).

61. In the bath, along with a copper tub and bidet, Mme Baudard kept a sofa and two armchairs upholstered in embroidered muslin (*Procès*, Biblio. Marm., Rés. 03020). Le Camus de Mézières sugggested that walls of a bathing room "might also be painted with trelliswork, so that in the bath one would see jasmine and honeysuckle all around" and that birdcages might be brought in "to dispel the ennui of the bath" (*Genius of Architecture*, 123–4).

62. AN, Z^{1j} 1171 (11-X-1787); Le Camus de Mézières also recommended canted corners with mirrored panels (and prints in simple frames) for *cabinets de toilette* (*Genius of Architecture*, 119–20).

63. In *L'Homme du monde* (1774), Blondel and Bastide still considered the *cabinet de toilette* part of a mistress's private apartment and did not mention that one might appear in the master's suite [II:39].

64. Dangé had a single *bureau* on the ground floor of no. 9.

65. *Procès*, Biblio. Marm., Rés. 03020.

66. On the Hocquart, see ch. 6, n. 39.

67. Formal gardens continued to be planted, especially in the Faubourg Saint-Germain [Monique Mosser, "The picturesque in the city: Private Gardens in Paris in the 18th Century," *Lotus International*, XXX (1982), 33].

68. Bachaumont et al., *Mémoires secrets*, XXXV:174–5.

69. Mme d'Oberkirch, for example, cited the "vast sums" Baudard spent on his houses as the cause of his ruin [*Mémoires sur la cour de Louis XVI et la sociéte française avant 1789* (Paris, 1853) II:273], but Baudard's dwellings were not a large enough element of his net worth to have caused his financial failure (Bosher, *French Finances*, 186).

70. Oberkirch, *Mémoires*, II:274.

71. Maurice Marquet (1683–1743) and his wife Marie-Anne Mercier, daughter of a bourgeois merchant in Bordeaux, had fourteen children; seven survived to adulthood, four of them sons. Each of the Marquet sons pursued a financial career.

72. Pâris Duverny, who loved "à la folie" the daughter he had with his Irish mistress, elicited the king's promise to place his son-in-law in the first open post (d'Argenson, *Mémoires*, III:293–4).

73. Cited in AN, Z^{1j} 926 (9-I-1769).

74. Bourgade also influenced Calonne, who wed his niece, Mont Saint-Père's daughter (Lüthy, *La banque protestante*, II:696–8; Bosher, *French Finances*, ch. 9; Bachaumont et al., *Mémoires secrets*, XVIII:238, 241).

75. Among twelve residents, the only woman was a *femme de charge* [AN, Y15091 (12-IV-1784)].

76. Bernard had an anteroom, a *salon* with furnishings (including four paintings) that were appraised at 1,540 *livres*, a *cabinet* (420 *livres*), a bedroom (188 *livres*), and a wardrobe [AN, MC LXV, 297 *bis* (17-IV-1784)].

77. AN, Y15091 (12-IV-1784).

78. He began acquiring the site shortly after his second marriage, to Catherine-Charlotte Gaulard, widow of two financiers [Durand, *Fermiers généraux*, 265, 476; DAAVP, *Le Faubourg Poissonnière: Architecture, élégance et décor* (Paris, 1986), 59, 62].

79. In 1779, Marquet de Peyre's house and parcel of 1,757 square *toises* were valued at 200,000 *livres* (Durand, *Fermiers généraux*, 476); in 1778, Joubert, Treasurer General of the Estates Languedoc, paid 300,000 *livres* for no. 9 Place Vendôme, on 483 square *toises* [Dumolin, "Place Vendôme," 40; Armand Brette, ed., *Atlas de la censive de l'archevêché dans Paris* (Paris, 1786; reprint, 1906), pl. XI].

80. *AR*, 1770.

81. Moreau later recalled that he had "discovered, at the corner of the Place Vendôme, on the side of the Capuchin convent, a house to lease, not far from his [Controller General of Finance Bertin's] house . . . [that seemed] marvelously suitable . . ." [*Mes Souvenirs* (Paris, 1898–1901), I:217].

82. Centralized *bureaux* had existed since the late seventeenth century, but a greater concentration began during the Seven Years War [Durand, *Fermiers généraux*, 54; Natacha Coquery, "Les hôtels parisiens du XVIIIe siècle: une approche des modes d'habiter," *Revue d'histoire moderne et contemporaine* XXXVIII (April–June 1991), 209–12].

83. AN, Y15369 (3-V-1764); MC II, 603 (14-V-1764)]. In the early fifties, he had devoted more space to *bureaux* [*Inventaire . . . Mme Hocquart*, AN, MC II, 534 (2-III-1752)].

84. As early as 1752, J.-B. Boucher, Treasurer General for French Colonies in America and receiver of the *capitation* tax, reserved considerable space at no. 23 for *bureaux*: one in the *entresol* and two more (one specifically for the *capitation*) on the second floor [AN, Y11769 (1-VIII-1752); MC CVII, 472 (7-VIII-1752)]. A decade later, Louis-Barthelemy Moufle de Georville, Treasurer General of the Navy and of the Order of Saint-Louis, installed the *bureaux* and *caisses* for those posts in three rooms on the second floor of no. 16 [AN, Y13390 (20-I-1764)].

85. They were Deville (no. 17) and Lavoisier's father-in-law Paulze (with his adjunct son, at no. 6) (*AR*, 1788).

86. The inscriptions are most conveniently found in Brice, *Description* (1752 ed.; reprint, 1971), 98–9.

87. Lüthy, *La banque protestante*, I:77, II:53.

88. *AR*, 1702, 1703. Rolland's brother-in-law Edme Pellé, a "bourgeois de Paris" active in finance, bought parcel no. 8 and commissioned a house from de Cotte in late 1690 [AN, MC CXVI, 92 (1 and 7-IX-1690)]; Pellé died in 1695, but the house remained in his family, and his son, Edme-Firmin, *conseiller au Châtelet*, resided at no. 1. Rolland's relation Solier (apparently his nephew Pierre), *agent de change*, resided at the square by 1703 (AR, 1704). Rolland and Cornette (who became Treasurer General of the *galères*) pursued strategies for advancement akin to those of financiers, each becoming a *secrétaire du roi* (as did Pierre Solier) [*Scellé . . . É.-P. Cornette*, AN, Y11070 (27-I-1755); F. de Saint Simon, *Place des Victoires*, 178, 288, 293, 296, 304; Favre-Lejeune, *SR*, 392, 1059, 1172, 1235; Marion, *Dictionnaire des institutions de la France*, 7].

89. *AR*, 1709, 1733, 1735, 1738, 1741, 1747, 1751, 1756, 1760, 1765, 1768, 1770, 1775, 1785. Baur remained until his death in 1770 [AN, MC XXIII, 709 (18-IX-1770)]; also operating from the square were *agents de change* Melchidor du Coulombier (in the fifties) and J. and L. Autran (during the seventies and eighties).

90. On Necker, see Lüthy, *La banque protestante*, II:ch. 4; Jean Egret, *Necker, Ministre de Louis XIV* (Paris, 1975); and Robert D. Harris, *Necker: Reform Statesman of the Ancien Régime* (Berkeley, 1979) and idem., *Necker and the Revolution of 1789* (Lanham, Md., 1986).

91. Bouchary, *Manieurs d'Argent*, III:111; see, too, Lüthy, *La banque protestante*, II: 300–14.

92. Cited in AN, MC XX, 767 (26 prairial, an III).

93. Mollet sublet a second-floor apartment (with a kitchen on the third story) from M. Sauvage, *grand audiencer* of France; Necker supervised Mollet's inventory [AN, MC L, 512 (I-1766)].

94. *AR*, 1775. He leased it from general tax farmer Nicolas Dedelay de la Garde, who also owned, and resided at, no. 7 (BN, Ms. Fr. 11671, f⁰ˢ189–234).

95. Cahouet de Villers, Treasurer General of the Maison du Roi and controller of wartime provisions, rented no. 14 in early 1774 and sublet it to Le Normand in 1777 [AN, MC XC, 468 (9-I-1776); MC LXXXVI, 797 (5-I-1778)]; see Bouchary, *Manieurs d'Argent*, II:115–21, III:256–8; Favre-Lejeune, *SR*, 865–6.

96. Berryer, *Souvenirs*, I:169–71.

97. See Lüthy, *La banque protestante*, II: ch. 4; Dumolin, "Place Vendôme," 34, 40, 50.

98. Magon apparently installed his *bureaux* in 1770 (*AR*, 1770), but the widow of François Beaumont, his former colleague at the tax farm, continued to occupy the dwelling until her death in 1772 [AN, Y10904 (29-I-1772)]; before her death, Magon does not seem to have resided in the house.

99. *Souvenirs*, I:167.

100. Ibid., I:173–4; see Marmontel, *Mémoires*, III: 328.

Conclusion

1. *Le Génie de l'Architecture ou l'analogie de cet art avec nos sensations* (Paris, 1780; reprint, Geneva, 1972), 85.

2. *Traité de la perspective*, 92.

3. *AF*, I:21.

4. See Bosher, "Chambres de Justice," 38–9.

5. See William Doyle, "Was There an Aristocratic Reaction in Pre-Revolutionary

France?" *Past and Present* 57 (1972), reprinted in D. Johnson, ed. *French Society and the Revolution* (Cambridge, 1976), 3–20.

6. It was a "baroque" space, in the sense that Jürgen Habermas has used that term in *The Structural Transformation of the Public Sphere*, trans. Thomas Burger (Cambridge, Mass., 1989), 10–11.

7. Boislisle, "Notices," 196, n. 7.

8. *Les Curiosités de Paris* . . . (Paris, 1771), 191; Robert M. Isherwood, *Farce and Fantasy: Popular Entertainment in Eighteenth-Century Paris* (Oxford, 1986), 131–2.

9. Boislisle, "Notices," 200, n. 3.

10. F. de Saint Simon, *Place Vendôme*, 82.

Contemporary Printed Sources

Aguesseau, Henri-François d'. "Discours sur la vie et la morte de M. d'Aguesseau, conseiller d'État; Par M. d'Aguesseau, Chancelier de France, son fils," *Oeuvres complètes du Chancelier d'Aguesseau*. Paris, 1819. XV:273–437.

Almanachs royaux (AR). Paris, 1699–1789.

Antonini, Annibale. *Mémorial de Paris et ses environs*. 2 vols. Paris, 1749.

Argenson, R. L. de Voyer, marquis d'. "Details sur l'Académie, ou club politique, connu sous le nom d'Entresol," *Lettres historiques, politiques, philosophiques et particulières de Henri Saint John Lord Vicomte Bolingbroke depuis 1710 jusqu'en 1736*. Paris, 1808. III: 451–8.

  Mémoires et journal inédit du marquis d'Argenson. Ed. C. R. d'Argenson. 5 vols. Paris, 1857–8.

Atlas des anciens plans de Paris. Ed. A. Alphand, L. Michaux, and L.-M. Tisserand. Paris, 1880.

Audiger. *La Maison réglée*. Paris, 1692. Reprinted by Alfred Franklin, *La Vie privée d'autrefois. La vie de Paris sous Louis XIV: Tenue de maison et domesticité*. Paris, 1898.

(Bachaumont, Louis Petit de.) *Mémoires secrets pour servir a l'histoire de la république des lettres en France depuis 1762 jusqu'à nos jours ou Journal d'un observateur*. 36 vols. London, 1780–9; reprint, Farnborough, 1970.

Barbier, Edmond. *Chronique de la Régence et du règne de Louis XV (1718–1763) ou Journal de Barbier, avocat au Parlement*. 8 vols. Paris, 1857.

Bastide, Jean-François. *La Petite Maison*. Paris, 1763; reprint, Paris, 1879. Translated with introduction by Rodolphe el-Khoury, preface by Anthony Vidler, as *The Little House: An Architectural Seduction*. Princeton, 1996.

Béat-Louis de Muralt. *Lettres dur les Anglais et les Français*. Reprint edition, Lausanne, 1972.

Bernstorffsche Papiere. Ausgewählte Briefe und Aufzeichnungen die Familie Bernstorff Betreffend aus der zeit 1732 bis 1835. 3 vols. Ed. Aage Friis. Copenhagen, 1904–13.

Berryer, Pierre-Nicolas. *Souvenirs de M. Berryer, doyen des avocats de Paris de 1774 à 1838*. 2 vols. Paris, 1839.

Blondel, Jacques-François. *Architecture française*. 4 vols. Paris, 1752–6; reprint, Paris, 1904.

  Cours d'architecture, ou traité de la décoration, distribution, & construction des Bâtiments contenant les leçons données en 1750, & les années suivantes. . . . 6 vols. Paris, 1771–7.

  De la distribution des maisons de plaisance, et de la décoration des édifices en général. 2 vols. Paris, 1737–8; reprint, Farnborough, 1967.

  Articles in *Encyclopédie ou Dictionnaire raisonné des sciences, des arts, et des métiers*. Paris, 1751–7, 1762.

Blondel, Jacques-François, and Jean-François Bastide. *L'Homme du monde éclairé par les arts*. Amsterdam, 1774; reprint, Geneva, 1973.

Boffrand, Germain. *Livre d'Architecture*. Paris, 1743; reprint, Farnborough, 1969.

Bois Jourdain, de. *Mélanges historiques, satiriques et anecdôtes de M. de B . . . Jourdain, écuyer de la grand écurie du roi (Louis XV); contenant des détails ou peu connus sur les événements et les premières années de celui de Louis XV, et de la Régence*. 3 vols. Paris, 1807.

Brette, Armand. *Atlas de la censive de l'archevêché dans Paris*. Reprint of 1786 ed., Paris, 1906.

Brice, Germain. *Description (nouvelle) de la ville de Paris*. Paris, 1685, 1694, 1698, 1701, 1706, 1713, 1717, 1725, 1752; reprint of 1752 ed., Geneva and Paris, 1971.

Briseux, Charles Étienne. *L'Art de bâtir des maisons de campagne où on trait de leur distribution, de leur construction, et de leur décoration . . .* Paris, 1761; reprint, Farnborough, 1966.

Buvat, Jean. *Journal de la Régence (1715–1723) par Jean Buvat écrivain de la Bibliothèque du Roi*. Ed. Émile Campardon. Paris, 1865.

Catalogue des livres de monsieur le président Crozat de Tugny. Paris, 1751.

Catalogue des tableaux, dessins, marbres, bronzes, terre cuites, pierres gravées, meubles précieux, lustres et autres objets de cristal de roche, porcelaines, laques, objets d'histoire naturelle &c du cabinet de M. * * * (Blondel d'Azincourt). Paris, 1783.

Catalogue des tableaux précieux, miniatures & gouaches; figures, bustes & vases de marbre & de bronze; armoires, commodes & effets précieux du célèbre Boule; un magnifique Lustre de crystal de roche . . . des porcelaines anciennes et modernes . . . qui composent le cabinet de feu M. Blondel de Gagny, trésorier-général de la caisse des amortissements. Paris, 1776.

Challes, Robert. *Mémoires de Robert Challes, écrivain du Roi*. Paris, 1931.

Chansonnier historique du XVIIIe siècle (Recueil Clairambault-Maurepas). Ed. Émile Raunié. 10 vols. Paris, 1879–84.

Cordemoy, J.-L. de. *Nouveau traité de toute l'architecture ou l'art de bastir; utile aux entrepreneurs et aux ouvriers*, 2nd. ed. Paris, 1714; reprint, Farnborough, 1966.

Correspondance administrative sous le règne de Louis XIV. Ed. Georges Bernard Depping. 4 Vols. Paris, 1850–5.

Courtin, Antoine de. *Nouveau Traité de la Civilité qui se pratique en France parmi les honnestes gens*. 6th ed., rev. Paris, 1682.

Courtonne, Jean. *Traité de la perspective pratique avec les remarques sur l'architecture*. Paris, 1725.

Créquy, marquise de. *Souvenirs de la marquise de Créquy de 1710 à 1803*. 5 vols. Paris, 1855.

Dancourt, Florent Carton. *Oeuvres choisies de Dancourt*. 5 vols. Paris, 1810.

Dangeau, marquis de. *Journal de marquis de Dangeau avec les additions inédits du duc de Saint-Simon*. Ed. E. Soulie and L. Dussieux. 19 vols. Paris, 1854–60.

(Darigrand.) *L'Anti-financier, ou relevé de quelques-unes des malversations dont se rendent journellement coupables les fermiers généraux, et des vexations qu'ils commettent dans les provinces*. Amsterdam, 1764.

Daviler, Augustin-Charles. *Cours d'architecture qui comprend les ordres de Vignole. . . .* 2 vols. Paris, 1691–3. Rev. eds. with supplements by Jean-Baptiste-Alexandre Le Blond, 1710; Pierre-Jean Mariette, 1738.

Deffand, Marie de Vichy-Chamrond, marquise du. *Correspondance complète de la marquise du Deffand avec la duchesse de Choiseul, l'abbé Barthélemy et M. Craufort*. Ed. M. le marquis de Sainte-Aulaire. 3 vols. Paris, 1867.

   Correspondance complète de la marquise du Deffand avec ses amis. Ed. M. de Lescure. 2 vols. Paris, 1865.

Delamare, Nicolas. *Traité de la police, où l'on trouvera l'histoire de son établissement, les fonctions et les prérogatives de ses magistrats, toutes les lois et les règlements qui la concernent.* 4 vols. Paris, 1705–38.

Dezallier d'Argenville, Antoine-Nicolas. *Voyage pittoresque de Paris.* Paris, 1765, 1778.

Dialogue ou entretien de Bourvalais & du Diable d'Argent enfermé dans son coffre-fort. N.p., n.d.

Dubois de Saint-Gelais. *Histoire journalière de Paris (1716–1717).* Paris, 1885.

Duclos, Charles Pinot. *Oeuvres de Duclos.* 3 vols. Paris, 1821.

Epinay, Louis Tardieu d'Esclavelles, marquise d'. *Mémoires et correspondance de Madame d'Epinay.* Ed. J.-P.-A. Parison. 3 vols. Paris, 1818.

Franklin, Alfred. *Les Anciens plans de Paris. Notices historiques et topographiques.* 2 vols. Paris, 1878–80.

   La Vie privée d'autrefois. La vie de Paris sous Louis XIV: Tenue de maison et domesticité. Paris, 1898.

Frémin, Michel de. *Mémoires critiques d'architecture.* Paris, 1702; reprint, Farnborough, 1967.

Gersaint, E. F. *Catalogue raisonné des bijoux, porcelaines, bronzes, lacqs, lustres de cristal de roche et de porcelaine, pendules du goût, & autres meubles curieux ou composés; tableaux, desseins, estampes, coquilles, & autres effets de curiosité & provenans de la succession de M. Angran, vicomte de Fonspertuis.* Paris, 1747.

Grimm, Friedrich-Melchior, et al. *Correspondance littéraire, philosophique, et critique.* Ed. Maurice Tourneux. 16 vols. Paris, 1877–82.

Hebert, (J.-A). *Dictionnaire pittoreque et historique.* 2 vols. Paris, 1766; reprint, Geneva, 1972.

Hénault, Charles-Jean-François. *Mémoires du Président Hénault.* Paris, 1911.

Hesseln, Robert de. *Dictionnaire universel de la France.* Paris, 1771.

Horace Walpole's Correspondence. Ed. W. S. Lewis. Vols. 3 to 8. New Haven, 1939.

Hurtaut, Pierre-Thomas-Nicolas and Magny. *Dictionnaire historique de la Ville de Paris et de ses environs.* 4 vols. Paris, 1779; reprint, Geneva, 1973.

Jaillot (Jean-Baptiste-Michel). *Recherches critiques historiques et topographiques sur la ville de Paris.* Paris, 1771–75.

Krafft, J. C., and N. Ransonette. *Plans, coupes, et élévations des plus belles maisons et hôtels construits à Paris et dans les environs.* Paris, 1800–2.

(Lacurne de Sainte-Palaye, J. B.) *Catalogue des Tableaux du cabinet de M. Crozat, Baron de Thiers.* Paris, 1755; reprinted with *Lettre a M. de B. (Bachaumont) sur le bon goût dans les arts et dans les lettres.* Geneva, 1972.

La Tournelle, Mme la Marquise de. "Essai sur la Vie de Mme la Comtesse de Chastel-lux" (1772) in *Lettres inédites du Chancelier d'Aguesseau.* Ed. D. B. Rives. Paris, 1823. I:1–64.

Laugier, Marc-Antoine. *Essai sur l'architecture.* Paris, 1753; reprint, 1979.

   Observations sur l'architecture. Paris, 1765; reprint, 1979.

Le Blond, Jean-Baptiste-Alexandre. Revisions to A.-C. Daviler, *Cours d'architecture qui comprend les ordres de Vignole. . . .* 2 vols. Paris, 1710.

Le Camus de Mézières, Nicolas. *Le Génie de l'Architecture ou l'analogie de cet art avec nos sensations.* Paris, 1780; reprint, Geneva, 1972.

   The Genius of Architecture; or, The Analogy of That Art with Our Sensations. Trans. David Britt. Introduction and notes by Robin Middleton. Santa Monica, 1992.

Lemonnier, Henry, ed. *Procès-verbaux de l'Académie royale d'architecture 1671–1793.* 5 vols. Paris, 1911–20.

Les Curiositez de Paris, de Versailles, de Marly, de Vincennes, de Saint Cloud et des environs. Paris, 1716, 1723, 1771.

206

Le Provincial à Paris ou État Actuel de Paris. 4 vols. Paris, 1787.

Les correspondants de la marquise de Balleroye. Ed. Édouard de Barthélemy. 2 vols. Paris, 1883.

Les relations artistiques entre la France et la Suède 1693–1718: Nicodème Tessin le jeune et Daniel Cronström Correspondance (extraits). Ed. R. A. Weigert and C. Hernmarck. Stockholm, 1964.

A Letter to a Member of the P--------t of G---t-B-----n, Occasion'd by the Privilege granted by the French King to Mr. Crozat. London, 1713; reprint, Boston, 1942.

Lister, Martin. *A Journey to Paris in the Year 1698.* Urbana, Ill., 1967.

Luynes, duc de. *Mémoires de Duc de Luynes sur la cour de Louis XV (1735–1758).* Ed. L. Dussieux and E. Soulié. 17 vols. Paris, 1860–5.

Maintenon, Madame de. *Lettres.* Ed. Marcel Langlois. 5 vols. Paris, 1939.

Marais, Mathieu. *Journal et Mémoires de Mathieu Marais, avocat au Parlement, sur la Régence et le règne de Louis XV (1715–1737).* Ed. M. de Lescure. 4 vols. Paris, 1863–8.

Mariette, Jean. *L'Architecture française.* 3 vols. Paris, 1727–38/39; reprint, Paris and Brussels, 1927–9.

Mariette, Pierre-Jean. *Abecedario et autres notes inédites de cet amateur sur les arts et les artistes. . . .* Eds. P. de Chennevières and A. de Montaiglon. 6 vols. Paris, 1853–62.

   Catalogue des tableaux et sculptures, Tant en Bronze qu'en Marbre, du Cabinet de feu M. le Président DE TUGNY, & de celui de M. CROZAT. Paris, 1751; reprinted in *Description de la Collection Crozat,* Geneva, 1973.

   Description sommaire des statues, figures, bustes, vases, et autres Morceaux de Sculpture . . . & des Modéles en terre cuite, Porcelaines & Fayences d'Urbin, provenans du Cabinet de feu M. CROZAT. Paris, 1750; reprinted in *Description de la Collection Crozat,* Geneva, 1973.

   Revisions to A.-C. Daviler, *Cours d'architecture qui comprend les ordres de Vignole. . . .* 2 vols. Paris, 1738.

Marmontel, Jean-François. *Mémoires de Marmontel.* Ed. Maurice Tourneux. 3 vols. Paris, 1891.

Maurepas, Jean-Frédéric Phélypeaux, comte de. *Mémoires du comte de Maurepas.* Paris, 1792.

Médailles sur la Régence; avec les tableaux symboliques du sieur Paul Poisson de Bourvalais, 1er maltôtier de Royaume, & le songe funeste de sa femme. Paris, 1716.

Mercier, Sébastien. *Tableau de Paris.* 12 vols. Amsterdam, 1782–8.

Molière. *Le Bourgeois gentilhomme.* Paris, 1670.

Muralt, Béat-Louis de. *Lettres sur les Anglais et les Français.* Postscript by Perrette Chappuis. Reprint ed., Lausanne, 1972.

Nouvelle ecole publique des finances ou l'art de voler sans aîles. 2nd ed. Paris, 1708.

Oberkirch, baronne d'. *Mémoires sur la cour de Louis XVI et la société avant 1789.* 2 vols. Paris, 1853.

Palatine, Elizabeth-Charlotte of Bavaria. *Correspondance complète de Madame duchesse d'Orléans née princesse Palatine, mère du Régent.* Trans. M. G. Brunet. 2 vols. Paris, 1869.

Les Partisans demasquez. Nouvelle Galante. Cologne, 1707.

Piganiol de la Force, Jean-Aymar. *Description historique de la Ville de Paris et de ses environs.* Paris, 1742, 1765.

   Nouvelle description de la France, Vol. 2. Paris, 1722.

Pluton Maltôtier, nouvelle galante. Cologne, 1708.

Recueil de Maurepas: chansons, épigrammes et autres vers satiriques sur divers personnages des siècles de Louis XIV et Louis XV. Paris, 1865.

Remy, P. *Catalogue des estampes, vases de poterie etrusques, figures, bas-reliefs & bustes de bronze, marbre & de terre cuite, ouvrages en marqueterie du célèbre Boule père, pieces de méchaniques, & autres objets curieux du cabinet de feu M. Crozat, Baron de Thiers. . . .* Paris, 1772.

    Catalogue raisonné des tableaux, porcelaines, bijoux et autres effets du Cabinet de feu M. Gaillard de Gagny, receveur général des finances de Grenoble. Paris, 1762.

Richelieu, maréchal de. *Nouveaux mémoires du maréchal duc de Richelieu.* Ed. M. de Lescure. Paris, 1869.

Restif de La Bretonne, Nicolas-Edme. *My Revolution: Promenades in Paris 1789–1794.* Trans. Alex Karmel. New York, 1970.

Roubo fils. *L'Art de Menuisier.* 4 vols. Paris, 1769–71; reprint, Paris, 1976.

Rousseau, Jean-Jacques. *Confessions.* Trans. J. M. Cohen. Harmondsworth, 1953.

Saint-Simon, Louis de Rouvroy duc de. *Mémoires de Saint-Simon.* Ed. Arthur de Bois-lisle. 36 vols. Paris, 1879–1928.

Savot, Louis. *L'Architecture française des bastimens particuliers.* Paris, 1624.

Savot, Louis, and François Blondel. *L'Architecture française des bâtiments particuliers,* reedition with supplement. Paris, 1685; reprint ed., Geneva, 1973.

Sourches, marquis de. *Mémoires du marquis de Sourches sur le règne de Louis XIV.* 14 vols. Ed. Arthur de Bertrand and Gabriel Jules de Cosnac. Paris, 1882–1912.

Thiery, Luc-Vincent. *Almanach du voyageur à Paris.* Paris, 1785.

Thrale, Hester Lynch, and Samuel Johnson. *The French Journals of Mrs. Thrale and Dr. Johnson.* Ed. Moses Tyson and Henry Guppy. Manchester, 1932.

Tiercelet. *Architecture moderne, ou l'art de bien bâtir pour toutes sortes de personnes. . . .* 2 vols. Paris, 1728.

Les Tours industrieux, subtils et gaillards de la maltôte. Nouvelles galantes. Paris, 1708.

Vigée-Lebrun, Mme. *Memoirs of Madame Elisabeth Louise Vigée-Le Brun, 1755–1789.* Trans. Gerard Shelley. New York, n.d. (1944?).

Villeneuve-Guibert, Gaston de, ed. *Le Portefeuille de Madame Dupin.* Paris, 1884.

Secondary Literature

AAVP. *De la place royale à la place des Vosges.* Paris, 1996.

Adams, Julia P. "One's Company, Three's a Crowd: Metropolitan State Building and East Indies Companies in the Early Modern Netherlands, France and England, 1600–1800." Ph.D. dissertation, University of Wisconsin–Madison, 1990.

Antoine, Michel. *Le Gouvernement et Administration sous Louis XV: Dictionnaire biographique.* Paris, 1978.

Ariès, Philippe. *Centuries of Childhood: A Social History of Family Life.* Trans. Robert Baldick. New York, 1962.

Babelon, Jean-Pierre. *Demeures parisiennes sous Henri IV et Louis XIII,* rev. ed. Paris, 1991.

    "Du 'Grand Ferrare' à Carnavalet: Naissance de l'hôtel classique," *Revue de l'art,* 40/41 (1978), 83–108.

    "Le passage du corps d'hôtel simple au corps d'hôtel double," *XVIIe Siècle* 162 (January – March 1989), 7–16.

Bailey, Colin B. "Aspects of Patronage and Collecting of French Painting in France at the End of the *Ancien Régime,*" Ph.D. dissertation, Oxford University, 1985.

    "Conventions of the Eighteenth-Century *Cabinet de tableaux*: Blondel d'Azincourt's *La première idée de la curiosité,*" *Art Bulletin* LXIX:3 (September 1987), 431–47.

    "Introduction," *Ange-Laurent de La Live de Jully. A Facsimile Reprint of the Catalogue Historique (1764) and the Catalogue Raisonné des Tableaux (March 5, 1770).* Reprint ed., New York, 1988.

Bailey, Colin B., et al. *Loves of the Gods: Mythological Painting From Watteau to David*. New York, 1992.

Baillie, Hugh M. "Etiquette and the Planning of the State Apartments in Baroque Palaces," *Archaeologia* 101 (1967), 169–99.

Baker, Keith M. *Inventing the French Revolution: Essays on French Political Culture in the Eighteenth Century*. Cambridge and New York, 1990.

Ballon, Hilary. *The Paris of Henri IV: Architecture and Urbanism*. Cambridge, Mass., 1991.

Ballot, Marie-Juliette. *Le Décor intérieur au XVIIIe siècle*. Paris, 1930.

Bauchart, Ernest Quentin. *Les Femmes bibliophiles de France (XVIe, XVIIe & XVIIIe siècles)*. 2 vols. Paris, 1886.

Bayard, Françoise. "Manière d'habiter des financiers de la première moitié du XVIIe siècle," *XVIIe Siècle* 162 (January–March 1989), 53–66.
    Le Monde des financiers au XVIIe siècle. Paris, 1987.

Beik, William. *Absolutism and Society in Seventeenth-Century France: State Power and Provincial Aristocracy in Languedoc*. Cambridge, 1985.

Benhamou, Reed. "Parallel Walls, Parallel Worlds: The Places of Masters and Servants in the *Maisons de plaisance* of Jacques-François Blondel," *Journal of Design History*, VII:1 (1994), 1–11.

Bertin, Jean-François. *Les mariages dans l'ancienne société française*. Paris, 1879.

Bien, David. "Manufacturing Nobles: The Chancelleries of France to 1789," *Journal of Modern History*, 61 (September 1989), 445–86.
    "Offices, Corps, and a System of State Credit: The Uses of Privilege under the Ancien Régime," in *The French Revolution and the Creation of Modern Political Culture*. Ed. Keith Baker. I:89–114. Oxford, 1987.
    "The *Secrétaires du Roi*: Absolutism, Corps, and Privilege under the Ancien Régime," in *Vom Ancien Régime zur Französischen Revolution*. Ed. Ernst Hinrichs et al. Gottingen, 1978.

Bier, Erich. *Från Ludvig XIV:s Paris—Pierre Bullets originalritningar i Nationalmuseum*. Stockholm, 1945.

Blanc, Charles. *Le Trésor de la curiosité*. 2 vols. Paris, 1857–8.

Bluche, François. *Les magistrats de la Cour des monnaies de Paris au XVIIIe siècle (1715–1790)*. Paris, 1966.
    L'Origine des magistrats du Parlement de Paris au XVIIIe siècle. Mémoires de la fédération des sociétés historiques et archéologiques de Paris et de l'Ile-de-France. V–VI (1953–4). Paris, 1956.
    Les magistrats du Parlement de Paris au XVIIIe siècle, 2nd ed. Paris, 1986.
    "The Social Origins of the Secretaries of State under Louis XIV, 1661–1715," in *Louis XIV and Absolutism*, pp. 85–97. Ed. Ragnhild Hatton. London, 1976.
    La vie quotidienne au temps de Louis XVI. Paris, 1980.
    La vie quotidienne de la noblesse française au XVIIIe siècle. Paris, 1973.

Boislisle, Arthur (de). "Notices historiques sur la place des Victoires et sur la place de Vendôme," *Mémoires de la Société de l'histoire de Paris et l'Ile-de-France*, 15 (1888), 1–272.

Boisnard, Luc. *Les Phélypeaux: une famille de ministres sous l'Ancien Régime: essai de généalogie critique*. Paris, 1986.

Bonfait, Olivier. "Les Collections picturales des financiers à la fin du règne de Louis XIV," *XVIIe Siècle* (April – June 1986), 125–51.
    "Les Collections des parlementaires parisiens du XVIIIe siècle," *Revue de l'art*, 73 (1986), 28–42.

Bonin, Hubert. *La banque et les banquiers en France du Moyen Age à nos jours*. Paris, 1992.

Bordeaux, Jean-Luc. "François Le Moyne et la décoration de l' hôtel Peyrenc de Moras (Musée Rodin)," *GBA*, 77 (February 1971), 65–76.

Bosher, J. F. " 'Chambres de Justice' in the French Monarchy," in his *French Government and Society 1500–1850: Essays in Memory of Alfred Cobban*. Ed. J. F. Bosher London, 1973.

    French Finances 1770–1795: From Business to Bureaucracy. Cambridge, 1970.

Bouchary, Jean. *Les Manieurs d'Argent à Paris à la fin du XVIIIe siècle*. 3 vols. Paris, 1939–43.

Bourdieu, Pierre. *Distinction. A Social Critique of the Judgement of Taste*. Trans. Richard Nice. Cambridge, Mass., 1984.

Bouvier, J., and H. Germain-Martin. *Finances et financiers sous l'ancien régime*. Paris, 1969.

Braham, Allan. *The Architecture of the French Enlightenment*. Berkeley and Los Angeles, 1980.

Braham, Allan, and Peter Smith. *François Mansart*. 2 vols. London, 1973.

Brejon de Lavergnée, Arnauld. "Plaidoyer pour un peintre 'de pratique': le séjour de Paolo de Matteis en France," *Revue de l'art*, LXXXVIII (1990), 70–79.

Broglie, Dominique de. *Les Broglie: leur histoire*. Paris, 1972.

Butler, Rohan. *Choiseul I: Father and Son*. Oxford, 1980.

Caisse Nationale des Monuments Historiques. *Jardins en France, 1760–1820*. Paris, 1978.

Caix de Saint-Aymour, Amédé. *Les Boullongne: une famille d'artistes et de financiers aux XVIIe et XVIIIe siècles*. Paris, 1919.

Campbell, Colin. "Understanding Traditional and Modern Patterns of Consumption in Eighteenth-Century England: A Character-Action Approach," *Consumption and the World of Goods*, 40–57. Ed. John Brewer and Roy Porter. London and New York, 1993.

Catheu, Françoise de. "Le Développement du faubourg Saint-Germain du XVIe au XVIIIe siècle," *BSHPIF*, LXXXVII–LXVIII (1955-6), 21–39.

Centre Culturel Suédois. *Le Marais, Place Vendôme, Les Invalides: Dessins d'architecture des XVIIe et XVIIIe siècles provenant des collections du Nationalmuseum de Stockholm*. Paris, 1972.

Champeaux, Alfred de. *L'art décoratif dans le vieux Paris*. Paris, 1898.

Chartier, Roger, ed. *Passions of the Renaissance*. Trans. Arthur Goldhammer. Ed. Philippe Ariès and Georges Duby. Cambridge, Mass., and London, 1989.

Chastel, André. "Les Vestiges de l'hôtel Le Gendre et le véritable hôtel de la Trémoïlle," *Bulletin Monumental*, CXXIV (1966), 129–65.

Chaussinand-Nogaret, Guy. *Les financiers de Languedoc au XVIIIe siècle*. Paris, 1970.

    Gens de finance au XVIIIe siècle. Paris, 1972.

    Histoire des élites en France du XVIe siècle au XXe siècle. Paris, 1991.

    La noblesse au XVIIIe siècle: de la féodalité aux lumières. Paris, 1976.

    La vie quotidienne des Français sous Louis XV. Paris, 1979.

Chéruel, Adolphe. *Histoire de l'administration monarchique en France depuis l'avénement de Philippe-Auguste jusqu'à la mort de Louis XIV*. Vol. 2. Paris, 1855.

Ciprut, Edouard-Jacques. "Ancienne Église du Couvent des Capucines de la Place Vendôme," *BSHAF* (1956), 259–69.

Cleary, Richard. "The Places Royales of Louis XIV and Louis XV," Ph.D. dissertation, Columbia University, 1986.

    "Romancing the Tome; or an Academician's Pursuit of a Popular Audience in 18th-Century France," *JSAH*, XLVIII (June 1989), 139–49.

Clermont-Tonnerre, E. de. *Histoire de Samuel Bernard et ses enfants*. Paris, 1914.

Coquery, Natacha. "Les hôtels parisiens du XVIIIe siècle: une approche des modes d'habiter," *Revue d'histoire moderne et contemporaine*, 38 (April–June 1991), 205–30.

Craveri, Benedetta. *Madame du Deffand and Her World*. Trans. Teresa Waugh. Boston, 1994.

Crousaz-Crétet, P. de. *Paris sous Louis XIV*. Vol. 1. Paris, 1923.

Crow, Thomas E. *Painters and Public Life in Eighteenth-Century Paris*. New Haven and London, 1985.

Darrow, Margaret H. *Revolution in the House: Family, Class, and Inheritance in Southern France, 1775–1825*. Princeton, 1989.

DAAVP. *Le Faubourg Poissonnière: Architecture, élégance et décor*. Paris, 1986.

  La Place des Victoires et ses abords. Paris, 1983.

  Le Quai Voltaire: études offertes à Colette Lamy-Lasalle. Ed. Bruno Pons and Anne Forray-Carlier. Paris, 1990.

  La rue du Bac: Le faubourg Saint Germain. Paris, 1990.

  La rue de Grenelle. Paris, 1980.

  La rue de Lille. Paris, 1985.

  La rue de l'Université. Paris, 1987.

  La rue Saint-Dominique: hôtels et amateurs. Paris, 1984.

  La rue de Varenne. Paris, 1984.

Dennis, Michael. *Court and Garden: From the French Hôtel to the City of Modern Architecture*. Cambridge, Mass., 1986.

Dent, Julian. *Crisis in Finance: Crown, Financiers and Society in Seventeenth-Century France*. Newton Abbot, 1973.

Desazars de Montgailhard, Marie-Louis baron de. *La Famille Crozat*. Toulouse, 1907.

Dessert, Daniel. *Argent, pouvoir et société au Grand Siècle*. Paris, 1984.

Dimier, Louis, *Les peintres français du XVIIIe siècle: histoire des vies et catalogue des ouvrages*. 2 vols. Paris and Brussels, 1928.

Doyle William. *Origins of the French Revolution*, 2nd ed. New York, 1988.

  Venality: The Sale of Offices in Eighteenth-Century France. Oxford, 1996.

  "Was There an Aristocratic Reaction in Pre-Revolutionary France?" *Past and Present*, 57 (1972), reprinted in *French Society and the Revolution* Ed. D. Johnson (Cambridge, 1976), 3–20.

Ducros, Louis. *French Society in the Eighteenth Century*. Trans. W. de Geijer. London, 1926.

Dulong, Claude. *La vie quotidienne des femmes au Grand Siècle*. Paris, 1984.

Dumas, Maurice. *Les cabinets de physique au XVIIIe siècle*. Paris, 1951.

Dumolin, Maurice. "La Place Vendôme," *Procès verbaux de la Commission du Vieux Paris*, mars 1927 (Paris, 1931), 3–52.

  "Les Propriétaires de la place Royale (1605–1789)," *La Cité*, 95–6 (July–October 1925), 273–316; 97–8 (April 1926), 1–30.

Durand, Yves. *Les Fermiers généraux au XVIIIe siècle*. Paris, 1971.

Egret, Jean. *Necker, Ministre de Louis XIV*. Paris, 1975.

Elias, Norbert. *The Civilizing Process*. Trans. Edmund Jephcott. New York, 1978.

  The Court Society. Trans. E. Jephcott. New York, 1984.

Etlin, Richard. "*Les dedans*: Jacques-François Blondel and the System of the Home, c. 1740," *GBA*, XCI (April 1978), 137–47.

  Symbolic Space: French Enlightenment Architecture and Its Legacy. Chicago and London, 1994.

Fairchilds, Cissi. *Domestic Enemies. Servants and their Masters in Old Regime France*. Baltimore, 1984.

Faure, Edgar. *La banqueroute de Law*. Paris, 1977.

Favre-Lejeune, Christine. *Les Secrétaires du roi de la grande chancellerie de France: Dictionnaire biographique et généalogique (1672–1789)*. 2 vols. Paris, 1986.

Féral, E. *Notice sur un très beau salon décoré par Lancret dont la vente aura lieu à Paris . . . le . . . 27 Mai 1896*. Paris, 1896.

Flandrin, Jean-Louis. *Families in former times: Kinship, household and sexuality*. Trans. Richard Southern. Cambridge, 1979.

Ford, Franklin. *Robe and Sword: The Regrouping of the French Aristocracy after Louis XIV*. Cambridge, Mass., 1953.

Forster, Robert. *The House of Saulx-Tavanes: Versailles and Burgundy 1700–1830*. Baltimore and London, 1971.

   The Nobility of Toulouse in the Eighteenth Century: A Social and Economic Study. Baltimore, 1960.

Fossier, François. *Les dessins du fonds Robert de Cotte de la Bibliothèque nationale de France*. Paris, 1997.

Frostin, Charles. "La famille ministérielle des Phélypeaux: esquisse d'un profil Pontchartrain (XVIe–XVIIIe siècle)," *Annales de Bretagne et des pays de l'ouest*, 86 (1979), 117–40.

   "Pouvoir ministériel, 'voies ordinaires de la justice' et 'voies de l'autorité' sous Louis XIV: Le Chancelier Louis de Pontchartrain et le Secrétaire d'État Jérôme de Pontchartrain (1699–1715)," in *107e Congrès National des Sociétés Savantes: Histoire Moderne et Contemporaine*. I:7–29. Brest, 1982.

Gallet, Michel. *Claude-Nicolas Ledoux, 1736–1806*. Paris, 1980.

   Les architectes parisiens du XVIIIe siècle: Dictionnaire biographique et critique. Paris, 1995.

   Stately Mansions: Eighteenth Century Paris Architecture. Trans. James C. Palmes. New York, 1972.

Gallet, Michel, and Yves Bottineau, eds. *Les Gabriels*. Paris, 1982.

Gallet, Michel, and Jörg Garms, eds. *Germain Boffrand 1667–1754: L'Aventure d'un architecte independant*. Paris, 1986.

Gibson, Wendy. *Women in Seventeenth-Century France*. New York, 1989.

Giraud, Marcel. *Histoire de la Louisiane française*. 4 vols. Paris, 1953–74.

Goncourt, Edmond, and Goncourt, Jules de. *The Woman of the Eighteenth Century*. Trans. Jacques Le Clercq and Ralph Roeder. London, 1928; reprint, Westport, Conn., 1981.

Goodman, Dena. "Enlightenment Salons: The Convergence of Female and Philosophic Ambitions," *Eighteenth Century Studies*, 22:3 (Spring 1989), 329–50.

   "Public Sphere and Private Life: Toward a Synthesis of Current Historiographical Approaches to the Old Regime," *History and Theory*, 31 (1992), 1–20.

   The Republic of Letters: A Cultural History of the French Enlightenment. Ithaca and London, 1994.

Gordon, Daniel. *Citizens Without Sovereignty: Equality and Sociability in French Thought, 1670–1789*. Princeton, 1994.

Goubert, Pierre. *The Ancien Régime: French society 1600–1750*. Trans. Steve Cox. New York, 1974.

Grasselli, Margaret Morgan, and Pierre Rosenberg. *Watteau 1684–1721*. Washington, D.C., 1984.

Gruder, Vivian R. *The Royal Provincial Intendants: A Governing Elite in Eighteenth-Century France*. Ithaca, N.Y., 1968.

Gutton, J.-P. *Domestiques et Serviteurs dans la France de l'Ancien Régime*. Paris, 1981.

Habermas, Jürgen. *The Structural Transformation of the Public Sphere*. Trans. Thomas Burger. Cambridge, Mass., 1989.

Harrington, Kevin. *Changing Ideals on Architecture in the Encyclopédie, 1750–1776*. Ann Arbor, Mich., 1985.

Harris, Robert D. *Necker. Reform Statesman of the Ancien Régime.* Berkeley, 1979. *Necker and the Revolution of 1789.* Lanham, Md. 1986.

Harsin, Paul. *Crédit public et Banque d'Etat en France du XVIe au XVIIIe siècle.* Paris, 1933.

Haskell, Frances. *Patrons and Painters: A Study in the Relations between Italian Art and Society in the Age of the Baroque,* 2nd, ed., rev. New Haven and London, 1980.

Hautecoeur, Louis. *Histoire de l'architecture classique en France.* 4 vols. Paris, 1943–57.

Hénard, Robert. *La rue Saint-Honoré.* 2 vols. Paris, 1908–9.

Herrmann, Wolfgang. "The Author of the 'Architecture Moderne' of 1728," *JSAH,* XVIII (1959), 60–2.

Hillairet, Jacques. *La rue de Richelieu.* Paris, 1966.

Himelfarb, Hélène. "Regards versaillais sur l'hôtel parisien: le silence des chroniqueurs et épistoliers de cour à la fin du règne de Louis XIV (1700–1715)," *XVIIe Siècle,* 162 (January–March 1989), 85–100.

Huppert, George. *Les Bourgeois Gentilhommes.* Chicago and London, 1977.

Iberville-Moreau, José-Luc d'. "Robert de Cotte: His Career as an Architect and the Organisation of the Service des Bâtiments," Ph.D. dissertation, University of London, 1972.

Isherwood, Robert M. *Farce and Fantasy: Popular Entertainment in Eighteenth-Century Paris.* Oxford, 1986.

Jal, Adolphe. *Dictionnaire critique de biographie et d'histoire.* 2 vols. Paris, 1872; reprint, Geneva, 1970.

Janet, Paul. "Une Académie politique sous le cardinal de Fleury de 1724 à 1731," *Séances et Travaux de l'Académie des sciences morales et politiques,* 5e série, IV (1865), 107–26.

Janzé, Alix de (Choiseul-Gouffier), vicomtesse de. *Les financiers d'autrefois. Fermiers généraux.* Paris, 1886.

Joudiou, Gabrielle. "Un architecte Parisien de 'bon goût': Contant d'Ivry," *BSHPIF,* 115 (1989), 81–106.

"Deux Réalisations de Pierre Contant d'Ivry à Paris et en Ile-de-France: les hôtels Crozat, place Vendôme" (1743–1747); le château de Chamarande et son parc (1739–1742), *BSHPIF,* 112 (1985), 115–33.

"Pierre Contant d'Ivry," in DAAVP, *Chevotet-Contant-Chaussard: un cabinet d'architectes au siècle des lumières,* Eds. Jean-Louis Baritou and Dominique Foussard, pp. 86–182. Lyon, 1987.

Kalnein, Wend von. *Architecture in France in the Eighteenth Century.* New Haven and London, 1995.

Kaplan, Marion A., ed. *The Marriage Bargain: Women and Dowries in European History.* New York, 1985.

Kaufmann, Emile. "The Contribution of Jacques-François Blondel to Mariette's *Architecture Françoise,*" *Art Bulletin,* XXXI (1949), 58–9.

Kimball, Fiske. *The Creation of the Rococo.* Philadelphia, 1943. *Le style Louis XIV: Origines et évolution du Rococo.* Paris, 1950.

Koselleck, Reinhart. *Critique and Crisis. Enlightenment and the Pathogenesis of Modern Society.* Oxford, New York, and Hamburg, 1988.

Kramick, Isaac. *Bolingbroke and his Circle: the Politics of nostalgia in the age of Walpole.* Cambridge, Mass., 1968.

Kretzschmar, Frank Joachim. *Pierre Contant d'Ivry: Ein Beitrag zur französischen Architektur des 18. Jahrhunderts,* Ph.D. dissertation, University of Cologne, 1981.

La Monneraye, Jean de. *Terrier de la censive d l'Archevêché dans Paris 1772,* Vol 2, 2nd ed. Paris, 1981.

Landes, Joan. *Women and the Public Sphere in the Age of the French Enlightenment.* Ithaca, N.Y., 1988.

Langenskiöld, Eric. *Pierre Bullet, the Royal Architect.* Stockholm, 1959.

Lanier, L. "Le Club de l'Entresol (1723–1731)," *Mémoires de l'Académie des Sciences, des Lettres et des Arts d'Amiens*, 3e série, VI (1880), 1–56.

Lavedan, Pierre. *Nouvelle Histoire de Paris.* Paris, 1975.

Lavisse, Ernest, et al. *Histoire de France illustrée depuis les origines jusqu'à la Révolution.* Vols. 6 to 8. Paris, 1900–11; reprint, New York, 1969.

Lebrun, François. *La Vie conjugale sous l'ancien régime.* Paris, 1975.

Leclercq, Dom H. *Histoire de la Régence pendant la minorité de Louis XV.* Paris, 1921–2.

Legohérel, Henri. *Les trésoriers généraux de la Marine, 1517–1788.* Paris, 1965.

Le Moël, Michel. "Archives architecturales parisiennes en Suède," in *L'Urbanisme de Paris et l'Europe 1600–1680*, 105–92. Ed. Pierre Francastel. Paris, 1969.

Lescure, M. de. *Les Maîtresses du Régent: études d'histoire et de moeurs.* Paris, 1861.

Lévy, C. F. *Capitalistes et Pouvoir au Siècle des lumières.* 3 vols. Paris-La Haye, 1969–1980.

Lilley, Ed. "The Name of the Boudoir," *JSAH*, LIII:2 (June 1994), 193–8.

Lion, Henri. *Le Président Hénault.* Paris, 1903.

Lordat, marquis de. *Les Peyrenc de Moras 1685–1798: Une famille cévenole au service de la France.* Toulouse, 1959.

Lougee, Carolyn. *Le Paradis des Femmes: Women, Salons and Social Stratification in Seventeenth-Century France.* Princeton, 1976.

Lucas, Colin. "Nobles, Bourgeois and the Origins of the French Revolution," *Past and Present*, 60 (August 1973), 84–126.

Ludmann, Jean-Daniel, and Bruno Pons. "Nouveaux documents sur la galerie de l'hôtel de Toulouse," *BSHAF* (1979), 115–28.

Lunsingh Scheurleer, Theo H. "Deux projets pour l'Hôtel de Thiers attribués à Contant d'Ivry," *BSHAF* (1934), 291–8.

Lüthy, Herbert. *La banque protestante en France de la révocation de l'édit de Nantes à la Révolution.* 2 vols. Paris, 1959–61.

Malros, Martin de. *Généologie de la famille Hocquart.* Auxerre, 1958.

Mandrou, Robert. *Louis XIV en son temps 1661–1715.* Paris, 1978.

Marion, J. "Molière a-t-il songé à Colbert encomposant le personnage de M. Jourdain?" *Revue d'Histoire Littéraire de la France*, 45 (1938), 145–80.

Marion, Marcel. *Dictionnaire des institutions de la France aux XVIIe et XVIIIe siècles.* Paris, 1923; reprint, New York, 1968.

  Histoire financière de la France depuis 1715, vol. I (1715–89). Paris, 1914; reprint, New York, 1965.

Marion, Michel. *Recherches sur les bibliothèques privées à Paris au milieu du XVIIIe siècle (1750–1759).* Paris, 1978.

Matthews, George T. *The Royal General Farms in Eighteenth-Century France.* New York, 1958.

Mauban, A. *L'Architecture française de Jean Mariette.* Paris, 1945.

Maza, Sarah. *Private Lives and Public Affairs: The Causes Célèbres of Prerevolutionary France.* Berkeley: 1993.

  Servants and Masters in Eighteenth-Century France. Princeton, 1983.

McQuaide, Rosalie. "The Crozat Concerts, 1720–1727," Ph.D. dissertation, New York University, 1978.

Meyer, Hélène. "La collection de Louis-Antoine Crozat, baron de Thiers," in *L'Age d'or flamand et hollandais: Collections de Catherine II, Musée de l'Ermitage* 49–56. Dijon, 1993.

Meyer, Jean. *Le Régent.* Paris, 1985.

La vie quotidienne en France au temps de la Régence. Paris, 1979.

Michaud, Claude. *L'Église et l'argent sous l'ancien régime: Les receveurs généraux du clergé de France aux XVIe et XVIIe siècles*. Paris, 1991.

Middleton, Robin. "The Abbé de Cordemoy and the Graeco-Gothic Ideal: A Prelude to Romantic Classicism," *Journal of the Warburg and Courthauld Institutes*, XXV (1962), 278–320; XXVI (1963), 90–123.

"Introduction" and notes to Nicolas Le Camus de Mézières, *The Genius of Architecture; or, The Analogy of That Art with Our Sensations*. Santa Monica, 1992.

Mignot, Claude. "De la cuisine à la salle à manger, ou de quelques détours de l'art de la distribution," *XVIIe Siècle*, 162 (January–March 1989), 17–36.

Moriarity, Michael. *Taste and Ideology in Seventeenth-Century France*. Cambridge, 1988.

Mosser, Monique. "The Picturesque in the City: Private Gardens in Paris in the 18th Century," *Lotus International*, XXX (1982), 29–35.

Mousnier, Roland. *The Institutions of France under the Absolute Monarchy*. Trans. Arthur Goldhammer. 2 vols. Chicago, 1979–84.

Neuman, Robert. "French Domestic Architecture in the Early 18th Century: The Town Houses of Robert de Cotte," *JSAH*, XXXIX (1980), 128–44.

Robert de Cotte and the Perfection of Architecture in Eighteenth-Century France. Chicago and London, 1994.

Normandy, Georges, and Fernand Mitton. *Quatre Maîtresses du Régent*. Paris, 1911.

Ozanam, Denise. *Claude Baudard de Sainte-James: Trésorier général de la Marine, 1738–1787*. Geneva, 1969.

Pardailhé-Galabrun, Annik. *La Naissance de l'intimité: 3000 foyers parisiens, XVIIe-XVIIIe siècles*. Paris, 1988. Trans. by Jocelyn Phelps as *Birth of Intimacy: Privacy and Domestic Life in Early Modern Paris*. Philadelphia, 1991.

Picard, Roger. *Les Salons littéraires et la société française, 1610–1789*. New York, 1943.

Pinon, Pierre. "Lotissements spéculatifs, formes urbaines et l'architecture à la fin de l'Ancien Régime," in *Soufflot et l'Architecture de Lumières*, Eds. Monique Mosser and Daniel Rabreau pp. 178–91. Paris, 1980.

Poëte, Marcel. *Une Vie de cité: Paris de sa naissance à nos jours*. 3 vols. Paris, 1931.

Pomian, Krzysztof. *Collectors and Curiosities: Paris and Venice, 1500–1800*. Trans. Elizabeth Wiles-Portier. Cambridge, 1990.

Pons, Bruno. "Les boiseries de l'Hôtel Cressart – 18 place Vendôme au J. Paul Getty Museum," *The J. Paul Getty Museum Journal* (1983) II: 67–88.

De Paris à Versailles 1699–1736: Les sculpteurs ornemanistes parisiens et l'art décoratif des Bâtiments du roi. Strasbourg, 1986.

Grands Décors Français 1650–1800. Dijon, 1995. Trans. by Ann Sautier-Greening as *French Period Rooms*. Dijon, 1995.

"L'hôtel de la Chancellerie," *Monuments historiques*, CLXXII (1990), 97–112.

Waddesdon Manor: Architecture and Panelling. London, 1996.

Rambaud, Mireille. *Documents du Minutier Central concernant l'histoire de l'art 1700–1750*. 2 vols. Paris, 1964–71.

Ravel, Pierre. *La Chambre de Justice de 1716*. Paris, 1928.

Riley, James C. *The Seven Years War and the Old Regime in France*. Princeton, 1986.

Ris, Clément de. *Les Amateurs d'autrefois*. Paris, 1877.

Roche, Daniel. *The People of Paris: An Essay in Popular Culture in the 18th Century*. Trans. Marie Evans and Gwynne Lewis. New York, 1986.

Rothkrug, Lionel. *Opposition to Louis XIV: The Political and Social Origins of the French Enlightenment*. Princeton, 1965.

Rule, John C. "Royal Ministers and Government Reform during the Last Decades of

Louis XIV's Reign," in *Consortium on Revolutionary Europe, 1750–1850: proceedings, 1972.* Gainesville, Fla., 1973.

Sabatier, Gérard. "Politique, histoire et mythologie: La galerie en France et en Italie pendant la première moitié du XVIIe siècle," in *La France et l'Italie au temps de Mazarin*, 283–301. Ed. Jean Servoy. Grenoble, 1986.

Saint-Germain, Jacques. *Les financiers sous Louis XIV: Paul Poisson de Bourvalais.* Paris, 1950.

Samuel Bernard, le banquier des rois. Paris, 1960.

Saint Simon, Fernand de. *La Place Vendôme.* Paris, 1983.

La Place des Victoires. Paris, 1984.

Saisselin, Remy. *Taste in Eighteenth-Century France.* Syracuse, 1965.

Samoyault, Jean-Pierre. *André-Charles Boulle et sa famille.* Geneva, 1979.

Schnapper, Antoine. "Antoine Coypel: La galerie d'Énée au Palais Royal," *Revue de l'art*, V (1969), 33–42.

Schneider, Robert A. *Public Life in Toulouse 1463–1789: From Municipal Republic to Cosmopolitan City.* Ithaca and London, 1989.

Scott, Katie. "Decoration and Cultural Distinction in Paris, c. 1680–c. 1750." Ph.D. dissertation, University of London, 1988.

"D'un siècle à l'autre: History, Mythology and Decoration in Early Eighteenth-Century Paris," in *Loves of the Gods: Mythological Painting from Watteau to David*, Ed. Colin B. Bailey, pp. 32–59. New York, 1992.

The Rococo Interior: Decoration and Social Spaces in Early Eighteenth-Century Paris. New Haven and London, 1995.

Ségur, Pierre de. *Le Royaume de la rue Saint-Honoré: Madame Geoffrin et sa fille.* Paris, 1897.

Sewell, William H., Jr. *A Rhetoric of Bourgeois Revolution: The Abbé Sièyes and "What is the Third Estate?"* Durham and London, 1994.

Shackleton, Robert. *Montesquieu: A Critical Biography.* London, 1961.

Shennan, J. H. *The Parlement of Paris.* London, 1968.

Philippe, Duke of Orleans: Regent of France 1715–1723. London, 1979.

Souchal, François. *French Sculptors of the 17th and 18th centuries: the reign of Louis XIV.* Collab. Françoise de la Moureye and Henriette Dumuis. Trans. Elsie and George Dumuis. 3 vols. Oxford, 1977.

"Le Portail de l'Église des Capucines à Paris," *GBA*, 73 (1969), 193–205.

Starobinski, Jean. *L'Invention de la liberté, 1700–1789.* Geneva, 1964.

Stern, Jean. *A l'ombre de Sophie Arnould, François-Josèph Bélanger.* 2 vols. Paris, 1930.

Storez, Isabelle. *Le Chancelier Henri François d'Aguesseau (1668–1751): monarchiste et libéral.* Paris, 1996.

Stourm, René. *Bibliographie historique des finances de la France au dix-huitième siècle.* Paris, 1895.

Strandberg, Runar. "Les dessins d'architecture de Pierre Bullet pour la Place Vendôme et L'Hôtel Reich de Pennautier-d'Évreux," *GBA* (1965), 71–90.

"Jean-Baptiste Bullet de Chamblain, Architecte du Roi (1665-1726)," *BSHAF* (1962), 193–255.

Pierre Bullet et J.-B. de Chamblain. Stockholm, 1971.

Stuffmann, Margret. "Les tableaux de la collection de Pierre Crozat: historique et destinée d'un ensemble célèbre établis en partant d'un inventaire après décès (1740)," *GBA*, 72 (1968), 1–143.

Swarte, Victor de. *Un Banquier du trésor royal au XVIIIe siècle, sa vie sa correspondance (1651–1739).* Paris, 1895.

Les financiers amateurs d'art aux XVIe, XVIIe et XVIIIe siècles. Paris, 1890.

Taton, René, ed. *Enseignement et diffusion des sciences en France au XVIIIe siècle.* Paris, 1964.

Tate, Robert S., Jr. *Petit de Bachaumont: His Circle and the Mémoires Secrets.* Geneva, 1968.

Thirion, H. *La vie privée des financiers au XVIIIe siècle.* Paris, 1895.

Thiry, Anne. "L'Hôtel Peirenc de Moras, puis de Boullongne, 23, place Vendôme," *BSHPIF*, 106 (1979), 51–84.

Thornton, Peter. *Authentic Decor: The Domestic Interior 1690–1920.* Avenel, 1993.
 Seventeenth-Century Interior Decoration in England, France and Holland. New Haven and London, 1978.

Vacquier, Jules. *Les vieux hôtels de Paris.* Série 3–13. Paris, 1908–37.

Verlet, Pierre. *Les Bronzes dorés français du XVIIIe siècle.* Paris, 1987.
 The Eighteenth Century in France: Society, Decoration, Furniture. Trans. George Savage. Rutland. Vt., 1967.
 French Furniture of the Eighteenth Century. Trans. Penelope Hunter-Stiebel. Charlottesville and London, 1991.

Vidler, Anthony. *Claude-Nicolas Ledoux: Architecture and Social Reform at the End of the Ancien Régime.* Cambridge, Mass., 1990.

Vossen, Franz. "Architecture et espace urbain au XVIIIe siècle," *Annales (Économies, Sociétés, Civilisations)*, 5 (October–November 1950), 440–7.

Wheaton, Barbara Ketcham. *Savoring the Past: The French Kitchen and Table from 1300 to 1789.* Philadelphia, 1983.

Whitehead, John. *The French Interior in the Eighteenth Century.* New York, 1992.

Wiebenson, Dora. *The Picturesque Garden in France.* Princeton, 1978.

Wildenstein, Georges. "Le goût pour la peinture dans le cercle de la bourgeoisie parisienne autour de 1700," *GBA*, série 6, XLVIII (1956), 113–95.
 Lancret. Paris, 1924.

Wilhelm, Jacques. "Le grand cabinet chinois de l'hôtel de Richelieu, place Royale," *Bulletin du Musée Carnavelet* (June 1967), 2–14.
 La vie quotidienne au Marais. Paris, 1966.

Yarrow, P. J. "M. Jourdain and Colbert," *Seventeenth-Century French Studies*, 9 (1987), 122–30.

Ziskin, Rochelle. "The Place de Nos Conquêtes and the Unraveling of the Myth of Louis XIV," *Art Bulletin*, LXXVI:1 (March 1994), 147–62.